Developing Consciousness for the Post-Capitalist Commons

Developing Consciousness for the Post-Capitalist Commons

Gregory Wilpert

BLOOMSBURY ACADEMIC
LONDON • NEW YORK • OXFORD • NEW DELHI • SYDNEY

BLOOMSBURY ACADEMIC

Bloomsbury Publishing Plc, 50 Bedford Square, London, WC1B 3DP, UK
Bloomsbury Publishing Inc, 1385 Broadway, New York, NY 10018, USA
Bloomsbury Publishing Ireland, 29 Earlsfort Terrace, Dublin 2, D02 AY28, Ireland

BLOOMSBURY, BLOOMSBURY ACADEMIC and the Diana logo are trademarks
of Bloomsbury Publishing Plc

First published in Great Britain 2026

Copyright © Gregory Wilpert 2026

Gregory Wilpert has asserted this right under the Copyright, Designs and Patents Act, 1988, to be identified as Author of this work.

Bloomsbury Publishing Plc does not have any control over, or responsibility for, any third-party websites referred to or in this book. All internet addresses given in this book were correct at the time of going to press. The author and publisher regret any inconvenience caused if addresses have changed or sites have ceased to exist, but can accept no responsibility for any such changes.

A catalogue record for this book is available from the British Library.

A catalog record for this book is available from the Library of Congress

ISBN: HB: 978-1-3505-9242-1
PB: 978-1-3505-9241-4
ePDF: 978-1-3505-9244-5
eBook: 978-1-3505-9243-8

Typeset by Newgen KnowledgeWorks Pvt. Ltd., Chennai, India
Printed and bound in Great Britain

For product safety related questions contact productsafety@bloomsbury.com.

To find out more about our authors and books visit www.bloomsbury.com
and sign up for our newsletters.

For Sofia

Contents

List of Figures viii
Preface ix
Acknowledgments xii

1. Introduction: Why Has Socialism Not Succeeded So Far? 1
2. The Biology and Psychology of Consciousness 13
3. Society, Ideology, and Class 35
4. Criticisms and Responses 69
5. The Challenge: Neoliberal Digital Capitalism 95
6. Commonist Consciousness and Commonist Institutions 131
7. Conclusion: Getting from Here to There 173

Bibliography 187
Index 199

Figures

1. The logic of consciousness development (according to Robert Kegan). 23
2. Base and superstructure. 39
3. Material and ideal. 39
4. Base vs. superstructure and interior vs. exterior. 40
5. Four dimensions of political ideology. 60
6. Circulation of money, goods, and knowledge between commons. 163

Preface

This book took a long time to write. I believe I began working on it in 2012. The difficulty with writing it was not so much the topic—I had been thinking about it already at least ten years earlier—but that I tried to work on it between other paying jobs, such as teaching political science at Brooklyn College and working as a journalist. Finding the time to work on it was difficult, which at times included years of interruption between focused work on it. The first draft was completed almost exactly ten years later, in January 2023.

Since then, my life and my outlook on this type of writing have changed significantly. When I started, I was still holding out hope that I might one day teach full time at the university and, as a result, I believed that I had to write in an academic writing style, backing up every single claim with at least one solid and credible reference. Also, much of the book tries to garner legitimacy for its arguments by referencing Marx. While I continue to believe that Marx was a genius, I no longer think it was necessary to legitimize my arguments by referencing Marx. On the other hand, I realize that part of the motivation for doing so is that referencing Marx serves as an argumentation shortcut, given that this book is directed toward a leftist audience that already believes that Marx was correct for the most part. In other words, referencing Marx makes it easier and faster to get a point across than if the argument had been made from scratch. This, of course, also goes for other major theorists mentioned in this book.

Another important related reason for referencing Marx is that I see this book as contributing to a major tradition in western thought, which is that of socialism and communism. Although this tradition remains very popular throughout the world, it has, unfortunately, suffered enormously from the discrediting of their practical implementation when socialist or communist movements came to power in countries such as Russia, China, Eastern Europe, North Korea, Cuba, and

Venezuela. I discuss some of these problems and how they motivated me to write this book in Chapter 1. Despite this discrediting, I continue to believe that working toward a humane, classless, ecological, and just post-capitalist society remains the only worthwhile goal for society. Whether we call this goal socialism or communism does not really matter to me. One reason, though, to perhaps change the term for this goal is that there are a lot of misconceptions surrounding the meaning of socialism and communism, leading to misunderstandings. A way to alleviate this misconception would be to come up with a related but slightly different new term. One writer who has tried to do this and whose effort I wholeheartedly support is Nick Dyer-Witheford, who, it seems, was the first to coin the term "commonism."[1]

The reason we might want to avoid the term communism in favor of commonism is that the former has been too closely tied to authoritarian forms of socialism, such as that of the Soviet Union. There still is some debate within the left about the extent to which Soviet-style state-socialism or communism was harmful for the vast majority of the population, but I am on the side of those who view this type of socialism/communism more negatively than positively. As Michael Albert likes to point out, it makes sense to see Soviet-style communism as being a manifestation of what he calls "coordinatorism," where instead of capitalists dominating society you have the coordinator class dominating. Given that Marx himself never really outlined what a communist society would look like but based on the little bit that he did write about the future communist society,[2] it could be argued that his vision was a lot closer to what Dyer-Witheford (and I, in this book) describe as commonism.

One thing that I did not discuss but which perhaps would deserve some consideration in this context is the difference between socialism and communism/commonism. Left thinkers tend to make two types

---

[1] Dyer-Witheford (2007). Also, I am inspired by my friend Raul Zelik, who made a similar argument in his book, "Nach dem Kapitalismus? Perspektiven der Emanzipation oder: Das Projekt Communismus anders denken" (2011).
[2] Such as in the "Critique of the Gotha Program" (1875).

of distinctions between the two. First, there is the more typically anti-communist distinction, which sees socialism as a democratic state-based system that organizes social relations, possibly with some market elements (as in market socialism), to create an economically egalitarian society. In this view, communism is often seen as a mostly totalitarian effort to give the state control over all aspects of society, perhaps in nominally democratic terms but not actually, to create a mostly classless, non-capitalist, centrally planned economy, but in which inevitably the coordinator class dominates. This distinction clearly takes the Soviet Union's implementation of communism at its word but sees it negatively.

The other type of distinction, which is the one that Marx argued for, sees communism as a positive goal (which the USSR never achieved according to more contemporary thinkers), where socialism is a transitional phase in which a democratic state implements communist institutions and relations on behalf of the working class, with the aim of ultimately dissolving the state (or, as Marx argued, in which the state would "wither away"), once all social relations and institutions are radically democratic, egalitarian, and classless (and ecological).

Some proponents of the second distinction might argue that the Soviet Union and similar projects aimed (or continue to aim) to implement the Marx-inspired version of communism but never were able to do so for a variety of reasons, primarily due to insufficient development of productive forces (technological inefficiency) or because of outside imperialist intervention, or a combination of the two.

However, as I intend to argue in this book, a third factor is usually forgotten, which is that consciousness, in the sense of how we see and make sense of the world and of what we value, was also insufficient for the establishment of institutions that communists hoped to ultimately achieve. In other words, the consciousness of the socialist and communist movements, as well as of the rest of the population, was not adequate to the new type of society they were hoping to create.

Acknowledgments

It is rather difficult to give credit where credit is due for this work, mainly because of the length of time it took to write it. Many different people influenced me at different phases of this book, and I need to apologize in advance if I forget anyone.

First and foremost, I am grateful to the work of Ken Wilber, who for me is perhaps the main pioneer in this type of thinking. I probably do not cite him as much as I could have mainly because he himself is someone who tends to synthesize other people's work and, in this book, I tried to cite the firsthand research more than the synthesizers. I am also very grateful to have had the opportunity to get to know Ken personally on several occasions in the early 2000s and he was very supportive of my thinking and writing at the time. Unfortunately, the book that I was working on back then never was completed and thus remains unpublished. I did publish a couple of articles through his *AQAL Journal*.

Another thinker who inspired me tremendously, shortly before I came across Wilber's work, is Rudolf Bahro. I was working on my dissertation in sociology at the time, on political consciousness among unemployed East Germans following German unification. Bahro was giving lectures at the Humboldt University of Berlin and tied eastern and western thinking, political philosophy, and psychology together in a masterful way.

The third theoretical and inspirational pillar for me was Jürgen Habermas, whom I unfortunately never got to know personally, but who also ranks for me among one of the greatest thinkers of the twentieth century and who, as the reader will see, was another primary inspiration for this book.

On a more personal level, I need to thank Carol Delgado who, in the earliest phase of this book, provided important support for me to work on it. I am also grateful to a variety of individuals who at various points took time to either listen to me ramble about the book's ideas, who might have read excerpts, or heard me give talks on this book and who provided me with feedback. Some of these include Michael Lebowitz, Michael Albert, Vera Weiler, Marta Harnecker, my mother, Czarina Wilpert, and three anonymous reviewers, to just mention a few of the main ones.

1

Introduction: Why Has Socialism Not Succeeded So Far?

The dream to create true socialism, in the sense of a true economic and political democracy with social justice for all members of society, has been frustrated many times and in many ways. The first sense in which it has been frustrated is that even countries that claimed to have achieved socialism, such as the Soviet Union and China, did not live up to the ideals and aspirations of most socialists (at least, of those who weren't vested in these systems). That is, these countries might have implemented some key ideals of socialism, primarily of achieving social equality and social justice, but they generally did not combine these with individual freedoms and economic and political democracy. The second sense in which the socialist dream has been frustrated is simply that it has never been achieved even in those countries that socialism's greatest theorist, Karl Marx, believed would become socialist first, the so-called advanced capitalist countries. At best, many of these countries implemented social democracy, which, in the face of neoliberal globalization, became hollowed out from the 1980s onward.

The explanations for these two failures are almost as varied as there are socialist or Marxist theorists. Most of these explanations refer to causes that one could label "external" or objective factors. These approaches focus on external causes, in that socialism's lack of success is external to the socialist movement itself, such as the overwhelming political and economic power of the ruling class, capitalism's seeming infinite adaptability to new circumstances, or capitalists' success in dividing and weakening the working class along race and gender lines. These types of external explanations can take an extremely wide variety of explanations in their details. When applied to the failure of established socialist states, theorists point to their initial economic poverty, to the movement's betrayal by certain leaders, or to the adverse international context of these states, whereby the United States and other powerful nations attempt to isolate and economically destroy socialist countries.[1]

The second set of explanations for the two failures of socialism refers to "internal" or subjective factors, which can be found within the socialist movement, such as the working class's lack of class consciousness, its "false" consciousness, or other forms of unpreparedness to either work toward a socialist revolution or to maintain one once it has been achieved. Again, the details of exactly why the consciousness of the working class or of the oppressed is not adequate for struggling for social change or why it cannot maintain that change once it has been achieved, are about as varied as the theorists who develop these explanations. Generally, though, these explanations all tend to argue that inadequate consciousness is the result of the dominant culture.[2]

An issue that these "internal" explanations rarely pay attention to, however, is that consciousness is not just a reflection of outside circumstances—that consciousness is not only determined by social conditioning. According to most critical or socialist theorists of consciousness, consciousness is a product of the internalization of external belief systems, whether of the dominant culture, mass media, popular culture, schooling, family dynamics, and the like.

---

[1] Practically all Marxist economic analyses of capitalism provide explanations for how capitalism stymies revolution.

[2] The perhaps best known and earliest theorist of this explanation for the lack of revolutionary consciousness is Antonio Gramsci. There is a long line of other theorists, though, including Georg Lukács and the "Frankfurt School of critical theory," whose members included Theodor Adorno, Max Horkheimer, Herbert Marcuse, Erich Fromm, Wilhelm Reich, and Jürgen Habermas. Other theorists who have focused on the role of ideology and culture in domination include the structuralists, post-structuralists, post-colonial theorists, and cultural theorists, such as Louis Althusser, Michel Foucault, Gilles Deleuze and Félix Guattari, Frantz Fanon, Gayatri Spivak, Raymond Williams, and Stuart Hall.

Such an approach, though, fails to consider that the human mind—consciousness—is not merely a "tabula rasa," that is, a blank slate that reflects whatever one attempts to pour into it. Parents know better than anyone else that their children often do not simply repeat back what their parents attempt to teach them. The same goes for any other medium by which society attempts to transmit ideology, culture, values, norms, and so on.

The reason that consciousness is not a blank slate has to do with several factors that socialist theorists of consciousness rarely take into consideration in their theories, such as human psychology, how humans learn, and how they build upon and develop their learning. Contemporary psychology and neuroscience argue that consciousness has a dynamic or developmental logic that causes it to change according to principles that cannot be simply deduced from the influence of outside forces. This is not to say that the formation of consciousness is autonomous or unrelated to outside forces. Rather, there is a constant interplay—a dialectic, if you will—between the logic of consciousness and the influence of outside factors, which ultimately shapes our consciousness. In effect, socialist theories of consciousness do not really examine the interior causes for the failure of socialism because they see the interior (consciousness and culture) as a mere reflection of outside forces, such as the mass media, pop culture, family life, schooling, and the like.

What I am suggesting is that for us to gain a fuller and better understanding of the failure of socialism, we need to understand not only the external social causes (such as class politics, flawed leadership, and economic dynamics) and the impact that cultural forces have on our interiors of consciousness (such as mass media, advertising, and educational systems), but that we also need to know how our consciousness reacts to these external forces. To gain a better understanding of how our consciousness reacts to and processes external forces, we need to take a closer look at the sciences that deal with the biology and psychology of consciousness.

Strangely, with the exception perhaps of psychoanalytical approaches, socialist theory and research rarely take empirical research of consciousness into account. One explanation for why socialist theorists do not take mainstream science much into consideration is that empirical science is often considered to be positivistic and therefore lends itself too easily to the reproduction of domination, rather than to its dismantling.[3] That is, positivistic (as opposed to critical) science tends to reproduce the status quo because it merely attempts to describe the world as it is, without considering its potential, thereby reinforcing the notion that the way things are is the way things will always be. While there is much validity to this critique of positivistic science, not all science reaffirms "what is" in this way. As a matter of fact, as I will argue in this book, much research into consciousness shows the emancipatory potential of the human mind far more vividly than notions of a utopian society could ever do.

In short, what this book sets out to do is to bring together research on consciousness development with socialist theory, to provide a fuller explanation for the failures of socialism—one that complements, not replaces, the external explanations. Such an explanation would also contribute to developing a strategy and a vision for achieving a socialist or post-capitalist society.

As mentioned earlier, the bringing together of theories of consciousness with socialist theory has a proud tradition, particularly in Gramscian and Frankfurt School critical theory, but Marx himself already suggested a need for such a combination. However, rather than use the term consciousness, Marx referred to the concept of individual development—an idea he adopted from his teacher, Hegel. Now, development can refer to a wide variety of phenomena, but applied to the individual it refers to the growth, learning, and maturation process of humans. Clearly, some of this development process is physical and some of it is psychological or mental. Marx, though, seems to mean the mental or psychological development process, which is also a process of

---

[3] A list of some of the most important critics of scientific positivism includes thinkers such as Theodor Adorno, Max Horkheimer, Herbert Marcuse, Jürgen Habermas, Paul Feyerabend, and Thomas Kuhn.

consciousness development. Human development for Marx could thus be considered synonymous with lifelong consciousness development. Michael Lebowitz, who focused on the dialectic between individual human development and societal development, shows how important this link was for Marx. For example, Lebowitz, citing Marx, writes, "In the very act of producing, Marx noted in the *Grundrisse*, 'the producers change, too, in that they bring out new qualities in themselves, develop themselves in production, transform themselves, develop new powers and new ideas, new modes of intercourse, new needs and new language' (Marx, 1973: 494)."[4] In capitalism, of course, the individual's development tends to be stunted or hindered because the emphasis is on the development of capital and not on the individual. "In capitalism, Marx commented, 'this complete working-out of the human content appears as a complete emptying-out, this universal objectification as total alienation, and the tearing-down of all limited, one-sided aims as a sacrifice of the human end-in-itself to an entirely external end' (Marx, 1973: 488)."[5]

In socialism, though, this relation would be reversed. According to Marx, capitalism "spurs on the development of society's productive forces, and the creation of those material conditions of production which alone can form the real basis of a higher form of society, a society in which the full and free development of every individual forms the ruling principle" (Marx, 1977, p. 739). Lebowitz goes on to quote Marx, saying, "The partially developed individual, he argued, 'must be replaced by the totally developed individual, for whom the different social functions are different modes of activity he takes up in turn' (Marx, 1977: 617-8)." Marx and Engels thus described the goal of this ideal post-capitalist society most succinctly in the *Communist Manifesto*, when they wrote that it is a society in which "the free development of each is a condition for the free development of all."

---

[4] Lebowtiz (2004, p. 3). See also, Lebowitz (2020).
[5] Lebowitz (2004, p. 4).

The problem, though, as Lebowitz points out, is that to get to such a society, people need to develop individually. That is, it is not enough for the productive forces of society to develop and for capitalism to collapse due to its own internal contradictions (as some Marxists would have it). Humans need to develop too, to create a new society. And, according to Lebowitz, they develop through social struggle. "[W]ithout practice, you cannot have the full development of human capacities. Without the protagonism that transforms people, you cannot produce the people who belong in the good society."[6]

Exactly what does this consciousness development process look like, though? To know what kinds of practices and what kind of consciousness development leads in the right direction—toward socialism—and what kind in the wrong direction (perhaps toward more capitalism or toward fascism), we need to have a clearer idea as to what consciousness development looks like. While Marx did outline a theory of the stages of political–economic development, from "primitive communism," to feudalism, capitalism, and socialism/communism, he never did theorize human consciousness development. As mentioned earlier, this is where developmental psychology research can help.

The first Marxist theorist (at the time) to outline a theory of the dialectic between human and societal development was the German philosopher Jürgen Habermas. In his effort to "reconstruct" dialectical materialism,[7] Habermas outlined a theory in which he showed the ways in which forms of social organization, such as feudalism and capitalism, are brought about by and reproduce structures of consciousness. These historical structures of consciousness correspond to stages of consciousness development of individuals, as studied and theorized by psychologists such as Jean Piaget and Lawrence Kohlberg. In other words, there is a direct relationship between the structures of individual consciousness development and historical socio-cultural forms, such as feudalism or capitalism (I will explain this parallel in much greater

---

[6] Lebowitz (2010, p. 15).
[7] Habermas ([1976] 1979).

detail in Chapter 3). For example, Habermas states, "the [human] species learns not only in the dimension of technically useful knowledge decisive for the development of [technologically] productive forces but also in the dimension of moral-practical consciousness decisive for structures of interaction."[8] Habermas identified these linkages, though, mainly to establish a theoretical foundation for critical theory. That is, he sought to explain how the potential and basis for social emancipation (from bureaucratic capitalism) could be found in human development.

The problem with Habermas's work, though, is that it was limited both by the developmental psychologists that he relied upon and to a rather truncated vision of socialism. His reliance on Piaget and Kohlberg limits his vision of post-capitalist forms of consciousness because these developmental psychologists did not delve much into the highest stages of consciousness. As a result, Habermas's vision of socialism seems to be quite social democratic in that his political and economic vision of a better society does not go beyond a deliberative and representative democracy and state regulation of a capitalist market economy.[9] However, if we take into account some of the latest research into the higher reaches of adult consciousness development, we can begin to identify a societal vision that more fully captures the Marxian ideal of a society in which the full development of each is a condition for the full development of all.[10]

A large part of my motivation for writing this book comes from my experience of living in Venezuela and studying the Venezuelan experience under President Hugo Chávez between 2000 and 2008. Beginning in 2005, Chávez declared that his intention is to introduce "21st-century socialism" in Venezuela, a project that, in my opinion, advanced in several important aspects. However, the project ran into serious problems in many areas, among the most difficult of which

---

[8] Habermas (1979, p. 127).
[9] Habermas's last major social theoretical work, *Between Facts and Norms* (1992), outlines this vision to a limited extent.
[10] My main inspiration for this approach comes from Rudolf Bahro ([1987] 1994) and Ken Wilber (2000a).

I believe were related to the country's political culture. Specifically, I identified three problematic aspects of Venezuelan political culture that create obstacles to the implementation of socialism: top-down management in the public administration, overdependence on a single leader for political direction, and clientelism.[11]

These three aspects of Venezuelan political culture combined to create the impression among ordinary Venezuelans, but especially among Chávez supporters, that one of the main obstacles in creating a truly participatory socialist democracy in Venezuela is the state bureaucracy. Repeatedly Venezuelans involved in communal councils and in worker-managed workplaces argued that bureaucrats in the public administration or in their own workplaces stymie their efforts at self-management.[12] In other words, Chávez supporters generally believe that Chávez genuinely wanted to create a participatory democracy in Venezuela but that there is a class of middle-level managers that is preventing its full realization.

If this is true, then one must ask, though, who are these middle-level managers or bureaucrats, where do they come from, and what makes them different from ordinary "chávistas" who want to create twenty-first-century socialism? One possible answer to these questions is to adopt Trotsky's analysis of the Russian Revolution and how Stalin betrayed the revolution. According to Trotsky,[13] Stalin empowered state bureaucrats against ordinary Russian citizens, so that in the end the bureaucrats constituted a new ruling class, interested in maintaining their position, with Stalin as their leader.

Most who adopt this analysis would not argue, however, that Chávez intentionally empowered the bureaucracy. If anything, through the creation of social missions, communal councils, communes, and worker-managed workplaces, Chávez took power away from the bureaucracy. Rather, the problem, according to the neo-Trotskyist

---

[11] I explore these problems in detail in my book *Changing Venezuela by Taking Power* (Wilpert, 2007).
[12] See Martinez et al. (2010).
[13] See Trotsky ([1937] 2004).

analysis, is that the state is still the old state, from Venezuela's so-called fourth republic and was not really transformed by the Bolivarian Revolution. In short, the battle for socialism in Venezuela is not only between ordinary Venezuelans and the bourgeoisie but also between ordinary Venezuelans and the state bureaucracy of the old regime.

While there is no doubt some truth to this analysis, I believe that one must also consider the possibility that these bureaucrats, who constitute a social class of their own,[14] are also ordinary Venezuelans. That is, they are recruited out of the general population and become bureaucrats not just because it is in their interest to become part of a particular social class that has power, but also because there is a predominant political culture in Venezuela that favors personalism, top-down management, and clientelism within the state administration.

As a matter of fact, there was widespread recognition in Venezuela that the political culture did not correspond to the highest ideals of twenty-first-century socialism. President Chávez himself talked about this on many occasions. For example, already in 2004, he referred to Victor Hugo's *Les Miserables*, saying, "The work is incomplete, I admit this. We have demolished the old regime in deeds, but we have not completely overcome it in ideas. It is not enough to destroy the abuses and it is necessary to modify habits—the windmill no longer exists, but the wind that moved it continues to blow." Chávez then added, "We must demolish the old regime on the ideological level."[15]

This issue received further recognition and legitimation in the Chávez government's "General Lines of the Social and Economic Development Plan of the Nation 2007-2013." Of the plan's seven sections, the first is devoted to the development of a "New Socialist Ethic." This document recognizes that creating twenty-first-century socialism in Venezuela requires an "ethical and moral re-founding of the nation" that has its roots in "the most advanced values and

---

[14] In the theory of participatory economics ("parecon," as developed by Michael Albert and Robin Hahnel) this class would be called the "coordinator class."
[15] Both quotes from "Taller de Alto Nivel," Ministerio de Comunicación e Información (2004, p. 17).

principles of the humanist and socialist currents and in the historical inheritance of the thought of Simón Bolívar." More specifically, the plan aims to inculcate values such as "human solidarity," "a state with honest functionaries," and "active militant tolerance in the midst of a plural environment." The section concludes by calling for "the construction of the new man of the 21st century" and that "there will be socialism when there is a new man."[16]

This conception of socialist ethics and of the new socialist "man" [sic] raises a whole host of issues that have been intensely debated within the left.[17] Ernesto "Che" Guevara probably coined the term "new socialist man" in 1965, when he wrote that socialism "requires the development of a consciousness in which there is a new scale of values. Society as a whole must be converted into a gigantic school."[18] The true revolutionary "new man," according to Guevara, would be "guided by great feelings of love." Exactly how such a revolutionary "new man" would be created is not clear, but it would involve education, civic participation, volunteer work, and incentives.

Guevara's admonition for a revolutionary socialist ethic subsequently inspired a debate within revolutionary Cuba, which has been replicated to some extent in Venezuela,[19] as to whether the incentives for citizens to create a socialist society should be mostly material, such as higher wages for more "socialist" behavior, or mostly moral, by appealing to socialist ideals. In Venezuela, this debate remained inconclusive, so that the government tended to apply both types of incentives.

---

[16] All quotes are taken from Section 1 of "General Lines of the Social and Economic Development Plan of the Nation 2007–2013," Ministerio de Comunicación e Información (2007; my translation).

[17] One of the main issues critics have raised is whether the creation of a "new man" is inherently a totalitarian project because it aims to transform not just social structures, but also the consciousness of the individual.

[18] Guevara (2003, p. 217). Mao Zedong also raised the issue of consciousness during China's Cultural Revolution (1966–76), but this approach to consciousness/culture was far cruder than Cuba's, in that it mainly aimed to remove individuals believed to embody capitalist culture from positions of power and "reeducating" them.

[19] See Ellner (2010, pp. 63–84).

The argument I present in this book is that neither type of incentive is going to be effective because both overlook how consciousness develops. That is, the materialist appeal sees individuals as being mostly motivated by material gain, while the moral appeal sees individuals motivated by ethical ideals. Both have elements of truth, in that material gain indeed motivates some people and ethical ideals motivate others. The crux of the problem, though, for supporting a new socialist consciousness is not how to best manipulate people to behave in the proper socialist way, but how to contribute to the development of their consciousness so that they actively create a socialist society without being manipulated via incentives or ethical guilt trips to do so.

My interpretation of Venezuela's experiment to create twenty-first-century socialism places equal emphasis on the social-structural obstacles (the old state, old capitalist economy, and external threats) and on the cultural obstacles (or consciousness). However, since most analysts of socialism's failures focus on the social-structural aspect of this process, this book focuses on the cultural/consciousness dimension. I do this not by taking a detailed look at Venezuelan culture, a project that would no doubt be useful, but by examining the more general logic behind consciousness development and the culture it would produce. To put it differently, culture is nothing other than shared consciousness, than social consciousness.

What I mean by consciousness is the topic of the next chapter. Then, Chapter 3, examines different conceptions of consciousness in socialist theory and how the developmental psychological approach proposed here can be integrated into those other approaches. Chapter 4 considers a wide variety of criticisms of this approach, given that it is closely related to what is known in sociology as "modernization theory," which has a long and very problematic history. Chapter 5 applies the ideas to our current situation, specifically that of neoliberal digital capitalism, as I call it. It examines how this form of capitalism came about, the obstacles it has run into, and what kind of consciousness problems— or psychological problems—it has created for the average member of today's society. Chapter 6 then takes a closer look at what kind of post-capitalist commons-based institutions a post-capitalist–socialist consciousness, or integral consciousness, would create. Finally, the conclusion, Chapter 7, summarizes the overall argument and points to some ideas for what types of real-world practices might promote an integral or commonist consciousness.

2

The Biology and Psychology of Consciousness

It is extremely difficult to dissect and discuss the concept of consciousness in a relatively short book. The concept has been one of the central issues of both Eastern and Western philosophy ever since ancient times and for psychology and biology since the development of these sciences in the twentieth century. As a result, I cannot present an in-depth discussion or overview of the topic here. Rather, I must limit myself to a very brief exposition of my approach to consciousness and hope that it is either convincing enough to be accepted by the reader or, at least, unobjectionable enough to make the rest of my argument about consciousness and socialism convincing. To help make the argument convincing, let's start with some commonly accepted notions about consciousness.

When we talk about the concept of consciousness there are usually at least two possible meanings we have in mind for the term. First, consciousness could merely mean awareness of something, as in, "I am conscious of the blue sky" or "I am conscious of a pain in my right foot." The second meaning, which tends to be more controversial among philosophers, psychologists, and biologists of consciousness, refers to awareness of oneself, to self-consciousness, that I am a distinct individual, with thoughts and feelings that are mine and that are different from those of other individuals. In short, the statement "I am conscious of myself" displays this meaning of the term.

The big debate within the study of consciousness has tended to focus on this latter meaning of consciousness, trying to explain exactly why and how we humans (and presumably only we humans) have (self-)consciousness since there generally is not much doubt that animals too are aware of their surroundings or of pain, for example. One of the main issues that students of consciousness have thus focused on is whether consciousness is the creation of human brain biology (the physicalist or materialist argument), whether consciousness is constitutive of everything else (the idealist argument), or whether it is both (the dualist argument). In Western philosophy and science, the materialist argument tends to predominate, while in the East it tends to be the idealist argument.[1] For most people, though, the commonsense view is the dualist argument, since we all clearly see that we have both a material body and immaterial consciousness and that the two appear to be distinct and irreducible to the other.[2] Which argument, if any, is the correct one cannot be discussed or resolved here, so I will stick to the commonsense view of dualism for now.[3]

For this study, I want to first focus on consciousness as awareness and only much later touch upon the concept of consciousness as self-awareness. The first thing to note about consciousness as awareness is that it is always an awareness of something else. Generally, we do not have "pure" awareness, but always an awareness of a blue sky, of feeling hungry, of anger, of an idea, and the like. What this means is that consciousness is always inextricably tied to perception—that is,

---

[1] Although, more recently analytic idealism, primarily led by Bernardo Kastrup, has gained much momentum (Kastrup, 2024).
[2] By neither being reducible to the other, I mean that we generally don't believe that our consciousness is only the creation of our biological brain, since most of us believe that we have some degree of free will (the essence of the self) that is not reducible to the electrical impulses in the synapses of our brain. Similarly, most people do not believe that the material world, including our body, is a creation of our consciousness.
[3] I believe that dualism is a sufficient explanation for now but realize that there are inherent contradictions and difficulties in this approach that many philosophers have pointed out (the so-called hard problem of consciousness, as David Chalmers (1996) called it). The bottom line is that this key philosophical problem cannot be resolved within everyday rational consciousness. For a fuller discussion of this issue that corresponds with my view, see Wilber (2000a), chapter 14.

perception not just with our five senses of an external world, but also the perception of our interior world, of what and how we feel and of what we are thinking (which is why Buddhists talk about there being six senses and not just five).

Once we recognize that consciousness is basically awareness of an exterior and of an interior world, we need to recognize that our awareness of these worlds is not necessarily the same as other people's awareness of these worlds. In other words, every consciousness is different from the consciousness of others, which means that everyone has different perspectives on and understandings of the interior and exterior worlds. The reason why we have different consciousnesses and different perspectives, aside from the fact that we are not all looking at the world from the same point in time and in space, is that our consciousness is fundamentally shaped by our past experiences, by our biography, which is unique for everyone. That is, our biology, our biography, our culture, our society, and our place in history shape our perspectives.

This is nothing new, of course, given that Marx famously declared a long time ago, "It is not consciousness that determines our social being, but our social being that determines our consciousness."[4] The key question—and the topic of most of this book—is, HOW does our social being, our life experience, determine our consciousness? As mentioned in the previous chapter, countless socialist theorists have already explored this issue to explain why socialism has so far failed to become a dominant ideology or a dominant perspective. What they generally did not refer to in their work, though, is actual research into the biology and psychology of consciousness. This research is not only useful for understanding the obstacles to achieving socialism but will also help us understand what type of consciousness would be most conducive to the creation of socialism. I will thus first look at research in neurobiology and then at research in developmental psychology.

---

[4] Marx ([1859] 1970, p. 21).

The Neurobiology of Consciousness Development

The history of the (at least, Western) understanding of the mind and of consciousness is torn between the "tabula rasa" conception of the mind, which believes that the mind is a blank slate that merely reflects all societal inputs, and the human nature conception, which believes that there is a particular human nature (usually either mostly good or mostly bad) that is practically impossible to change. Both conceptions seem quite compelling. The tabula rasa conception is compelling because we can clearly see the incredible diversity of human individuals, cultures, and ways of being, ranging from the most barbaric to the most sublime. This diversity would seem to indicate that there is no human nature. On the other hand, it is tempting to believe that given the persistence of certain human behaviors, such as the tendencies toward violence and selfishness, this type of conduct constitutes a certain baseline of human nature.

The amazing thing is that brain biology can help us understand why both conceptions of the human mind might be at least partially correct. First, it is important to note that our skills, habits, ways of thinking, and our consciousness are closely related (but not entirely determined) to the ways in which our brain is "wired."[5] That is, experimental research clearly shows that the ways we think are closely related to the way our brain cells, our neurons, are connected to each other. And when we develop new skills, new ways of thinking, and new experiences, our brain neurology changes with these new skills, thoughts, and experiences.

For example, Bruce Wexler, a noted neuroscientist, states that a series of animal studies conducted in the 1960s and 1970s showed that "our brains (and minds) develop concrete perceptual structures, capabilities,

---

[5] The use of a "wiring" metaphor for the brain is extremely common nowadays, but it is misleading because it gives the impression that the brain is a machine that once created does not change. However, the brain is part of a living organism that constantly reorganizes itself, or "rewires" itself. A perhaps better metaphor would be that of a landscape, in which rivers and streams continuously adapt to a changing landscape.

and sensitivities based on prominent features of the environment in which we are reared, and then are more able and more likely to see those features in the sensory mix of new environments we encounter."[6] This sensitization of senses is well known in the case of blind people who develop keener senses of hearing and of touch.

The high correlation between neurology and mind, between our brain and our consciousness and awareness, helps us understand why both conceptions of the mind—as tabula rasa and as fixed human nature—have some truth.

To put it simply, supporting the tabula rasa conception, the human brain is clearly capable of creating an extreme diversity of individuals. This comes from the fact that early in an individual's life, during childhood and into early adulthood, the brain is extremely malleable and capable of being shaped in a wide variety of ways. In the field of neurology, this is known as "neuroplasticity." That is, during the first years of an individual's life new neurological connections are created with relative ease and quite rapidly. Certain experiences and practices create certain neurological connections in the infant's brain, which stay with this infant for the rest of their life. Certain experiences and practices will then create certain types of connections and therefore certain perceptual sensitivities and propensities of thinking.

However, supporting the fixed nature conception, as the individual gets older, the brain becomes increasingly slower in the process of creating new neurological connections, which explains why it becomes increasingly more difficult for people to learn new skills and assimilate new experiences as they get older. According to Wexler,

> Once brain organization evolves, and the individual reaches sexual maturity, existing structures tend to be enduring and resistant to change. This is due in part to changes in brain chemistry that reduce neuroplasticity. It is also because as long as input pathways and neuronal ensembles remain active, the existing organization is stabilized. While activity-related functional reorganization is possible

---

[6] Wexler (2006, p. 47).

in adult mammals, it is much slower, much more limited, and achieved with much greater physiological demands.[7]

In short, if members of a society are exposed to similar childhood experiences, then they are likely to forge a certain group "nature" that appears to be fixed and that could be confused with a particular human nature.

While neuroscience took for granted for a long time that the human brain hardly changed at all once an individual reached adulthood, more recent research has shown that this is false. Rather, neuroplasticity continues to be an important factor throughout an individual's lifetime. True, the brain is no longer as "plastic" or malleable as it was during childhood, but neurons continue to be capable of forging new pathways and new connections as new skills are developed and new experiences are made. The clearest proof of this is the ability of stroke victims, who lose the ability to use a limb or to speak can recover almost completely, even though the neurons that used to control these areas were killed by the stroke.[8] This is not to say that adult neuroplasticity comes easy—far from it, it is generally difficult.[9] The key insight for the purpose of the analysis presented here, though, is that it is possible and, if we want to achieve socialism, it is something we need to be aware of.

Another reason why neuroplasticity is difficult in adulthood, according to Wexler, is that once our brain's plasticity decreases due to changes in brain chemistry, we try to change our environment so that it fits with our by-now ingrained habits and ways of thinking, rather than the other way around. The reason we try to change the environment rather than our neurons is that familiar stimuli are experienced as being pleasurable, while unfamiliar stimuli, especially stimuli that directly contradict ingrained views or perceptions, are experienced as

---

[7] Wexler (2006, pp. 58–9).
[8] For a detailed review of numerous case studies and neuroscientists who have pioneered this area, see Doidge (2007).
[9] Recent research has shown that psychedelic substances, such as LSD, psilocybin, ketamine, and DMT, can significantly enhance neuroplasticity for a short amount of time, usually for between several days and several weeks (de Vos et al., 2021).

stressful.[10] As a result, we also tend to ignore or avoid experiences that are not consonant with existing neuronal structures and to seek out those experiences that are.

As we will see later, when I discuss developmental psychology, this neuroscientific explanation for the persistence of ways of thinking and of seeing the world might also help explain why psychological development moves in fits and spurts, or in stages, rather than in a smooth and continuous fashion. That is, neural networks might develop ways of thinking, or a type of consciousness, that is adequate to its environment, but as the environment changes beyond the individual's control, the crisis of a lack of fit between consciousness and environment gets ever larger, provoking a sudden shift at some point, as new structures are created to adapt the brain (and one's worldview) to this new environment. As we will see later, this generally happens several times in an individual's lifetime.

This neuroscientific approach also helps explain why we generally do not forget our old ways of thinking or of doing things, just as we don't forget how to ride a bicycle, even if we have already moved on to new ones. This is because the old neural structures can remain in place, even while new and presumably superior ones have developed on top of the old ones. I will develop this point and other principles of psychological development in greater depth in the next section.

On the Relationship Between Psychology and Biology, Internal and External

As we examine both the biology and psychology of consciousness development, we enter into terrain that is closely related to that of cognitive science, and it would be good to take a brief look at how one of the leading approaches in cognitive science handles the relationship between biology and psychology. Similar to the previously discussed

---

[10] Wexler (2006, pp. 155–69).

relationship between materialism and idealism in philosophy, cognitive science tends to focus on "external" factors, such as biology and environment, for the shaping of learning and development. It generally either completely ignores the "internal" lived subjective experience or sees it merely as an effect of causative biological and environmental factors.

A major challenge to this one-sided approach has been that of Varela et al. (2016), who introduced the concept of enactment, as a bridge between the internal and external. That is, according to them,

> The environment of a given living body of whatever degree of complexity can only be what is knowable and known to its sense organs and cognitions, and that environment is in turn constantly changed by the organism's actions on it— ... neither side is pregiven. The lived body, lived mind, and lived environment are all thus part of the same process, the process by which one enacts one's world.[11]

Thompson, puts it this way:

> [A] cognitive being's world is not a prespecified, external realm, represented internally by its brain, but a relational domain enacted or brought forth by that being's autonomous agency and mode of coupling with the environment.[12]

In other words, our internal processes and decisions fundamentally shape how we interact with the external world, our environment, which, in turn, shapes what we perceive and how we react—and this also shapes our biological processes, such as the functioning of our brain. In effect, the internal processes of perceiving, identifying, meaning making, and acting in the world both shape and are shaped by our external environment and our biology (which is internal to the body, but external to our mind). The philosopher Ken Wilber uses the concept of enaction as well, explaining, "[P]henomena are enacted, brought forth, disclosed, and illumined by a series of behaviors of a

---

[11] Varela et al. (2016, p. xxxviii).
[12] Thompson (2007, p. 13).

perceiving subject. ... Subjectivity ... brings forth a phenomenological world in the activity of knowing that world."[13]

In a sense, subjective experience is the flip side of objective biological and environmental factors, where neither one is prior to the other. Conceiving the relationship between subjective experience and objective factors as a process of enaction is important in order for individual and social agency to bring about social change. After all, if biology and environment were the only ultimate causative factors, agency would have no role in changing social conditions nor in changing consciousness and thereby in changing society. However, at the same time, we need to recognize the ways in which biology and social environment can impede or shape consciousness. This, to me, is why Marx stated, "Men make their own history, but they do not make it just as they please; they do not make it under circumstances chosen by themselves, but under circumstances directly encountered, given and transmitted from the past. The tradition of all the dead generations weighs like a nightmare on the brain of the living."[14]

Now that we have established the constraints that biology imposes on our consciousness and our actions, we can take a closer look at how consciousness develops from the perspective of subjective experience within these constraints.

The Psychology of Consciousness Development

Psychologists have intensely researched the development of childhood consciousness for over a century. The perhaps most important figure in this area is Jean Piaget (1896–1980), who conducted thousands of studies to identify exactly how children's minds develop. But already before Piaget, one of the founders of psychology in the United States James Mark Baldwin (1861–1934) had proposed many of the

---

[13] Wilber (n.d., p. 41).
[14] Marx ([1885] 1963).

ideas that inspired Piaget a few decades later. Since then, the field of developmental psychology has become one of the cornerstones of psychological research, particularly regarding children. However, as we will see later in this section, more recent research has shown that consciousness development does not have to end when people reach adulthood—rather, it can be a lifelong process. The argument of this book is that it is this adulthood development that is crucial for achieving socialism within one generation. In short, it is not possible to build a new society by adopting merely the "correct" ideology and ignoring the psycho-logical and neuro-logical limitations and potentialities of the human mind.

Before we can get to a better understanding of what a socialist consciousness that is informed by developmental psychology might look like, we need to take a brief look at the developmental logic of childhood and adulthood consciousness development. As I stated in the previous section, each new developmental phase builds upon and maintains the previous phase. This is true not only for neurological reasons but also because each new phase needs the capabilities developed in the previous phase to develop a new phase. A good analogy for this is that we need to have learned and understood addition before learning and understanding multiplication, and we need to understand multiplication before we can understand exponentials. In short, as Ken Wilber, one of the main exponents of consciousness development, puts it, each new level "transcends and includes" the previous level.[15] Similarly, Robert Kegan, the chair of Harvard University's Institute for Management and Leadership in Education and pioneer in adult development research, writes,

> Each successive principle subsumes or encompasses the prior principle. That which was subject becomes object to the next principle. The new principle is a higher order principle (more complex, more inclusive) that makes the prior principle into an element or tool of its system.[16]

---

[15] Wilber (2000a).
[16] Kegan (1994, p. 33).

Similarly, according to Wilber "each new growth in consciousness is not just the 'discovery' of more of a pregiven world, but the co-creation of new worlds themselves, what Popper calls a 'making and matching' of new epistemological domains, a discovery/creation of higher and wider worlds."[17] Returning to the previously mentioned concept of enactment, we can also see this as a process by which each new stage of consciousness enacts a new world by acting upon the previous stage of consciousness.

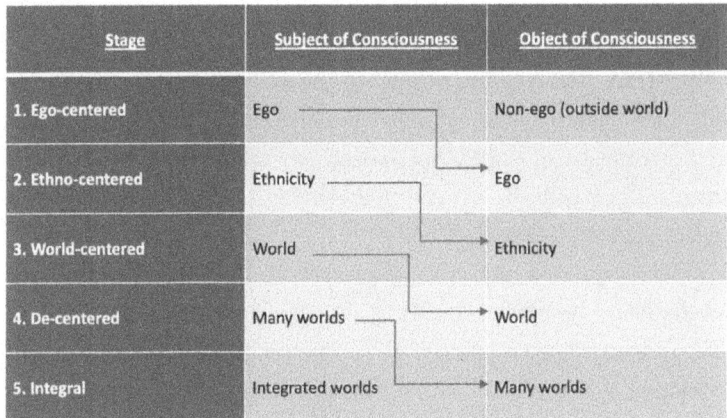

Figure 1. The logic of consciousness development (according to Robert Kegan).

Figure 1 summarizes this developmental logic for each stage. That is, in the first stage the subjectivity—the perspective from which the world is seen—is from the undifferentiated ego and views as its object everything that is non-ego. At the next stage, the object of consciousness becomes the ego, and the perspective or subjectivity of consciousness is from that of the social or ethnic group. Next, the ethnic group becomes the object of consciousness, which is seen from the larger perspective or subjectivity of the world in general. Then, as one recognizes that

---

[17] Wilber (2000a, p. 163).

the world is actually many different worlds, it becomes the object of consciousness and the subjectivity from which the world is seen is one of many worlds. Finally, many worlds become the object and the integration of many worlds is the subjectivity from which one sees.

One of the main criticisms of developmental psychology, especially of the Piagetian kind, is whether the stages or phases of development are universal or merely culturally specific. However, one of the main textbooks on cross-cultural analysis of developmental psychology finds no cultural differences, except for the highest of Piaget's stages: "While systematic cultural differences were found in the rates of cognitive development that could be related to eco-cultural factors, there is no indication from this body of research that there could be any reversals in the sequence of stages, nor indeed any culture-specific cognitive processes."[18] (I will discuss this and other criticisms of the theory in greater detail in Chapter 4.)

Before outlining the main stages of childhood and adulthood development in greater detail, it is important to point out that recent research has shown that psychological or consciousness development is not unilinear and monolithic, contrary to what many early developmental psychologists believed. That is, as Howard Gardner, another Harvard University psychologist, has theorized, humans develop intellectually along a variety of intelligences or lines (to use Wilber's term for almost the same thing). Gardner identifies eight intelligences: linguistic, musical, logical-mathematical, spatial, bodily-kinesthetic, interpersonal, intrapersonal, and naturalist.[19] Ken Wilber, though, argues that there may be as many as twenty-four separate "lines" of psychological development, whereby each line of consciousness develops more or less independently from the others.[20] It is thus possible for an individual to have a highly developed cognitive intelligence or line, and a less developed interpersonal intelligence.

---

[18] Friedlmeier et al. (2005). A textbook on cross-cultural research in developmental psychology, Gardiner and Kosmitzki (2010) makes almost exactly the same argument.
[19] Gardner (2006).
[20] Wilber (2000b).

In the past few years, much has also been made of Daniel Goleman's thesis that emotional intelligence is a crucial intelligence for people to succeed in today's world.[21]

Given the controversies surrounding exactly which kinds of intelligences or developmental lines are relevant, it might make sense to simply stick with the main ones that developmental psychologists have studied. For example, one can identify the following five lines of psychological development according to existing research: cognition (Jean Piaget), morality (Lawrence Kohlberg), affect/emotion (Daniel Goleman), self-perception/identity (Jane Loevinger, Susanne Cook-Greuter, and Robert Kegan), and values (Clare Graves).[22] As I go over the main levels of childhood development, the reader should keep in mind that each level might be reached at a different time in different lines of development. That is, just because I describe each line of each level simultaneously does not mean that an individual will be at that same level in each line of development at any given time in their life.

Childhood Development

1. <u>Sensorimotor (0–2 years)</u>: At this first stage it does not make much sense yet to divide development into different lines because the only processes at work are those of impulses and sensory perceptions. Since the infant does not distinguish between self and other, it does not make sense to talk about morality, interpersonal relations, or self-perception. Robert Kegan describes this stage as one where,

---

[21] Goleman (1995). Goleman (2005) later developed the idea that social intelligence was also crucial.
[22] I am not suggesting at all that these are the five most relevant or important ones. It seems plausible that intelligences develop according to how people are socialized and what people do. For example, a culture that emphasizes socializing in particular contexts might develop individuals with a high intelligence in that area, but not in other areas. Although, related practices and experiences could lead to higher intelligence in all the related areas. So, for example, someone who develops a high musical intelligence with a particular instrument can carry some of that intelligence over to other instruments, but not to the same extent as they achieved with their main instrument.

All developmental theories consider the infant to be "undifferentiated," the essence of which is the absence of any self-other boundary (interpersonally) or any subject-object boundary (intrapsychically) ... The infant is believed to consider all of the phenomena it experiences as extensions of itself. The infant is "all self" or "all subject" and "no object or other."[23]

Similarly, Piaget describes this stage as one where, "the small child can only perform motor actions, without thought activity, but such actions display some of the features of intelligence, as we normally understand it."[24]

2. Preoperational/ego-centric (2–7 years): Cognitively, as the child learns to create mental images of the outside world and of his or her own emotions and inner world, to "hold an object in memory" (Kegan), when there is "object permanence," the child also learns that he or she "has" emotions or impulses and that objects and individuals in the outside world, such as a toy or the parent, generally continue to exist even when they cannot be perceived. In short, the child learns to differentiate between "me" and "not-me." "The initial lack of differentiation between internal and external, between interpersonal and intrapsychic, gives way to the experience of feelings directed toward others separate from the self."[25]

This also means that the child develops the ability to recognize and think in terms of symbols. "As a result of the symbolic function, 'representation formation,' that is to say, the internalization of actions into thoughts, becomes possible. The field in which intelligence plays a part becomes considerably enlarged."[26] However, since the child still cannot take the role of the other and thus cannot realize that the other's perspective on things is different from his/her own, the child can also be

---

[23] Kegan et al. (1982, p. 109).
[24] Piaget (1995, p. 456).
[25] Kegan et al. (1982, p. 110).
[26] Piaget (1995, p. 457).

said to take an ego-centric perspective on the world. "Though the child has become differentiated enough to recognize that the whole world is not an extension of herself, she remains embedded in her impulses and perceptions and confuses real others with these. ... other people are not seen to have a point of view of their own; feelings of their own, even a mind completely separate from one's own."[27]

Later in this stage (or what some developmental psychologists consider to be a subsequent stage), the child can join symbols together to form concepts. This is also a stage filled with magical beliefs because the child confuses fantasy and imagination with reality.

In terms of morality, the child at this stage differentiates right from wrong solely based on whether an action is pleasurable or harmful. "Actions are judged in terms of physical consequences rather than in terms of psychological interests of others. Authority's perspective is confused with one's own," writes Lawrence Kohlberg.[28]

Finally, the child also begins to form a self-image. "The child becomes increasingly interested in and identified with the classes and groups to which he belongs ... The self at this stage is composed of the subject that organizes impulses and perceptions—now the contents or objects of experience—according to stable needs and enduring habits."[29]

3. Concrete operational/ethno-centric (7–12 years): At this stage, the child begins to realize that the world is governed by rules, whether natural or social. Piaget called this stage concrete operational because the child can perform logical operations on concrete objects. That is, "logical operations result from the coordination of the actions of combining, dissociating, ordering, and the setting up of correspondences, which then acquire the form of reversible systems."[30] This means that the child moves from recognizing objects (and the self) as distinct, from

---

[27] Kegan et al. (1982, p. 111).
[28] Kohlberg (1981, p. 410).
[29] Kegan et al. (1982, p. 112).
[30] Piaget (1995, p. 458).

developing a self–other distinction, to a situation in which he or she thinks about how these objects and the self relate to each other. In the process, the individual can identify that patterns or rules govern the relationships between self, others, and objects. However, the rules are intimately bound up with the objects on which they are based because the individual cannot think about the rules themselves, apart from their objects. According to Piaget, "The formal operations are not yet completely dissociated from the concrete data to which they apply. In other words, the operations develop separately field by field, and result in progressive structuralization of these fields, without complete generality being attained."[31]

This stage is also sometimes known as "ethno-centric" because the self's center is no longer solely in the (ego-centric) emotional body, but now revolves more around rules and norms derived from one's social group. One's identity is thus also not bound up solely in the highly individualized self, but in one's group membership, one's ethnic/social background. Jane Loevinger, who studied the changes in the sense of self, writes, "A momentous step is taken when the child starts to identify his own welfare with that of the group, usually his family for the small child and the peer group for an older child."[32] Furthermore, "While he observes group differences, he is insensitive to individual differences. The groups are defined in terms of obvious external characteristics, beginning with sex, age, race, nationality, and the like. Within groups so defined, he sees everyone as being pretty much alike, or at least he thinks they ought to be."[33]

Kegan describes the transition from the ego-centric to the ethno-centric stage as one in which "the individual emerges from an embeddedness in her needs, or she 'has' them rather than 'is' them."[34] In

---

[31] Piaget (1995, p. 460).
[32] Loevinger (1976, p. 17).
[33] Loevinger (1976, p. 18).
[34] Kegan et al. (1982, p. 114).

other words, the individual is now able to see their needs "objectively" rather than being immersed in them.

Regarding morality and what is right and wrong, Kohlberg says, "This stage takes the perspective of the individual in relationship to other individuals. A person at this stage is aware of shared feelings, agreements, and expectations, which take primacy over individual interests."[35]

4. <u>Formal operational/world-centric (13/14–? years of age)</u>: Cognitively the individual gradually can think about things not only in their concrete form but also in a hypothetical form. According to Piaget, "such hypothetico-deductive reasoning is characterized, inter alia, by the possibility of accepting any sort of data as purely hypothetical, and reasoning correctly from them."[36] And, "Instead of just coordinating facts about the actual world, hypothetico-deductive reasoning draws out the implications of possible statements and thus gives rise to a unique synthesis of the possible and necessary." In short, the individual develops logical and formal-rational patterns of thought at this stage.[37]

Self-identity at this stage is based on the individual's ability to think about the group to which one belongs and to question its rules and norms. As a result, "People at this stage can 'step back' and look at themselves as objects for the first time and begin to self-reflect. This 'third person' perspective enables the person to deal with abstract concepts and develop multiple solutions to problems."[38] This also means that "one starts to explore the nature of oneself in terms of traits through more ongoing introspection."[39]

---

[35] Kohlberg (1981, p. 409).
[36] Piaget (1995, p. 461).
[37] Some developmental psychologists who have continued Piaget's research have identified an important substage within this general stage, which they call "systematic order" (see Commons and Richards, 2003). However, other researchers would argue that systematic order belongs into the next stage, the "pluralistic."
[38] Ingersoll and Cook-Greuter (2007).
[39] Cook-Greuter (1999, p. 263).

Kegan describes self-awareness at this stage where,

> In separating itself from embeddedness in the interpersonal, the person authors a self that maintains a coherence across a shared psychological space and so achieves an identity. This authority, sense of self, self-dependence, or self-ownership is the hallmark of a new psychologic. In moving from "I am my relationships" to "I have relationships," there is a new subject organizing the new contents of experiences.[40]

In short, once again, the subject of the previous stage (being in relationships) becomes the object of the new stage (making sense of relationships).

For morality, this means that the individual can reflect on the group's rules and norms and can question these. According to Loevinger, an individual at this stage has internalized rules after having evaluated them objectively and not just because the group told him or her to accept them. Someone at this stage thus "evaluates and chooses the rules for himself. ... Thus rules are no longer absolutes, the same for everyone all the time; rather exceptions and contingencies are recognized."[41]

Some refer to this stage as "world-centric" because the self's center no longer is in the (ethnic) group, but an abstract world society of all humans. This stage is thus also a universalistic stage. As such, it is generally a stage that for a long time was seen as the maximum stage to which humans could develop psychologically and which would generally be reached by adulthood. However, as we will see in the next section, more recent research has shown that adults can develop beyond this stage, and I would even argue that it is necessary for them to do so if we are to move toward a more humane socialist society.

Adult Development

Just as with the development of neurobiology, the assumption that individual consciousness development ends with adulthood is false.

---

[40] Kegan et al. (1982, p. 114).
[41] Loevinger (1976, p. 21).

Many researchers have identified at least two more stages that lie beyond the formal operational or world-centric stage: the pluralistic and the integral.

5. Pluralistic/de-centered: Cognitively the individual at this stage begins to realize that the abstract rules, principles, and deductions that were arrived at through rational thought in the previous stage are still embedded in particular systems—systems of thought, of society, or of nature. That is, the individual realizes that different systems produce different abstract regularities. Another way of putting this is that the person realizes the context-boundedness of their thinking. As Cook-Greuter puts it, "The same thing means different things to different people. Self and context (object) form an interdependent system. There are as many truths as there are individuals. No truth can therefore be better than any other. Everything seems relative, undecidable, context-dependent."[42]

The relativization of what previously seemed to be universal truths can lead to relativism. For self-identity this means,

> Own sense of self is fluctuating, often seen as contradictory, inconsistent, made up of different subpersonalities. Since all is uncertain, [they] often concentrate on enjoying the experience of the here and now. They turn inward and are increasingly able to understand themselves in complex ways. ... Discovery of cultural and personal "assumptions" and own tendency towards defensive moves. [They] realize that reality is not out there, separate from the viewer as previously felt, but connected to the person who experiences it. Increasing ability to see how things are related and influence each other in non-linear ways.[43]

This is essentially the self that theorists of postmodernity describe, a self that is de-centered, context-bound, and relative.

For morality this means, according to Kohlberg, "What is right is being aware of the fact that people hold a variety of values and opinions,

---

[42] Cook-Greuter (1999, p. 263).
[43] Cook-Greuter (1999, p. 263).

that most values and rules are relative to one's group. These 'relative' rules should usually be upheld, however, in the interest of impartiality and because they are the social contract. Some nonrelative values and rights such as life, and liberty, however, must be upheld in any society and regardless of majority opinion."[44]

6. Integral/a-centric: Some developmental psychologists (particularly Clare Graves and Ken Wilber), argue that the transition from the pluralistic to the next stage, the integral, is a far more important and qualitatively different leap than any of the previous transitions because it is a stage at which the individual both recognizes the relativity of world views (that none is absolute) but also how they relate to each other and thus has a firmer footing in his or her own world view. Cognitively this expresses itself, according to Michael Commons and Francis Richards, in the creation of "new fields out of multiple metasystems."[45] Loevinger describes a person at this stage as someone who "is able to unite and integrate ideas that appear as incompatible alternatives to those at lower stages; there is a high toleration for ambiguity."[46] Similarly, Cook-Greuter also argues that this stage has to do with the overcoming of dualisms: They "know empirically and intuitively that there is no clear subject/object separation, no either/or, yet they are stymied by trying to transcend this state of affairs."[47]

For one's self-identity this means that one recognizes that one's self is the result of a developmental process, just as the self of others is. A person at this stage "sees himself and others as having motives that have developed as a result of past experiences. The interest in development thus represents a further complication of psychological causation. Self-fulfillment becomes a frequent goal, partly supplanting

---

[44] Kohlberg (1981, p. 409).
[45] Commons and Richards (2003, p. 199).
[46] Loevinger (1976, p. 23).
[47] Cook-Greuter (1999, p. 88).

achievement."[48] An important aspect of this thus is the integration of body and mind, of animal self and rational human self, which is why Wilber refers to this stage as being "centauric," based on the mythological creature that is part horse and part human.[49] Another consequence is relatively high self-esteem, according to Cook-Greuter, because they "have found relative balance between inner and outer, body and mind, thought and feelings."[50]

Regarding morality, universalism makes a comeback in a relativized form, in that persons at this stage are "guided by universal ethical principles. Particular laws or social agreements are usually valid because they rest on such principles. When laws violate these principles, one acts in accordance with the principle not the law. Principles are universal principles of justice: the equality of human rights and respect for the dignity of human beings as individuals."[51] Another principle, which is derived from the recognition that we are all beings enmeshed in a process of development and the conviction "that higher development is better and closer to truth (...). They are therefore often invested in helping others to grow."[52] Ken Wilber thus describes the "Basic Moral Intuition" of this stage as one that is guided by the principle of fostering the "greatest development for the greatest number of beings."[53] This principle is also echoed in Marx and Engels' ideal of communism as being a society in which "the full development of each is a condition for the full development of all."[54]

In practical terms, at the integral/a-centric stage individuals apply universalistic principles in their actions while evaluating the outcomes in accordance with the context in which the actions take place and adjusting their actions, if necessary, in case these outcomes violate

---

[48] Loevinger (1976, p. 26).
[49] Wilber (1981).
[50] Cook-Greuter (1999, p. 83).
[51] Kohlberg (1981, p. 410). Gandhi, Martin Luther King Jr., and Ralph Waldo Emerson expressed this type of morality in their writings on civil disobedience.
[52] Cook-Greuter (1999, p. 83).
[53] Wilber (2000c, p. 306).
[54] Marx & Engels ([1848] 1998), *The Communist Manifesto*.

their principles. Another way putting this is that actions are guided by both universal principles and context-bound assessments. Here we can see how this stage (just as the ones before it) creatively enacts a new morality in the process of transcending but including the previous (very context-bound) stage.

Now that we have established how consciousness changes or transforms itself according to neurobiological and psychological research, we have a basis for figuring out how consciousness relates to social institutions and to society more generally. After all, the whole point of this analysis is to figure out what kind of consciousness can bring about post-capitalist "commonism." But before we do that, it makes sense to take a brief detour into how this approach to the issue of consciousness relates to more typical Marxist approaches to consciousness, which usually emphasize the role of material interests, class consciousness, and ideology when discussing how consciousness fits into the problem of revolutionary social change.

3

Society, Ideology, and Class

The key to understanding how consciousness development relates to social change or social evolution is to realize that just as humans develop their consciousness through an individual learning process, so do societies, through a social learning process. In short, the social learning process parallels the individual learning process. This is not to say that the two are identical but that they correspond to one another. That is, when a critical mass of individuals reaches a particular level of consciousness, this can—but does not have to—provoke changes in social structure and organization and in the larger culture, which end up reinforcing this new level of consciousness through the education and socialization of many more individuals into this consciousness.[1]

The main sociological question in this process is, what drives or moves changes in consciousness forward? Also, from a socialist perspective—a perspective that is interested in overcoming domination

---

[1] Many social theorists have proposed this type of theory of social change, perhaps beginning with Herbert Spencer and carried on with Freud's application of the biological theory that "ontogeny recapitulates phylogeny" (one of the perhaps easiest to discredit approaches to social change). Other, far more sophisticated approaches have been proposed by Elias ([1939] 2012), Gebser ([1949] 1991), Habermas ([1976] 1979), and Wilber (1981, 2000a), among many others. This approach is also echoed in what is known as the "great chain of being" (see Lovejoy ([1936] 2009)), which has been espoused in one form or another by philosophers since the time of Aristotle and Plotinus, up to Hegel and beyond. This theory of social evolution has received plenty of criticisms, especially in the twentieth century and particularly from postmodernist thinkers. I will explore some of these criticisms in Chapter 4 and argue that while many of the criticisms are valid, there are ways of conceiving this theory so that it avoids the problems of many earlier attempts to theorize the connection between individual development and social evolution.

and oppression—we need to ask, what is the relationship between power and the transformation of consciousness?

In the previous chapter, I suggested that a crucial catalyst for the advance in consciousness development is crisis: when a particular form of consciousness confronts a crisis that it cannot resolve and thus provokes either a reorganization of consciousness at the next higher level, or a downshifting of consciousness to a previous level (which generally provides for a far more temporary resolution). So, for example, if a child gradually begins to realize that the needs of others are irreconcilable with his or her own needs, a higher-level resolution must be found, which lies in abiding by societal norms. This would constitute the transition from pre-conventional to conventional moral consciousness. In effect, it is the clash between consciousness (the realm of the ideal) and the material reality that provokes changes in both. This type of crisis, of course, can take place not only in childhood but also at any time in adulthood and on a societal level.

Marx and the Relationship Between Material Reality and Consciousness

There is a lot of confusion in socialist literature about exactly what Marx meant by the relationship between the material and the ideal. On the one hand, he seemed to argue that the economy is primary and that all other social formations and institutions are derivative of economic processes. This conception of Marx's materialism comes out in his concepts of "economic base" and "superstructure," where he argues that it is the base that "conditions" the superstructure:

> In the social production of their existence, men inevitably enter into definite relations, which are independent of their will, namely [the] relations of production appropriate to a given stage in the development of their material forces of production. The totality of these relations of production constitutes the economic structure of society, the real

foundation, on which arises a legal and political superstructure, and to which correspond definite forms of consciousness. The mode of production of material life conditions the general process of social, political, and intellectual life.[2]

On the other hand, Marx also seemed to argue that it is not just economic processes that are primary, but material reality (or social being) as a whole that is primary and that consciousness is derivative of material reality, which is why Marx is generally considered to be a "materialist" philosopher who was opposed to the "idealism" of Hegel. The next sentence in the section quoted above Marx states, "It is not the consciousness of men that determines their being, but, on the contrary, their social being that determines their consciousness."[3]

Marx's argument that economic processes are primary has often been distorted to make it sound like Marx was an economic determinist. This, however, is clearly false, since Marx merely says that the economy *conditions* everything else and that each generation creatively modifies the economic conditions it finds:

> [E]ach stage [of history] contains a material result, as sum of productive forces, a historically created relation to nature and of individuals to one another, which is handed down to each generation from its predecessor; a mass of productive forces, capital funds and circumstances, which on the one hand is indeed modified by the new generation, but on the other also prescribes for it its conditions of life and gives it a definite development, a special character. It shows that circumstances make men just as much as men make circumstances.[4]

One of the foremost interpreters of Marx, István Mészáros, explains that the relationship between base and superstructure cannot possibly be a deterministic one because that would make the argument for socialist revolution incoherent:

---

[2] Marx ([1859] 1970, p. 20).
[3] Marx ([1859] 1970, p. 21).
[4] Marx ([1846] 1970, p. 59).

The relative autonomy of superstructural complexes establishes the possibility of breaking the stranglehold of direct material/economic determinations under favorable circumstances. Without the relative autonomy that arises out of the interplay of superstructural mediations upon which the possibility of a break is founded, the Marxian discourse on socialism—which stipulates the necessity of such a break—would be totally incoherent.[5]

In effect, it is absurd for a Marxist or socialist to argue that social change or transformations occur first and primarily on the level of the base, since it would make class consciousness and class struggle completely superfluous. This, in turn, would completely negate Marx's dictum that history is the history of class struggle.

However, what seems to be more ambiguous in Marx's work is the relationship between material or social reality and mental reality or consciousness. With regard to this relationship Marx appears to postulate more of a one-sided relationship between the two ("social being determines consciousness"). Part of the reason for this ambiguity lies in Marx's apparent conflation of social being with economic reality or institutions.

While it is probably true that economic institutions and processes have an important impact on all other institutions in society in one way or another, this does not mean that economic material reality alone determines consciousness and culture. Economic institutions are just one set of institutions that are part of the material reality of any given society. Also, economic institutions themselves are shaped by the consciousness of the individuals that make them up. For example, it would be extremely difficult, if not impossible, to maintain feudal institutions with individuals who adhere to capitalist consciousness. Similarly (and this is the larger point of this book), it would be practically impossible to maintain socialist institutions with individuals who adhere to capitalist consciousness.[6] In short, as I outlined in Chapter 1,

---

[5] Mészáros (2011, p. 61).
[6] Maurice Godelier (1986) makes a similar argument, while still maintaining a Marxist perspective.

we ought to conceive of societies as having an exterior (material) and an interior (consciousness, culture) dimension, where neither dimension "determines" the other but where each influences the other in a dialectical process. To put it in terms described in Chapter 2, one could also say that the external material reality and internal reality of consciousness and culture take form in a process of enactment, whereby institutions shape consciousness and consciousness shape institutions.

As a matter of fact, this enactivist or dialectical conception fits with Marx's critique of both Hegel's idealism, which took only consciousness to be ultimate source of reality, and of Feuerbach's materialism, which saw material reality as the ultimate source. When Marx refers to "social being" as the determining factor of consciousness, he actually does not mean merely material reality. Rather, by "social being" Marx refers to the socially constituted individual, who becomes an acting and thinking subject through his or her activity in society (through social *praxis*). The sociologist Anthony Giddens explains Marx's position this way: "Human consciousness is conditioned in the dialectical interplay between subject and object, in which man actively shapes the world he lives in at the same time as it shapes him."[7]

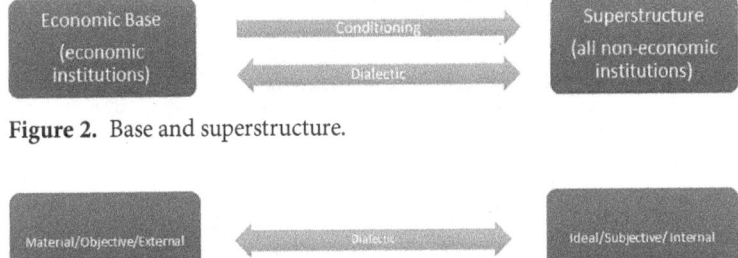

Figure 2. Base and superstructure.

Figure 3. Material and ideal.

To repeat, this enacting dialectic of subject and object is very different, though, from the dialectic between economic base and

---

[7] Giddens (1971, p. 21).

superstructure. Not only are we talking about different concepts in the two dialectics, but in the relationship between base and superstructure, the base, because of its fundamental life-supporting nature, shapes or "conditions" the superstructure (Figure 2). However, in the subject–object dialectic, the relationship is more reciprocal (Figure 3).

In short, we need to think of the economic base as the set of institutions that have both an interior/subjective and an exterior/objective dimension. That is, the interior (values and meaning systems) and the exterior (objective relationships) are in a dialectical relationship with one another where neither "determines" nor "conditions" the other. However, the economic base (economic institutions), which has an interior and an exterior dimension (both an economic culture and an economic structure), does shape or condition (but does not determine) the rest of society's institutions (which also have interior and exterior dimensions). We can thus diagram the relationships as follows (Figure 4).

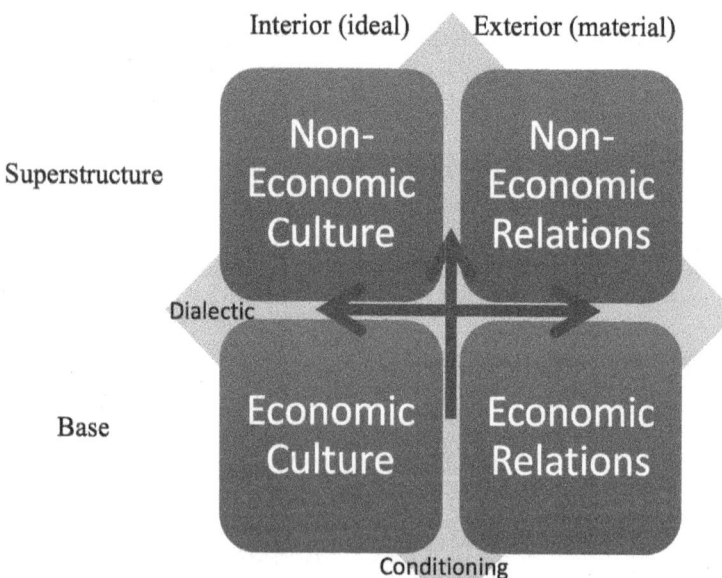

Figure 4. Base vs. superstructure and interior vs. exterior.

Technical and Moral Crises as Drivers of Social Transformation

According to Habermas, however, Marx's conception of social change does not provide much detail as to exactly how crises lead to revolutionary change, especially regarding transformations of consciousness.[8] Ultimately, Marx's explanation for this process relies on transformations in the production process, that is, in the "forces of production" (technology), which involve changing cognitive capacities. While it is certainly true that impasses or crises in technical knowledge (in science and technology), such as an inability to solve a technical problem, can provoke changes in cognitive capabilities, this does not explain how moral and practical capabilities are transformed. More than that, the crises that we confront as a society are not only of a technological or scientific nature but require transformation of moral and practical consciousness for the resolution of the crisis.[9] Habermas:

> [T]he [human] species learns not only in the dimension of technically useful knowledge decisive for the development of productive forces but also in the dimension of moral-practical consciousness decisive for structures of interaction.[10]

These problems or crises occur to a large extent in the economic realm:

> In its developmental dynamics, the change of normative structures remains dependent on evolutionary challenges posed by unresolved,

---

[8] Habermas ([1976] 1979).
[9] One could argue that in Marx's conception of social transformation the relations of production, which Marx says enter into contradiction with the forces of production (production technology), essentially represent the moral–practical dimension that Habermas talks about. If this is an accurate interpretation, Habermas merely provides greater detail to Marx's more general outline. One should also note that Marx focuses on this process relatively little in his later work, suggesting that he did not consider it as important as many of his followers have made it out to be.
[10] Habermas ([1976] 1979, p. 148).

economically conditioned, system problems and on learning processes that are a response to them. (Emphasis mine)[11]

For example, in our current situation, we could attempt to solve the global warming crisis with purely scientific and technological means (applying our cognitive capacities), but a better and more lasting solution would require a moral and practical transformation in the way we relate to each other and to nature. Similarly, we could try to solve the problems of increasing inequality and increasing poverty with an economic–technical fix (e.g., higher interest rates, changing money supply or exchange rate, lower taxes, etc.), but a long-term solution would require a reorienting of practical social behavior in general, toward, for example, greater solidarity with the poor.[12] What these examples also demonstrate is a more general point that Habermas makes about the "dialectic of progress," whereby every advance in technological and scientific (or cognitive) capabilities also tends to bring with it greater and possibly deeper crises, which, in turn, are only resolved in the longer term through a transformation of moral–practical capabilities. That is, "The dialectic of progress can be seen in the fact that with the acquisition of problem-solving abilities new problem situations come to consciousness."[13] This in turn means that, "With each evolutionarily new problem situation there arise new scarcities, scarcities of technically feasible power, politically established security, economically produced value, and culturally supplied meaning; and thus new historical needs come to the fore."[14]

Once we recognize that moral–practical change is essential for solving societal crises and for real and lasting social change, largely to resolve crises that first present themselves as being of a technical-cognitive nature, we can start to decipher in greater detail the different stages through which societal change appears to move. Before we do

---

[11] Habermas ([1976] 1979, p. 98).
[12] In Chapter 6 I will return to these examples in detail.
[13] Habermas ([1976] 1979, p. 164).
[14] Habermas ([1976] 1979, p. 166).

so, however, it is necessary to highlight some important caveats about this process.

First, social evolution is not an inevitable process, but there can be long periods of standstill or even reversals to earlier stages. Second, whether a society advances, stagnates, or even reverses in its evolutionary process, this ultimately depends on historical circumstances and contingencies—that is, progress is not inevitable. Third, just as there are a wide variety of "lines" of consciousness development (cognitive, moral, interpersonal, etc.), there may be several "lines" of social evolution, beyond merely the technical-cognitive and the moral–practical, which can evolve independently of one another and at different speeds in different societies. Fourth, while there are parallels or correspondences between levels of consciousness development and levels of social evolution, they are not identical because the external pressures on an individual and on a society are different. Fifth, just because a society has evolved to a higher stage than another society does not mean (as it has all too often in theories of social evolution) that this gives the more evolved society the right to dominate the other society. As a matter of fact, such domination of one society over another generally contributes toward reversing or slowing social evolution (more on this in Chapter 4).

Finally, and perhaps most importantly for a theory on consciousness and socialism, the modern capitalist stage of social evolution is not the highest social stage possible, just as the post-formal or world-centric stage of consciousness development in the individual is not the highest stage possible.[15] However, before we can examine the higher, possibly socialist, stages of societal evolution, it makes sense to briefly review the earlier stages and how they correspond to the stages of consciousness development.

---

[15] This is an aspect that Habermas never seriously considers in his theory of social evolution. As a result, his theory ends up not only explaining but also justifying and supporting the latest developmental stage of the existing capitalist society.

While I will conduct this review along the economic "line" of social evolution, it is important to remember that the number of lines or tracks of societal evolution increases, the higher the evolutionary stage. This increase in the number of evolutionary lines (or tracks or subsystems) occurs because as a society becomes more complex, it develops more and more specialized and relatively autonomous institutions to deal with different aspects of society. For example, while early societies tend to be relatively non-differentiated so that economic, political, familial, educational, institutions are all meshed, in more complex societies each of these becomes more independent and autonomous ("differentiated" in the sociological jargon).

Another key factor to keep in mind is that there is absolutely nothing inevitable or necessary about a society's evolution. Societies probably have an equal probability of advancing as they do stagnating or returning to a previous stage. These stages merely allow us to identify certain common tendencies in societal development, in their rough outlines, while also keeping in mind that the particulars and specifics in each society can be vastly different.

Stages of Societal Evolution
(Culture – Polity – Economy)

The terminology for the following stages of societal development are largely based on the work of the Swiss philosopher Jean Gebser (1991), but very similar stages can be found in most accounts of societal evolution.[16] Also, the end of each era represents when a majority of the world's societies moved on to the next stage, but this of course means

---

[16] The two other philosophers on whom much of this book is based and who also outline stages of societal evolution are Jürgen Habermas ([1976] 1979) and Ken Wilber (1981). While there is nearly universal agreement in the social sciences about the unfolding of these different stages in the course of human history, there is plenty of disagreement about the details of this unfolding and exactly what the causal factors are in moving it forward. Some of the explanations are thus based on my own inferences of others' research.

that there still are plenty of societies and individuals that continue to function at an earlier stage.

According to Gebser's conception of cultural evolution, worldviews passed from what he called magical, to mythic, to mental, and to integral. Two things to keep in mind about the first stage mentioned, the magical. First, it is rather difficult to know much about the worldview or thinking of prehistoric tribal cultures precisely because they did not leave a written record of their culture. And we cannot assume that today's tribal cultures are the same as those that existed thousands of years ago, since they likely have changed and evolved since then. Second, some anthropologists would argue that some prehistoric tribal cultures were more advanced than the feudal societies that replaced them—that feudalism was a regression to a more primitive way of thinking.[17] Whether this is true is difficult to answer, but it could very well be the case in many cases precisely because some tribal or hunter-gatherer societies might have developed their culture beyond the mythic-feudal ones in the cognitive and moral lines of development, even if they did not develop feudal-agricultural technology. I will return to this question later, when I discuss the importance that later stages integrate earlier stages of development.

Magical – Clan – Hunter-Gatherer (50,000 BC–5,000 BC)[18]

Since the emergence of the human species—homo sapiens—into what anthropologists call "behavioral modernity" about 50,000 years ago, humans began to develop a cultural worldview that Gebser and others call "magical." In this worldview, which is similar to the psychological developmental stage known as the ego-centric or preoperational stage, these cultures tend to see the world as an extension of their will. In other words, the self and the environment are not yet fully differentiated and so individuals believe that they can control the world, at least to

---

[17] See, for example Graeber and Wengrow (2021), who make this argument.
[18] The first term in each of these subheadings captures the culture, the second the politics, and the third the economics of each phase.

a limited degree, by mere willpower or incantation. Since this is the stage at which humans begin to develop images and symbols of their surrounding world, they also tend to believe that these images and symbols not only represent objects but embody an aspect of these. Wilber thus states,

> [E]arly images and symbols are *not differentiated* clearly from the objects they represent. Thus, it seems that to manipulate the image is to actually change the object. If I make an image of you and stick a pin into the image, something bad will actually happen to you. ... Mind and world are not clearly differentiated, so their characteristics tend to get fused and confused, "magically."[19]

This explains why during this stage humans often drew their prey before hunting, believing that the image of the hunted and slain animal would help them in the actual hunt.[20]

The political dimension in this type of culture is usually organized along clan-based lines, of relatively small cooperatively organized groups,[21] in which all members had equal status, even between men and women.

The economy in such societies was based on hunting and gathering, which is why it supported only relatively small groups. While this stage lasted for a very long time, relative to the human existence on earth, for at least 45,000 years for the vast majority of the human population, gradually populations grew too large for the amount of food available to hunter-gatherers in a particular territory and consciousness developed in response to these pressures. Humans thus learnt to plant and turned toward horticulture, which meant working with small tools

---

[19] (Wilber, 2000a, p. 157).
[20] At this point, some readers might notice that there is a close parallel between the magical worldview and the one that is predominant in contemporary "new age" spirituality, with its emphasis on the individual being able to "manifest" their desires through the so-called law of attraction. One could argue, though, that this contemporary spirituality integrates magical thinking within an integral worldview. Whether this is indeed the case is an open question, though, and would need to be examined on a case-by-case basis. If it does integrate the magical, this could be an example of "re-enchanting" the world, as some theorists, such as Silvia Federici (2018), have called for. I will discuss this question in greater detail in Chapter 6.
[21] Bowles and Gintis (2011).

and settling down in a particular region for a longer period of time than was previously the case. The transition toward the horticultural mode of production coincided with a transition in consciousness toward a mythical culture.

Mythic – Feudal – Horticultural/Agricultural

With the onset of the so-called Neolithic revolution, humans began to conduct small-scale agriculture, domesticate animals, and set up more permanent settlements. In the first phase, the primary form of agriculture was horticultural, using a hoe and other small handheld tools. Humans began to appeal to otherworldly beings that could interfere on their behalf and developed elaborate mythologies around these beings, spirits, or deities. This type of society resembles the ethnocentric or what Piaget called concrete operational stage of individual development, when a child learns that it is not in control and that it must appeal to others, mainly to the parents, in order to get what it wants. This, in turn, leads to identification with the parents and the following of the parents' rules and norms. Similarly, in the mythic worldview people identify with their group and learn to follow the group's rules, norms, and mythology.

Political organization at this stage takes on a wide variety of forms but is generally one based on status differences, where the leaders have some sort of special status that is justified via mythology, that is, via religion and tradition. Chieftains, kings, emperors, pharaohs, and the like derive their power from religiously justified status differences, with which they are born or anointed by religious leaders. The production of an agricultural surplus brought about greater material inequality and therefore also greater differences in political power among the members of the society. As agriculture was developed with the invention of the plow, the surplus grew, and political and economic inequality grew even more.

The combination of increasing political and economic inequality with the failures of effective appeals to mythological deities for the alleviation of suffering eventually led to a questioning of these mythologies as well as of political authority. This then opened the path toward the next worldview, the rational or world-centric. It is no coincidence that Enlightenment philosophy and the French Revolution coincided.

Modern Rational – Liberal Democratic – Industrial Capitalist and Industrial State-Socialist

The first flowering of the rational worldview and the rejection of mythology, around 500 BC, both in ancient Greece and in ancient India, did not result in capitalism, however, nor was it initiated by perceived injustices. Rather, it was centered on a privileged elite in both regions. Exactly what caused the flowering of ancient Greek and Indian philosophy is not known. But the Enlightenment philosophers of the seventeenth and eighteenth centuries, who were inspired by ancient Greek philosophy, Martin Luther's revolt against Catholic injustices, and the church's reaction during the Counter-Reformation, gave an important new impetus to the development of the rational worldview. One could thus say that the transition toward the rational worldview lasted more than 2,500 years and is still continuing.

As the rational worldview became increasingly consolidated in the general population, it provided a rationale for the demand for democracy in the political sphere and formed the behavioral basis, as well as justification, for capitalism. More and more people, especially in the cities and towns, began to reject their lot in life and worked on building successful businesses (and, according to Max Weber, initially with the religious justifications that the protestant ethic gave them). Also, with the deepening of Enlightenment philosophy came the development of empirical science and a tremendous boost to the development of technology. This, in turn, fed into the industrial revolution, which formed the main economic basis for the transition from agricultural feudalism toward industrial capitalism (and industrial state socialism). Finally, with the gradually increasing triumphs of the increasingly wealthy capitalist class over the aristocracies and monarchies in Europe and in North and South America, capitalist class governance, in the form of (initially very limited) representative democracy, was eventually consolidated in the political sphere.

In some parts of the world, state socialism gained the upper hand, which is also the result of a quintessentially rational worldview, but which is oriented around collective solidarity instead of individualism. Instead of organizing production and distribution in accordance with market rationality, it sought to organize them in accordance with state rationality, that is, with a centralized state plan. That this type of society did not result in liberal representative democracy in the political sphere had something to do with both historical circumstances (the assault from capitalist societies) and with the ways in which centralized planning and control undermined democratic decision-making. Eventually, the lack of even the limited form of representative democracy and an increasing bureaucratic inefficiency contributed to the collapse of these regimes and their joining the capitalist "mainstream" (whereby China has taken a more gradual route than the Soviet Union by slowly embracing aspects of market rationality, while still holding on to many socialist ideals).

Pluralist/Postmodern – Neoliberal Digital Capitalism

Almost since the start of the emergence of the rational worldview (especially in the Eastern philosophy of Buddhism), but particularly since Marx and Nietzsche in the West, philosophers realized that Enlightenment philosophy was not all it claimed to be. That is, it established universal rights and promised progress and justice for all, but at the same time, it became increasingly clear that this worldview could not fulfill its promises. More and more critics of modern rationality came to realize that the universalizing rational self was merely universalizing its own perspective on the world and thereby excluding everyone who was not able to disseminate their own perspective. More than that, with the help of the rational worldview some of the greatest atrocities mankind has ever known were committed, always under the guise of progress and rationality.

The pluralistic or postmodern worldview, though, did not come into its own until the late 1960s, when more and more people rebelled against the supposed rationality of war, sexism, racism, and ecological destruction. This worldview eventually became quite strong in the humanities and social sciences in academia in the 1980s and 1990s. It expressed itself as a profound critique of the Enlightenment paradigm of representation[22]—the idea that we can know the world simply by looking at it and describing it. These critics pointed out how we have no unmediated knowledge of the world because all our knowledge is always mediated by language and by relationships of power and domination. Taken to an extreme, this pluralist worldview ("pluralist" because no perspective is privileged) often ended up endorsing forms of relativism.

Just as with previous stages, the shift toward the new worldview was accompanied by changes in politics, technology, and the economy. In the economy, these changes have often been described as the transition toward "late capitalism" (sometimes also known as "postindustrial society"), which shifts the focus of capitalism away from industrial mass production toward more personalized "just in time" production. Along with this, work becomes more "flexible," finance capital becomes dominant over other forms of capital, and service industry employment outnumbers manufacturing employment. Most importantly, though, is that information technology enables this transition and in effect transforms all aspects of society. I refer to this phase as "neoliberal digital capitalism."

While political structures themselves have so far not changed much since the introduction of liberal democratic regimes, mainly because the constitutions on which these regimes are based tend to be relatively

---

[22] Buddhist philosophy already developed a critique of representation since the very first emergence of the rational worldview, around 500 BC, when the Buddha spread his teachings. For example, a popular Buddhist saying admonishes followers "not to confuse the moon with the finger that is pointing at the moon."

fixed and inflexible, the modality in which politics is conducted has changed quite a bit. In the postmodern or late capitalist era, politics has become more influenced by global economic pressures. That is, the late capitalist state is being retooled, so to speak, to support a more flexible and globally financialized economy.[23] Also, since ecological crises do not recognize borders, these crises have an impact on nation-states even when these do not contribute to the crises themselves. This leaves national governments with relatively little power to resist economic and ecological pressures and without meaningful global political tools to do much about the crises.

Despite having laid out some of the outlines of the pluralist political, economic, and cultural domains, it is too early to provide a full account of what this stage looks like since we are only at the beginning of this stage. It is even possible that this stage will never come to full bloom because the ecological, economic, and political crises that the world faces will force a rapid transition to a new stage or toward a regression to an earlier stage.[24]

Integral – Post-Capitalism – Participatory Society/Participatory Socialism

The realization that the postmodernist–pluralist worldview cannot solve the global crises that humanity faces ought to serve as a spur to the development of the integral worldview, which is not only explicitly global in outlook but is also a worldview that integrates the diversity of previous perspectives while keeping the best of what they all have to offer.[25] However, since we know this worldview only through the observation of individuals and small groups, and not on a society-wide scale, we can only speculate what a society might look like where integral consciousness is dominant. I will return to this central issue in

---

[23] See especially Robinson (2004) and a vast array of literature on globalization.
[24] I provide a fuller account of this stage in Chapter 5.
[25] This is a key argument that both Rudolf Bahro ([1987] 1994) and Peter Sloterdijk ([1983] 1988) have made, that the existential crisis facing humanity is something that could raise people's consciousness to a new level.

Chapter 6. It is my contention, though, that integral consciousness is the form of consciousness that is necessary for realizing a truly socialist—that is, a more just, democratic, participatory, and free—society.

The Question of Ideology

But what about ideology? For over a century, many socialist theorists have argued that one of the key subjective factors that prevents the emergence of socialism is the lack of a socialist ideological hegemony. How does the concept of ideology relate to the theory of consciousness development?

There are a wide variety of conceptions of what ideology means, but despite this wide variety, what they all seem to have in common is the notion that ideology is a kind of "lens" through which we view the world around us that either distorts our view of reality or gives us a better or worse view of this world than we would have with a different ideological lens. In other words, the theories of ideology fall into two general categories: ideology as necessary and unavoidable distortion versus ideology as unnecessary and avoidable distortion.

For example, Marx conceived of ideology in the latter sense, as something avoidable, which gives workers a false—even inverted—view of society. According to Marx, capitalist ideology gives workers the impression that not they, but the capitalist is the creator of wealth and value. Workers are thus tricked into believing in the necessity and inevitability of the capitalist-worker relationship. In his later work, Marx departed from the use of the concept of ideology and instead referred to an even more insidious dynamic, the "fetishism of commodities," whereby the capitalist production process itself (rather than a crude capitalist propaganda machine) creates the illusion that social relationships between people are the same as the relationship between things. In other words, due to workers' alienation in the production process, because they are involved in only one small part of it, they do not realize that the things they produce are the result of a societal process and come to believe it is objective or unrelated to them. Marx thus wrote, "A commodity is a mysterious thing, simply because in it the social character of men's labor appears to them as an objective character stamped upon the product of that labor." He went on to say, "It is a definite social relation between men which assumes, in their eyes, the form of a relation between things."[26] In short, socially and historically developed relationships come to appear to be eternal, fixed, and unchangeable in capitalism. Another word for this is reification.

While Marx's conception of ideology was mostly pejorative (but not always so, as he seemed to be slightly inconsistent in his use of the term) and contrasted it with science, Lenin developed a more neutral conception of ideology, where ideology simply stood for the ideas and belief systems that people have. The key, for Lenin, was to promote the right kind of ideology, the socialist ideology, which represents the best interests of the working class and to oppose capitalist ideology, which represents the ideology of the bourgeoisie. According to Lenin, "[T]he *only* choice is bourgeois or socialist ideology."[27] Lenin came to this realization because the working class clearly did not embody socialist ideology on its own, and so it needed an outside force, an avant-garde party of professional revolutionaries, to carry this ideology into the working class. Workers on their own would only develop "trade union consciousness," which means "the ideological enslavement of the workers by the bourgeoisie."[28]

This class-bound and neutral conception of ideology came to dominate nearly all socialist thinking of the twentieth century. However, some, such as Georg Lukács, introduced a new issue, which is the idea that some ideologies or forms of class consciousness could be "true" and others "false," where their truth value depended on whether the ideology espoused is in the material interest of the class that holds it. In the case of Lukács and in many other theorists thereafter, though, the

---

[26] Marx (1977, p. 436).
[27] Lenin ([1902] 1961, p. 156).
[28] Lenin ([1902] 1961, p. 157).

problem remained as to how workers would acquire socialist ideology and class consciousness.

Another key socialist theorist, Antonio Gramsci, shared this neutral notion of ideology but tried to overcome the problem of how to develop and promote socialist ideology by arguing that it had to come from within the working class, via its own "organic" intellectuals. Since bourgeois ideology had become so dominant in capitalist societies as to be hegemonic and even took on the appearance of common sense, the working class and its organic intellectuals would have to launch an ideological offensive in society in general, not just among workers, to gain the upper hand. This ideological counter-hegemony would have to be created via new media outlets, new educational institutions, and new cultural traditions (folklore).[29]

The work of Herbert Marcuse took a closer look at the ways in which ideological reification processes in the broader culture hinder consciousness transformation. Marcuse illustrated the many ways in which capitalism changes the culture in such a way as to project the impression that the present is eternal; that real social change is impossible because the society that which currently exists is its most rational form. To put it slightly differently, as one Marcuse commentator explains, "Where before workers' obedient behavior was exacted by imposing on them an ideological conception of dutiful behavior, today they are kept in harness in a culture that purges all memories and visions of transcendental possibility."[30] In short, capitalist culture becomes "one-dimensional" in that nothing within capitalist culture points to transcendent possibilities. Examples of this one-dimensionality can be found in political concepts, such as "liberty" or "democracy," whose meanings become identical with social reality so that the concept of democracy refers to US democracy and nothing more or beyond the currently existing forms of democracy. As a result, to eliminate the possibility of a different future, such a one-dimensional society must

---

[29] Gramsci ([1947] 2011).
[30] Agger (1992, p. 136).

also banish any understanding of the past, or at least make the past look as much like the present as possible.

The theory of science known as positivism models this one-dimensionality because positivism argues that the only things we can consider real or that we can consider for scientific analysis are those that we observe and quantify through a set of operations on the material world. Anything that cannot be operationalized in this way is not valid. So, for example, the study of democracy only has validity if the concept of democracy and its analysis is whittled down to specific procedures (operations) for its analysis, such as how many people vote, how many political parties there are, how transparent the electoral process is, and so on. Such an operationalization of the concept of democracy, however, eliminates its potentially explosive meanings, of establishing real emancipation and self-determination. "The concept is synonymous with the corresponding set of operations," wrote Marcuse.[31]

This one-dimensional culture comes about, according to Marcuse, because culture itself has become commodified. Capitalism does not sell only material commodities, but also symbolic or cultural commodities. It needs to do so to create false needs that help continue to drive consumption. As a result, "advanced industrial culture is *more* ideological than its predecessor, inasmuch as today the ideology is in the process of production itself."[32]

> The means of mass transportation and communication, the commodities of lodging, food, and clothing, the irresistible output of the entertainment and information industry carry with them prescribed attitudes and habits, certain intellectual and emotional reactions which bind the consumers more or less pleasantly to the producers and, through the latter, to the whole. The products indoctrinate and manipulate; they promote a false consciousness which is immune against its falsehood. ... Thus emerges a pattern of one-dimensional thought and behavior in which ideas, aspirations, and objectives that,

---

[31] Marcuse (1964, p. 13).
[32] Marcuse (1964, p. 11; emphasis in the original).

by their content, transcend the established universe of discourse and action are either repelled or reduced to terms of this universe. They are redefined by the rationality of the given system and of its quantitative extension.[33]

Marcuse's concept of one-dimensionality represents a deepening of the concept of reification in that he examines the many ways in which social processes and concepts have become objectified in that their multiple and self-transcendent potentials have been stripped by the capitalist consumer culture. Marcuse in effect equates one-dimensional consciousness with false consciousness, which is false in the sense that it falsely believes that the given social world is the best and only possible world.

Modern technology and what he called "technological rationality" further deepens this process of one-dimensionalization because technology has been developed primarily for the domination of nature and of society. Science and technology, as a result, come to serve this purpose, again reinforcing the notion that this is the only thing that science and technology are good for.

> The industrial society which makes technology and science its own is organized for the ever-more-effective domination of man and nature, for the ever-more-effective utilizations of its resources. It becomes irrational when the success of these efforts opens new dimensions of human realization.[34]

With the so-called linguistic turn of post-structuralism in philosophy and in the social sciences during the last twenty-five years of the twentieth century, the issue of ideology became increasingly moot. All interpretations of reality came to be seen as discourses that bear little or no relation to reality because we cannot know reality outside of our language and our discourses about it. All we can say is that different discourses and ideologies are effects of power, whereby the

---

[33] Marcuse (1964, p. 12).
[34] Marcuse (1964, p. 17).

more powerful manage to impose their preferred discourses on the less powerful. In effect, the neutral sense of ideology, as something that we always carry with us, becomes not only all-pervasive and unavoidable, but it is also impossible to evaluate whether one discourse or ideology is better or worse than another, since all discourses are merely different claims to power.[35]

Leaving aside for a moment the epistemological implications and problems of the postmodern position, one can see why the contemporary analysis of ideology has largely turned away from the issue of socialism and emancipation and toward what is known as "identity politics." In the postmodern conception, the issues of socialism and emancipation are far too entwined with western meta-narratives that have historically led to new forms of domination. Instead, the postmodern position turned toward a much more neutral examination of the different dominant discourses in society and toward a critique of the many ways in which western culture dominates various marginalized groups.

A social philosopher who more recently tried to reinvigorate the false consciousness approach toward ideology is Peter Sloterdijk. Sloterdijk[36] in a sense rescues Marx's original notion of ideology as being an inversion of a real state of affairs but argues that in contemporary societies people have come to recognize the falsity of the dominant ideology, all the while they still believe that they cannot do anything about it. Sloterdijk thus calls this form of consciousness "enlightened false consciousness," in that the critique of bourgeois ideology has been successful in clearing up people's illusions about capitalism, but that it also failed because they continue to believe that they are powerless

---

[35] This is, admittedly a bit of a caricature of the postmodern philosophy, but in its extreme forms, this is the view that came to be endorsed by many in the humanities and social sciences in the 1980s and 1990s. One of the strongest arguments in favor of this conception of discourse and ideology is presented by the "post-Marxist" theorists Ernesto Laclau and Chantal Mouffe (1985).

[36] Sloterdijk (1983). It should be noted, though, that in contrast to the other theorists discussed here, Sloterdijk is a decidedly nonsocialist (even anti-socialist) theorist. This does not mean that he is a bourgeois theorist, though, since his work resists conventional classification.

to change it. The result is a profound cynicism, which has become the predominant ideology in most capitalist societies. In effect, the reification of social relations that commodity fetishism implies has become even more entrenched because not even a general agreement with the critique of capitalism can overcome capitalism anymore. More than ever, according to Sloterdijk, Western societies have thus solidified the notion that "there is no alternative." The only hope for escape from this cynical ideology is a confrontation with our existential crises due to the possibilities of nuclear or ecological catastrophe.[37]

All these approaches to the problem of ideology focus on the different ways in which the hegemonic ideology of our time enables capitalism in one way or another. Indeed, the ways in which the dominant ideology supports capitalism are manifold. However, what all these approaches fail to do is to examine the *structure* of the different ideologies, which line up quite closely with the structures of consciousness that developmental psychologists have identified. Focusing merely on the ways in which the dominant ideology supports capitalism does not allow us to differentiate sufficiently between different ideologies and thus also makes it difficult to understand how the ideologies relate to each other and how capitalist ideology might be overcome with more than just ideology critique.

Historically speaking, political ideologies did not really develop until the time of the French Revolution, which represents a key date or high point in the separation or differentiation of politics, economics, and religion. Certainly, people disagreed over political ideas before this, but the development of coherent systems of ideas about politics to which groups adhered is a relatively recent phenomenon. I have already outlined the basic structures of these ideologies and how they correspond to different stages of consciousness development. However, as noted above, some ideologies, such as those of state socialism and of

---

[37] It is the predominant cynicism and the confrontation with this existential crisis that has caused the alter-globalization movement, as gathered in the World Social Forum, to proclaim as its slogan, "another world is possible." This happened, though, well after Sloterdijk first wrote his analysis of cynicism.

liberal democratic capitalism are quite different, even though they share the same stage in consciousness development. How might we further distinguish these two ideologies in terms of their basic structures?

One way to do this is to add more dimensions to the structures of ideology besides the vertical one of levels of consciousness development.[38] A second dimension would thus be the extent to which ideologies focus more on the individual or focus more on the collective. While both are eminently world-centric ideologies, liberalism tends to focus more on the individual, while state socialism tends to focus more on the collective. A third dimension would be the extent to which an ideology focuses more on interior explanations for resolving social issues, versus exterior explanations. That is, are social phenomena more the result of cultural or individual belief systems (the interior), or are they more the result of social, political, or economic structures (the exterior)? Traditional conservatives, for example, tend to argue that it is the interior values and belief systems of groups or individuals that are the cause of their good or bad fortune, while social democratic and socialist approaches tend to argue that it is the exterior structures and opportunities that are to blame. Finally, the fourth dimension for political ideologies would be how they evaluate the present—as positive and worth maintaining, as something that must be overcome in the direction of a new and unprecedented future, or as a deviation from a more positive and better past. In other words, is the present to be maintained, overcome via progress, or overcome via regress? These four dimensions of ideology can be combined into a diagram as in Figure 5.

Beginning at the bottom of Figure 5, at the ego-centric level, we cannot talk about coherent ideologies because the nature of the belief system is such that it is ego-centric, that is, centered on largely emotional control-oriented needs, which generally precludes world-centric rational elaboration (except in the form of post hoc rationalization).

---

[38] For elaboration of this section on the dimensions of ideology I owe a great debt to the philosophy of Ken Wilber (2000a) and his "all quadrants, all levels" approach. The ideas presented here are also published in Wilpert (2006).

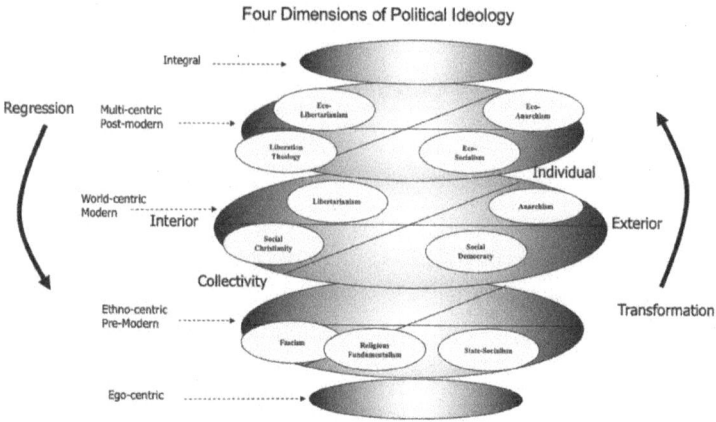

Figure 5. Four dimensions of political ideology.

As such, at this stage, the belief system does not fall into the interior–exterior or individual–collective dimensions mentioned above.

With the emergence of world-centric reasoning that is still embedded in a socio-centric societal context, ideologies begin to form and provide elaborate explanations for their ways of thinking. These ways focus on the importance of the collective since this is the context in which they emerge. Conservative religious thinking is particularly representative of this type of ideology. However, later, regressions from more modern thought emerge, such as fascism, which combines pseudoscientific (and thus irrational) racist reasoning and nationalism. Also, state-socialism, which began as a preeminently world-centric ideology of liberation devolves into collective groupthink where what the party and the leadership says is more important than individual rational thought.

Ideologies come into their own with the full emergence of the world-centric stage of consciousness development, where people rationally elaborate political and economic belief systems from different perspectives, with some emphasizing the collective, some the individual, some interior causation (culture), and some exterior causation (social structure). Since the ego returns in the world-centric stage, after having integrated its social and emotional dimensions, more individually oriented ideologies, such as liberalism, libertarianism, and anarchism emerge. Here libertarianism tends to focus on the interior and individual, believing that everyone must rely on themselves and that their success or failure is mainly determined by their individually held values. Most forms of anarchism (but certainly not all) argue that libertarianism's hyper-individualism can only result in a dog-eat-dog world and thus incorporate insights about the need to pay attention to social structures and organization, even while anarchism tends to reject the collective action of the state apparatus.

More collectively oriented ideologies develop as well of course, such as social Christianity, which is less dogmatic and more universalistic (or world-centric) than the earlier religious fundamentalism and focuses more on solidarity with the less fortunate. Its religious foundation, though, points to its belief in interior causation, in the importance of (Christian) culture and values. Rejecting the interior causation perspective are various forms of socialism, but particularly important here is social democracy (since state-socialism tended to devolve to an earlier stage once in power), which pays particular attention not only to the collective dimension of social well-being and solidarity but also to social structure and the exterior impediments and opportunities that society poses. It thus places a stronger emphasis on the role that the state must play in overcoming social-structural obstacles and in providing opportunities, via redistribution and public education.

The emergence of the pluralistic stage of consciousness means that earlier ideologies start to pay more attention to the larger social and ecological context in which societies exist. This means that social Christianity evolves into liberation theology as it takes the marginalized, particularly the poor, women, minorities, and the environment, as a central theme and incorporates an analysis of the systemic–structural causes of marginalization. A similar transformation occurs with other ideologies as they enter the pluralistic stage. Eco-anarchism (and its cousin, anarcho-feminism), eco-libertarianism, and eco-socialism (and its cousin, feminist socialism), all begin incorporating a multi-perspectival approach that includes previously marginalized views and beings. In effect, a convergence of ideologies takes place at this level, even though they all still maintain their identity due to their different origins.

Finally, at the integral stage, ideologies would converge even more because consciousness at this stage recognizes the need to overcome the dualisms of individual and collective and of interior and exterior causation, and becomes aware of the cumulative and developmental nature of perspectives.

Using this model of the dimensions of ideology, we can see that even though some of the ideologies at the world-centric stage tend to be anti-capitalist, such as anarchism and social democracy, they can easily fall back or support capitalism because structurally they reinforce the world-centric perspective of capitalism. It is only the post–world-centric ideologies, such as eco-socialism, eco-anarchism, and integral socialism that are both structurally and analytically post- or anti-capitalist.

The Problem of Class Consciousness and Class Struggle

Given the preceding analysis of the role of ideology, where does the issue of class consciousness, class struggle, and of class more generally fit in? After all, many Marxist theorists, such as Lenin and Lukács, posited that the correct ideology would help bring about class consciousness, which would then, in turn, provide the basis or rationale for class struggle. To help us make sense of the role of class consciousness, we first need to provide a clear definition of this concept, which, just as ideology, has been used in a wide variety of ways.

A traditional or orthodox Marxist conception of class consciousness, such as that of Bertell Ollman, identifies five elements of working-class consciousness.[39] First, members of a social class are class-conscious when their objective and subjective interests coincide. Second, workers

[39] Ollman (n.d.).

need to understand the functioning of capitalism and their place in it. Third, workers need to act and feel in solidarity with other workers and be in opposition to the capitalist class. Fourth, workers need to have a vision that a more just and democratic society is possible. Fifth, a group that belongs to the working class collectively shares class consciousness.

There are two problems with Ollman's conception of class consciousness. First, it assumes that we can identify objective class interests. But how would we identify such objective interests? Who is to say which interests are objective and which interests are merely ideological impositions? Such an approach that subscribes to objectively (or scientifically) identifiable interests is wide-open to dogmatic and authoritarian manipulation. Ollman describes objective interests as the practices and changes that serve the workers. No doubt he means practices and changes that lead to the emancipation or liberation of workers. The problem here isn't with the goal of emancipation, but rather that figuring out how to go about achieving this goal is unspecified. If this figuring out is left up to a revolutionary vanguard party, the result would almost inevitably mean that this party reserves the right to be the ultimate arbiter of what is in the objective interest of the working class.

Second, while the goal of emancipation is certainly worthwhile for the working class, it begs the question of what the achievement of this goal might mean for other classes. This depends, first, on how one defines the working class. It also implies that anyone who is not working class is potentially excluded from this emancipation. This, in turn, could easily lead to a justification for a new class society where merely the class that is on top has changed. For orthodox Marxists, however, this is not supposed to happen because the working class represents a "universal class," that is, a class that embodies the interests of humanity as a whole, or at least of the "immense majority."[40] This hypothesis, though, is also highly problematic and questionable.

---

[40] Marx (1998, p. 49): "All previous historical movements were movements of minorities, or in the interest of minorities. The proletarian movement is the self-conscious, independent movement of the immense majority, in the interest of the immense majority."

Nonetheless, even if we dismiss the orthodox Marxist conception of class consciousness, the issue of class consciousness remains an important one because for Marxism it answers the question of who the revolutionary subject or agent is, that is, which societal group drives the revolutionary socialist project forward. If we were to give up on working-class consciousness as the driving force for revolutionary or at least transformative change, we need to provide an answer to the question of who or what is the transformative agent or agency.

For Marx, there are both transformative (or revolutionary) dynamics and a revolutionary agent that make revolution possible. The transformative dynamics are several, according to Marx. First, there is the previously mentioned dialectic between the forces of production and the relations of production. Second, there is the dialectic between base and superstructure, and third, there is the class struggle between workers and the bourgeoisie. Each of these dynamics contributes to transformative or revolutionary change, which produces revolutionary class consciousness within the working class and this revolutionary consciousness, in turn, reinforces class conflict. This is what Marx means when he writes in his "Theses on Feuerbach," "The coincidence of the changing of circumstances and of human activity or self-change [*Selbstveränderung*] can be conceived and rationally understood only as revolutionary practice."[41]

I have already discussed the different ways in which the dynamic of relations and forces of production—reinterpreted in terms of Habermas's dynamic of moral–practical versus cognitive development—contribute to transformation. However, exactly who in Habermas's reconceived dialectic is the transformative agent? The answer is that it can be any group that has reached a stage of development in a given society and is in a position to transform society as whole. This usually means that it must be a group that has a certain "critical mass" that is large enough to bring a significant number of others, through societal learning

---

[41] Marx (1978, p. 144).

processes such as formal education and child rearing, into the new and higher stage as well.

However, if groups that belong to non-marginalized or dominant classes lead a consciousness transformation to the next higher level, it is unlikely that the transformation will result in a society that achieves social justice and includes marginalized and disenfranchised individuals and groups of society. This helps explain why the transition from feudalism to capitalism resulted in the exchange of one dominant class—the aristocracy—for another dominant class—the bourgeoisie. That is, the bourgeoisie represented a higher-level consciousness than the aristocracy, a world-centric consciousness, but did so from a position of privilege relative to other marginalized sectors of feudal society. Similarly, it could be argued that socialist transitions that resulted in the dominance of a state bureaucracy or coordinator class did not lead to true socialism because marginalized sectors did not play a leading role and thus did not contribute to the abolition of class domination.

Therefore, for a real socialist transformation or revolution to be possible, one that indeed strives for abolishing domination of all kinds, whether of class, gender, or race, the group that is leading this transformation process, because it represents a critical mass of individuals at the leading edge of consciousness development, would also have to include those who are affected by marginalization and domination and those who are in solidarity with them. In effect, the discussion of class and of class consciousness is essential for the achievement of socialism because it adds the elements of power and of solidarity to considerations of socialism and of consciousness.

Conclusion

Now that I have reviewed the different elements that need to be included in a comprehensive theory of consciousness and society, I can summarize how these elements fit together. First, stages of socio-cultural evolution correspond to specific stages of consciousness development because of social learning processes. Socio-cultural evolution, as well as consciousness development, can advance or retrocede in reaction to either cognitive or moral crises. These crises can take a wide variety of forms, whether economic, ecological, scientific, or social, for example. According to Marx, though, it is the economic crises that are more likely to drive revolutionary transformations of social conditions and of consciousness. According to others, such as Bahro and Sloterdijk, it is the existential ecological crisis that is most likely to push consciousness and thereby societal organization into the next (integral) level.

Second, capitalist ideology maintains capitalism and thereby presents an obstacle to further consciousness development. According to Marcuse, the one-dimensional ideology of late capitalism is particularly insidious because it denies the possibility of transformation, inoculates our minds so to speak, seducing us into believing that the way things are is the way they have always been and always will be, at the very least in terms of qualitative changes. However, a shift toward a more critical and less capitalist ideology is not enough for a real shift in consciousness that could resolve the multiple crises we face today. Rather, the shift in ideology and thus of consciousness must be toward a qualitatively new level if we are to resolve these problems.

Third, shifting consciousness to a higher level by itself is also not enough for fulfilling the ideals of socialism, if this shift is not accompanied by an understanding of how power disparities, such as those based on class, race, and gender, prevent or hinder consciousness development for the less powerful. Given that integral consciousness is generally focused on promoting the greatest degree of consciousness development for the greatest number of beings, it should exhibit a greater degree of solidarity with the less powerful and embody an effort to find systemic solutions to overcoming the obstacles they face to their full development. This solidarity and the accompanying insight into systemic solutions, however, are not going to come about with the development of integral consciousness but also require insights and understanding of how power dynamics function in society. In other words, consciousness development by itself is not sufficient for the development of socialist consciousness, if ignorance about social, political, and economic dynamics persists.

4

Criticisms and Responses

The developmental psychological approach to socialism that I have presented so far is—despite the many volumes of social science research to back it up—a highly controversial one. Social scientists and social theorists have challenged this type of approach by raising a wide variety of criticisms. After all, the historic-developmental theory that human consciousness develops in stages, that it is the result of a socialization process whereby people generally reach the stage of consciousness that predominates in their social environment, and that therefore societies also develop an average predominant consciousness that evolves from one stage to another through history, makes a wide variety of claims, each of which can be challenged.

To counter at least some of the objections to this theory, I will present seven of the most common criticisms and my responses, moving from the most sweeping rejections of the approach presented here to the more sympathetic and smaller criticisms. The seven arguments against the historic-developmental theory of consciousness may be summarized under the following headings: ontogenetic fallacy, Eurocentrism, totalitarian tendency, teleological fallacy, stagelessness, idealism, and lack of class and power dimensions. In the process of reviewing each of these arguments, I will try to make the best opposing argument that I can and try to avoid so-called straw man arguments since a rebuttal of the most convincing criticism is ultimately going to be more convincing.

The Ontogenetic Fallacy

The ontogenetic fallacy, according to several critics, is the false assumption that the logic of individual development (also known as ontogenesis) is repeated in social evolution. Strydom, for example, says, "The ontogenetic fallacy consists in drawing a conclusion from ontogenesis in respect of the change and development of culture or collective symbolic systems which can be accounted for only with reference to supra-individual learning processes."[1] Other theorists, such as the prominent anti-evolutionary sociologist Anthony Giddens, argues that such a theory "imagines that there is a homology between the stages of social evolution and the development of the individual personality."[2] Similarly, the evolutionary sociologist Stephen K. Sanderson says Habermas "confused individual ontogenesis and social evolution."[3]

The problem with these criticisms is that they fundamentally miss or misinterpret the reason why theorists draw a parallel between individual development and social evolution. The critics seem to believe that the social evolutionary argument is based on a faulty assumption. However, assumption is not the basis for drawing a parallel between individual development and societal evolution, rather it is based on a logical argument and on empirical research.

The logical aspect of the argument is that, first, humans are socialized into a certain stage of psychological development. That is, they will generally not reach a stage of development that is higher than the average level of the people who raise and educate them. Exceptions to this rule take place all the time, of course, which is the reason that consciousness development often does continue beyond the average level of one's social surroundings. But, as a rule, if one's surrounding members of society are at the socio-centric (or conventional) stage of

---

[1] Strydom (1992, p. 82).
[2] Giddens (1984, pp. 239–41).
[3] Sanderson (2007, p. 220).

development, then those socialized or raised into that society will not go beyond that stage unless they confront crises that this stage cannot resolve.

Second, if we accept the logic of the previous point, then we must accept that the first human societies did not start with the ability to socialize their newborns into the highest levels of consciousness that predominates today, that is, the post-conventional or world-centric stage of development. In other words, if we generally reach our highest stage of consciousness mainly through socialization, then how do those who do the socializing reach that stage themselves, if not through their own socialization to that stage? Only through a process of social learning, when a critical mass of individuals goes beyond the average level—due to their confrontation with crises—and socialize a new generation to that higher level, does social learning and consciousness development to a new level take place.

In addition to the logical argument above, there is also an empirical argument that this approach makes, which is to carefully analyze the structures of consciousness of individuals in their development and compare these to the structures of consciousness that societies exhibit historically. A wide variety of detailed studies have been conducted that make such comparisons, and criticism of the parallels that they discover between individual development and social evolution would have to start there, with this empirical research, rather than with simply dismissing the comparison as being based on an assumption, imagination, or confusion.[4]

Finally, there are at least two misunderstandings of the theory that can make it relatively easy to dismiss the comparison between individual development and social evolution. First, it is easy to mistakenly believe that those who argue in favor of the developmental–historical approach believe that the stages of individual development and the stages of social evolution are identical. However, as Habermas and others have pointed

---

[4] The perhaps more prominent such studies include those of Elias ([1939] 2012), Gebser ([1949/1953] 1985), Wilber (1981), Oesterdiekhoff (2009), Dux (2000).

out, this would be a false conclusion. That is, while there is a parallel or similarity (a "homology") between the two, they are different in that the individual must resolve different types of problems and approaches the world in a different manner than a social group does. That is, group dynamics are different from individual dynamics.

Second, it is easy to mistakenly believe that this theory argues that hunter-gatherer societies of today remain at the same stage of socio-cultural development as those that existed tens of thousands of years ago. This too would be a false assumption about the theory because while hunter-gatherers' technological capability might be relatively unchanged from ten thousand years ago, this does not mean that their culture and their consciousness have not developed significantly since then.

Eurocentrism

The criticism that developmental psychology, social evolutionary theory, or historical–genetic theory are Eurocentric (or "value-laden" in favor of European values) is the perhaps most common criticism leveled against these types of theories. Whether these types of theories are Eurocentric depends to a large extent on what is meant by the term. If it means that there is an implicit assumption that all societies and all individuals are evolving or ought to evolve toward the Western European type of culture and consciousness, then these theories would indeed be Eurocentric if this were the type of consciousness and culture that these theories were advocating. However, developmental psychology has mostly been quite explicit about finding universal patterns in psychological development that are not specific to Western European culture. That is, it is an argument about the deep structures of thinking and of consciousness, not about its more superficial values or attachments.

For example, the world-centric stage of development could be interpreted as being supremely European in origin because the

Enlightenment philosophy of Western Europe celebrated this type of rationality. But, as I argued in Chapter 3, world-centric consciousness already appeared on a worldwide scale during what the philosopher Karl Jaspers called the "Axial Age," around 500 BC, not just in ancient Greece, but also in India, Persia, and China. Also, while each of these regions developed a similar deep structure or world-centric consciousness, the details of these cultures were vastly different from each other. The fact that the Western European version of rationalism and of world-centric consciousness ended up dominating the world, does not make this type of consciousness unique to Western Europe. As I mentioned earlier, cross-cultural developmental psychology has established quite well that the developmental stages it describes are universal.[5]

Some, however, argue that the theory is Eurocentric because it either believes that some stages—those that are more closely identified with Western European norms—are higher and more evolved or developed than others. In other words, the mere theorization of a hierarchy of consciousness development is itself Eurocentric according to this argument.[6] Certainly, it is important to be sensitive to Eurocentric biases when developing such a theory. But this does not mean that because there is a danger of including such biases one should discard developmental psychology as a whole. Denying the validity of developmental psychology altogether because of its possible Eurocentrism would be to deny that human learning occurs in a particular ontological developmental sequence. In effect, it would suggest that a person could engage in world-centric thinking before they ever learned to think egocentrically or ethnocentrically. An understanding of exactly how these different types of consciousness build upon one another and thus require each other, though, shows that a reverse or random developmental sequence is impossible.[7]

---

[5] See Friedlmeier et al. (2005) and Gardiner and Kosmitzki (2010).
[6] One example of this type of criticism is that of Blaut (1993).
[7] Robert Kegan's developmental psychology provides one of the strongest arguments for the ontological nature of the development process, whereby each new stage represents a broadening of one's perspective (Kegan, 1994; Kegan and Lahey, 2009).

Similarly, many critics argue that all existing notions of social evolution are inherently Eurocentric, mainly because they all see Western European societies as being the most evolved and therefore as being superior to all other societies. Several issues end up getting mixed up in this argument. First is whether history represents some sort of progress or directionality. Another is whether Western European societies represent the highest or most advanced degree of progress in this presumed scale.

First, responding to the question of whether human history represents progress or directionality, are two different but related questions. It seems practically impossible to deny that there is a directionality involved in human history, in the sense of the existence of long-term social learning trends. For example, as Gerhard Lenski, one of sociology's foremost social evolutionary theorists, points out, social evolution refers to "the cumulation of heritable or transferable information within populations and its attendant consequences."[8] This makes the cumulative development of science and technology central to social evolution. One could also point to the increasing relevance and expansion of human rights—expansion both in terms of the categories of people covered and in terms of the types of rights granted to people.

But do these trends or this historical directionality represent progress, in the sense of improvement? Answering this question is a matter of values. If one values progress in science and technology and/or progress in human rights, then there is progress—at least in some of the trends that one might consider important. The theory thus would indeed be "value-laden" in the sense that it sees the cumulation of knowledge/information and the development of universal principles or of human rights as something positive.

The observation that there appears to be progress, however, comes with at least two important caveats. First, progress is not uniform and constant. In the short run, there are reversals, stagnations, and harmful complications. By complications, I refer to what Wilber calls the

---

[8] Lenski (2005, p. 43).

"hijacking" of advanced cognitive capabilities by less advanced moral reasoning.[9] For example, while Germany's Weimar Republic represented an advance over the previous political system in Germany, while Hitler's Third Reich, which followed, represented a moral regression that took over the advanced technological and cognitive capabilities of that time, to produce more efficient mass killing and genocide, both in warfare and in concentration camps, than were possible in previous eras.

The second caveat relating to the long-term trend of progress is what Habermas calls the "dialectic of progress."[10] That is, while progress means improvements in the cognitive and moral aspects of social life, one must also recognize that this progress can result in greater problems in other areas. The clearest example of this is the development of the atomic bomb, which represents a milestone in our cognitive ability to harness the forces of nature, but also results in a far more dangerous and potentially catastrophic weapon of war. Another example of the dialectic of progress is how modern science and technology make our lives easier, giving us far more freedoms than we previously enjoyed, but at the same time bringing us closer to a global ecological crisis than ever before. Habermas presents this dialectic of progress as one in which, "A higher stage of development of productive forces and of social integration does bring relief from problems of the superseded social formation. But the problems that arise at the new stage of development can—insofar as they are at all comparable with the old ones—increase in intensity."[11]

Returning to the question of whether the notions of progress in social evolutionary theory and in developmental psychology are Eurocentric, we need to examine the second question that I posed earlier, of whether Western European societies are supposed to represent the most "advanced" or "evolved" societies. At least three responses are possible to this type of charge of Eurocentrism.

---

[9] Wilber (2000c, p. 284).
[10] Habermas ([1976] 1979).
[11] Habermas ([1976] 1979, pp. 163–4).

First, if we recognize that there are many different dimensions of progress, this complicates the picture as to which societies are more or less "advanced" than others. For example, we could think of progress in terms of the degree of freedom that its members enjoy on average, the degree of social justice that has been achieved, the degree of happiness that its members express about their lives, or the sophistication of its science and technology. Any one of these dimensions could represent a measure of progress and a society could be at different degrees of advancement in each of them. In other words, referring to Chapter 2, where I emphasized that individual development could be at different levels in different "lines" of psychological development (cognitive, moral, interpersonal, aesthetic, etc.), the same can be said about societies and their cultures.

Second, the dialectic of progress implies that societies whose average level of social evolution across different dimensions (or lines) is relatively "advanced" compared to other societies can also be more dangerous and oppressive than less "advanced" societies. This is particularly true regarding societies that have advanced technological capabilities combined with large economic resources since they can use these for war or the threat of war. Also, a high level of scientific and technological capability generally implies greater economic power, which, if combined with a less evolved moral dimension, increases the likelihood that these societies will use their technological and economic superiority to oppress or dominate less powerful societies. This aspect of domination ought to be considered too when evaluating a society's supposed degree of advancement or progress. More than that, while Western Europe has been more "advanced" in many dimensions of social evolution for the past five centuries, this is largely a result of its ruthless domination and exploitation of the rest of the world, beginning especially with the exploitation of the Americas, which, according to some historians, gave it a significant advantage in promoting its own development and in its domination of the rest of the world in the past five centuries.[12]

---

[12] One of the historians who has made this argument particularly persuasively in my opinion is J. M. Blaut (2000).

Finally, another reason why the social evolutionary theory proposed here is not Eurocentric is that it also argues that these (in some dimensions of progress) advanced societies could lose their position relative to other societies relatively quickly and easily at any point soon. The best indication for this is the ongoing economic decline among Anglo-European societies and the rise of China.[13]

A related argument that developmental psychology is value-laden and Eurocentric is that the research of its main representative, Jean Piaget—and thus also of elaborators of his such as Jürgen Habermas and Norbert Elias—embodies liberal values. That is, according to the developmental psychology critic Erica Burman, Piaget's conception of childhood development "is deeply imbued with liberalism," where "a hierarchical model of 'cognitive structures' emerges whereby a more mature logic arises from and supersedes earlier and less adequate structures." Also, Piaget's highest stage of development "treats scientific rationality as the pinnacle of psychological development."[14]

I do not mean to say that Piaget's writing does not display elements of cultural chauvinism or Eurocentricity, but this does not justify dismissing the enormous body of research that he and countless other developmental psychologists have conducted into the stage-like nature of human development as long as it takes into account gender differences (as, for example, Carol Gilligan's work emphasizes) and the varieties of lines of development that I have brought up earlier.

Totalitarian Tendency

The perhaps best-known and most sweeping criticism that social evolutionary theory leads to totalitarianism was made by the philosopher Karl Popper, in his criticism of the social theories of Plato, Hegel, and

---

[13] The person who has perhaps developed this argument to its fullest is Gunder Frank (1998).
[14] Burman (1994, pp. 158-9).

Marx.¹⁵ While the theory presented here is different from the theories of the philosophers that Popper criticizes, there are distinct parallels and no doubt Popper would have leveled the same criticism against this theory. The essence of Popper's argument is that social evolutionary theories or theories of history, as he refers to them, are dangerous and lead toward authoritarianism and totalitarianism because they provide the theoretical foundation for efforts to force individuals and society to conform to the historical preconceptions and predictions of those who espouse the theory.

Popper's criticism of historicism (theories of history) has been thoroughly debated, but it remains perhaps one of the most prevalent liberal criticisms of Marxism and of any revolutionary and social theory-based attempt to change the world. The fact that the billionaire financier and philanthropist George Soros named his foundation after one of Popper's main works that develops this line of argument, the Open Society Foundation, testifies to the ongoing use of this critique. Defendants of Marx and of historicist social theory, however, have developed several responses to Popper.

One response is that Popper largely misinterprets the historicist theories of Plato, Hegel, and Marx because he falsely claims that they all believe that the evolution of history is inevitable. Leaving aside whether this is an accurate interpretation of Plato and Hegel (and there are those who say Popper is wrong about them¹⁶), with regard to Marx this is a very common but also somewhat serious misinterpretation.¹⁷ Marx's point of trying to identify the "laws of motion" of society isn't to make a deterministic prediction about an inevitable future development, as Popper claims, but to figure out where and how the working class can best intervene in social affairs so it can make a revolution.

Marx's previously quoted statement that "Men [sic] make their own history, but they do not make it as they please; they do not make it

---

¹⁵ Popper ([1945, 1947] 2013).
¹⁶ See Hook (1951) and Bhargava (1994).
¹⁷ Cornforth (1968) presents a through book-length critique of Popper from a Marxist point of view.

under self-selected circumstances, but under circumstances existing already, given and transmitted from the past,"[18] perhaps best displays Marx's position regarding determinism versus free will. This is also the point of view of my approach to history.

That is, there is nothing inevitable about the development of consciousness or the evolution of society. Whether we progress as individuals or as a society is entirely up to us and could just as well not happen or even end up in a reversal and a regression. However, in the process of figuring out which way to proceed, which direction in consciousness development and in social evolution is better, and how these developments build upon one another, it helps to understand one's own and society's past, as well as the *potential* for progress inherent in individuals and in society.

This argument, however, leads to a second objection that is closely related to Popper's totalitarianism critique of Marxism, which is that the consciousness approach to socialism ends up attempting to control people's minds. Kołakowski's criticism of Herbert Marcuse's psychoanalytic Marxism[19] and similar critiques of Guevara's notion of creating a "socialist man" emphatically reject the idea that socialists should or could develop recommendations about what forms of consciousness are better and therefore worth promoting. Taking such a strong stand against consciousness development in the name of avoiding totalitarianism implies taking a stand against any type of learning that produces cumulative and qualitative changes in how we think about things, which ultimately implies taking a stand against intellectual growth altogether.

These critics are probably not opposed to the quantitative increase in knowledge but are against intentional qualitative changes. The roots of this criticism and this avoidance of qualitative change lie in the notion that once we reach adulthood, we are all the same in terms of our consciousness development and that any deviation from the mature

---

[18] Marx ([1852] 1978, p. 595).
[19] Kołakowski (2005, pp. 1104–23).

stage of rational world-centric thinking must be the result of a form of mind control. However, as we can see from the research referred to earlier, consciousness development does not end at the world-centric stage, and it does not end with the onset of adulthood. In addition, consciousness development implies greater freedom, not less, because moving beyond the world-centric stage of consciousness enables us to act from greater awareness and greater understanding, which gives us more freedom due to the greater insight that we achieve.

Teleological Fallacy

The critique that a developmental psychological approach to socialism is linear and teleological is similar to Popper's critique of its totalitarian tendency. However, rather than focusing on the dangerous totalitarian consequences that are inherent in a supposedly preconceived notion of history, the critique of linearity and teleology focuses on the theory's supposedly false presuppositions.

According to this critique, the developmental approach to socialism embodies a false linear assumption in its positing of a stage-like process of societal development because such an approach cannot account for the reversals and the horrors of historical developments, such as the Holocaust.[20] A variant or continuation of the linearity criticism is that the supposed linearity of the theory is rooted in a false teleological assumption that the development of humanity is heading toward a predefined end point, such as a state of complete freedom and/or the reconciliation of opposites. Here again, the specter of Hegelian philosophy rears its head in that Hegel posited precisely such a goal-oriented end point for human historical development. The problem, according to this critique, is that such teleology represents an unproven

---

[20] Walter Benjamin made the perhaps most eloquent argument in favor of this perspective (Benjamin, 1968), which Terry Eagleton has contested to some extent (Eagleton, 2021).

and unknowable a priori assumption, one that can also have dangerous consequences.[21]

There are several responses possible to the criticism that the theory is too linear. First, as argued in previous chapters, this critique is essentially false because no claim within this theory posits an inevitable linear advance or progress. Rather, the theory lays out a method for observing or identifying advances and states that in the past, generally speaking, have represented developmental advances. This does not mean that this theory denies or fails to account for reversals. As a matter of fact, it is only on the basis of theoretical criteria—such as that of a developmental approach—that we can even distinguish between advance and regression. In other words, it is only as a result of having criteria for identifying why a world-centric worldview is more "advanced" than an ethnocentric one that we can even talk about possible regressions. For example, we can thus clarify that, as a political system, Nazi Germany represented a regression relative to its predecessor, the Weimar Republic.

Linearity thus exists only in the sense that the theory postulates societies advance in a process of individual and societal learning, where one stage builds upon the earlier stage; that stages cannot be skipped or entered in random order. However, this does not mean that under some circumstances—usually crises—regressions don't happen or are not possible. Rather, regressions to earlier stages are always a possibility and have indeed taken place throughout history. Progress in the future is only postulated as a possibility based on the observation of experience. This also means that there is no inevitable teleological outcome.

The second response to the critique of linearity is that just because there is progress or advancement, following certain criteria, such as increased freedom and greater complexity, this does not mean that there is advancement according to the criterion of overcoming social problems. As Habermas points out, there is a "dialectic of progress"

---

[21] That teleology has dangerous consequences is, again, precisely Popper's critique of Hegel and of Marx.

at work, whereby advances imply the overcoming of some sets of problems, but that also create new sets or types of problems that did not exist before. For example, the transition from hunter-gatherers to agricultural societies meant the overcoming of scarcity problems caused by population growth but created new problems, such as increasing inequality. Similarly, the transition from ethnocentric cultures to world-centric cultures meant the potential to overcome overt racism in favor of more universalistic norms but eventually created the realization that this still has not solved the problems of persistent inequality and exploitation. The perhaps most familiar example of the dialectic of progress is the progress of science, which keeps solving one scientific problem after the other, only to create the next problem, such as the invention of the atomic bomb.

The perhaps most common critique of developmental-evolutionary approaches to society has its roots in a misplaced assumption of Darwinism in this theory. That is, these critics, such as Stephen J. Gould,[22] argue that arguments about progress are nonsense because humans are no better adapted to their environment than cockroaches or other, normally considered more "primitive" creatures (such as bacteria) or more "primitive" societies. This criticism, however, makes the false assumption that adaptation is the only or best criterion for evaluating progress. Understandably, critics would make this false assumption because the founder of evolutionary theory, Charles Darwin, and his intellectual sociological heirs, Herbert Spencer (1820–1903) and Talcott Parsons (1902–1979), made precisely this argument.

However, if we consider progress along the criteria of increasing complexity and of increasing relative freedom, it is much more plausible that societal evolution or development have a directionality. The term "progress," though, might be an unfortunate one to use because of its loaded connotations of "better," which never provides us with clear criteria as to what "better" means. Also, while it might be easy to agree that increasing complexity is a relatively uncontroversial directionality

---

[22] Gould (1996).

in human development and evolution, it might not always be clear why increasing complexity should represent progress or something better.

A perhaps more controversial but also unambiguously evaluative criterion of directionality is relative freedom, meaning that each advance or progress in development represents an increase in the subject's ability to act upon and within its given environment. For example, someone at the world-centric stage of development has a greater degree of autonomy or freedom than someone at the ethnocentric stage because at the ethnocentric stage, the individual is subject to the group's norms and customs, while at the world-centric stage, they are freer to come up with their own norms. Similarly, the integral stage represents greater freedom than the world-centric because at the integral stage, the individual is more conscious of how presumably autonomously conceived norms are still embedded in cultural presuppositions and embeddedness. This awareness, in turn, allows for greater freedom to overcome these presuppositions.[23]

A final issue that needs to be taken into account when considering the supposed linearity of the developmental approach to socialism is the argument first made in Chapter 2, that both individual and societal development occur along a variety of different "lines," along which development can take place at a variety of different paces. So, for example, just as an individual might be at different stages along the cognitive, interpersonal, and value lines, a society could also be at a variety of different stages in different lines. However, the different developmental lines of a society are not necessarily the same as within individuals. That is, the differentiation of societal functions into different social subsystems is different for societies than it is in

---

[23] The issue of freedom is an extremely complicated one that philosophers have debated for centuries and which I can only outline in the most general form. Good references to the claim that evolution and development imply greater freedom are, in the natural sciences, Laszlo (1996), and in the social sciences, Jantsch (1980). The argument that human development and evolution imply greater freedom mainly applies to individuals and not necessarily to societies as a whole, since it is always possible that one segment of any given society (often a minority) dominates another segment of that same society, which makes general statements about the relative freedom of the society as a whole practically impossible.

individuals. In a society, the main differentiation of lines falls into the economic and the political. These are quite different than the main personal developmental lines for individuals, which are generally considered to be the cognitive and the interpersonal/moral lines.

Problems with Stage Identification and with Developmental Psychology

A common criticism of developmental-psychological approaches to socialism is that developmental psychology is either such an incoherent field that there is no theoretical advantage to basing a theory on it,[24] or they argue that developmental psychology as a whole is a pseudoscience and that there are no such things as sequential developmental stages.[25] There are several responses possible to these criticisms, but let me start with the one that is more easily rebutted, which is the denial of the validity of developmental psychology as a whole.

It is practically impossible to find anyone who makes the argument that there is no such thing as psychological development. This is perhaps because it is undeniable that a newborn does not have the same intellectual capacities as an adult. Thus, more commonly, the variant of this argument against the usage of developmental psychology for a theory of socialism is, first, yes, there might be something we can call psychological development between infancy and adulthood, but since all adults reach the same level of competency and since societies are generally governed and organized by adults, there is no advantage to the use of developmental psychology for a socialist social theory. Second, some critics would also argue that even if there is psychological development, it is culturally specific and nonuniversal, and therefore one cannot identify common or invariant developmental sequences.

---

[24] This is the argument that Blunden (2012, pp. 318–24), for example, makes.
[25] I have not been able to find any academic psychologists who make this rather extreme claim, but it is a common claim I have encountered among nonacademics.

My main response to both arguments against developmental psychology would be to refer to the psychological research literature that I have already referred to in this book. That is, according to this research, there is psychological development during adulthood, which is precisely why the approach to socialism presented here makes use of this research. This response, though, leads us straight to the second argument against developmental psychology, which is that there simply is no consensus within the field of developmental psychology, neither over the types and number of stages and how they should be characterized, when they take place in a person's biography, nor what causes shifts from one stage to another and that therefore the approach is not particularly useful.

Indeed, according to one developmental psychologist,

> [T]here is no dominant theory of cognitive development. The limitations of the major theories in the area - Piagetian, neo-Piagetian, Vygotskian, information processing, social learning, ethological, and neo-nativistic - are sufficiently large and apparent that none of them can claim the adherence of anything like a majority of investigators. In all likelihood, the greatest number of developmentalists see themselves as eclectic, borrowing concepts from many theories, but not being entirely comfortable with any one of them.[26]

Granted, there is very little consensus in the field of developmental psychology and the developmental psychologists I have cited in this book represent only one slice within this rather broad school of thought. However, this fact alone should not be a reason to dismiss the theory out of hand. After all, one could say the same thing about Marxism or pretty much any other approach within the social sciences. Rather, the point ought to be to critically examine developmental psychological theories and their supporting evidence and evaluate them on their merits according to one's own standards of whether the

---

[26] Siegler (1996, p. 20).

different arguments for or against developmental psychology are based on sound research.

When examining this research and theory, however, one should always keep in mind that the whole approach is a contested realm and that we cannot be rigid in our appropriation of one approach over another. We must always keep an open mind, particularly in light of criticism that a particular approach or application of a developmental theory might reinforce one form of domination or another, such as Eurocentrism, sexism, racism, or classism.

Having said that, the main debate today within developmental psychology seems to be between the Piaget-inspired approaches and those inspired by Lev Vygotsky. The Piagetian approach tends to argue that there are universal and invariant stages of development (although there is plenty of disagreement as to how far they go). The Vygotsky-inspired approaches, in contrast, tend to argue that development is far more indeterminate and context and culture-specific and nonuniversal. Based on my reading of the literature on these approaches, my feeling is that they do not have to be mutually exclusive and can both be useful for socialist theory.[27]

Developmental Psychology Is Idealism, Not Materialism

Most theorists of social evolution would tend to criticize the developmental psychological approach to social evolution by arguing that it places far too great an emphasis on transformations of consciousness as an explanation for social change, instead of on material factors, such as changes in the functioning of the economy or of the environment. That is, the most prominent social evolutionists,

---

[27] See, for example, Ratner et al. (2017). In my opinion, a unification of the Piaget-inspired and Vygotsky-inspired theories is possible, but has, to my knowledge, not been done so far.

such as Gerhard Lenski, Marvin Harris, Robert Carneiro, or Stephen Sanderson, consider themselves to be materialists because they argue that social evolution advances based on "the material conditions of human existence, that is, the demographic, ecological, technological, and economic forces at work in social life."[28] The reason that such material forces are so important in shaping social evolution is quite simple and is the same reason that Marx supported a materialist approach, which is that material factors are ontologically the most important factors for human survival. That is, all other factors pale in importance compared to factors involving the acquisition and maintenance of food, shelter, and reproduction. The most common and persuasive illustration of this argument is that the transition from hunter-gatherer societies to horticultural and then to agricultural societies took place because hunting and gathering gradually became unviable in the face of growing population pressure and declining resources to hunt and gather.

The materialist approach, however, does not deny the importance of noneconomic factors in social evolution. Sanderson, for example, argues that allowance must be made for "superstructural feedback," meaning, just as Marx wrote, that the institutions that societies create on top of the economic "base" can also act as causal factors once they are in place. Sanderson mentions, for example, that "Christianity arose, at least in part, out of the exploitation and oppression of Jews in the Roman Empire, but once it evolved it gradually began to exert its own force as a significant causal agent in the world."[29]

Sanderson, however, dismisses the developmental psychological approach to social evolution out of hand, arguing—as mentioned already at the beginning of this chapter, regarding the ontogenetic fallacy—that there is no evidence that there is a correspondence between the cultures of a particular social formation and the average level of psychological development. He goes on to argue, "Societies are

---

[28] Sanderson (2007, pp. 290-1).
[29] Sanderson (2007, pp. 292-3).

not just networks of ideas, information, or discourse, but of contrasting and conflicting *material interests*, and in my judgment, it is these, far more than anything else, that shape social evolution."[30]

It is extremely difficult to sort out what, ultimately, are the causes of social change and some might even argue that this is a rather academic debate without too many real-world consequences. The problem with Sanderson's (and by extension most social evolutionists') argument, though, is not whether it is material interests or ideas that are the main causal factors, but that this is a false dichotomy—one that prevents us from understanding the role that ideas, consciousness, and developmental stages play in society. That is, Sanderson here conflates the two types of materialism that need to be distinguished, as I already argued in the previous chapter. On the one hand, there is Marx's materialism of the "conditioning" effect that the economic base has on social formations, and, on the other hand, there is the false materialism of the supposed priority of material or biological needs over ideas (Feuerbach's materialism).[31]

The mistake here is to believe that ideas and material reality and material interests can be neatly separated so that the material gives rise to ideas. Rather, as I already pointed out earlier, it makes far more sense to think of this as a dialectical process of enactment, where each shapes the other. To put this differently, it makes little sense to argue that material interests—beyond the basic survival level—are what shape our motivations, without realizing that it is our *perception* of reality, especially what we *perceive* to be important that shapes what our interests are. And our perception of reality and our values (which help shape what we pay attention to) are, in turn, a function of our level of consciousness. In other words, a developmental approach to socialism can be every bit as materialist as Marx's materialism. What it is not, though, is materialism in Sanderson's (or Feuerbach's) sense,

---

[30] Sanderson (2007, p. 221; emphasis in the original).
[31] I call this "Feuerbach's materialism" because this was the type of materialism that Marx criticized in his "Theses on Feuerbach."

that ideas are merely a function or an effect of material (or biological) interests or needs.

Returning to the earlier example of the transition from hunter-gatherer societies to agricultural societies, it is probably true that material survival interests motivated this transition. However, a more complete account of this transition would also include an account of how hunter-gatherers' perception of their environment changed—in a dialectical relationship with their changing environment—when they gradually realized that animistic rituals were apparently not helping with the provision of food and that they perhaps could play a larger role in manipulating and shaping their environment by planting crops. This changing realization about their impact on the natural world changed their worldview fundamentally, making a transition from hunter-gathering toward agriculture and a mythological or sociocentric worldview possible. More than that, such a transition of worldviews is necessary for a transition in production regimes to become possible. Without a change in worldviews, societies would neither perceive nor conceive of new ways of doing things.[32]

Insufficient Consideration of Class and Class Struggle

The final common argument against a developmental psychological approach to socialism is similar to the previous one, regarding its lack of materialism, but emphasizes the lack of a class and power dimension to the approach. There are at least two varieties of this argument, one, which is quite sweeping in its indictment of this type of theory, has its roots in the Marxist structuralism of Louis Althusser,[33] and the other, which is more specifically directed against Habermas and against some

---

[32] Owen (2002, p. 95) describes Habermas's approach similarly: "So while the problems that generate crises originate in the domain of material reproduction, evolutionary steps only occur when (and if) developments occur in the domain of symbolic reproduction."
[33] The most concise summary of his argument against Marxist humanism, which would no doubt include the approach I present here, is formulated in Althusser (1969).

forms of Frankfurt School critical theory, has been formulated by the Marxist philosopher István Mészáros. Beginning with Althusser's sweeping criticism, his argument opposes any conception of subjectivity and of consciousness—concepts that are central to the developmental psychological approach to socialism. According to Althusser, subjectivity and consciousness are merely an effect of economic, political, and ideological structures.

> Ideology is indeed a system of representations, but in the majority of cases these representations have nothing to do with "consciousness": they are usually images and occasionally concepts, but it is above all as structures that they impose on the vast majority of men, not via their "consciousness". They are perceived-accepted-suffered cultural objects and they act functionally on men via a process that escapes them.[34]

Socialist humanism, which emphasizes the role of the individual human and his or her consciousness and freedom, according to Althusser, forgets or ignores the extent to which capitalistic and class-based economic, political, and ideological institutions determine the very concept of what it means to be human (as a subject with consciousness). "The couple human/inhuman is the hidden principle of all humanism which is, then, no more than a way of living-sustaining-resolving this contradiction. Bourgeois humanism made man the principle of all theory," writes Althusser.[35] Socialist humanism is thus actually part of the ideology of the ruling class.

Althusser's rejection of humanism and thereby of subjectivity, of consciousness, and also of individual freedom, is based on the total determinism of his Marxist structuralism. In short, according to this approach, there can be no real conception of humanism, consciousness, and freedom that is free from bourgeois ideology as long as there is capitalism because under capitalism these concepts are irredeemably entwined with bourgeois ideology.

---

[34] Althusser (1969, p. 233).
[35] Althusser (1969, p. 237).

It is no doubt important to be aware of the extent to which one's concepts are "contaminated" or shaped by an ideology that justifies oppression and exploitation, such as the ideology of capitalism. Our concepts must thus be sensitive to this possibility. However, simply rejecting all bourgeois concepts because of their contamination throws out the conceptual baby with the ideological bathwater. More than that, Althusser's wholesale rejection of bourgeois humanism could end up justifying a different oppressive and exploitative system, simply because it is anti-capitalist, such as totalitarian socialism (an oxymoron, no doubt, but a term that can be used to indicate the social system Stalin created in the Soviet Union).

On a deeper philosophical level, though, the theory advocated here—the developmental psychological approach to socialism—indeed sees consciousness as being the result of social, political, and economic structures, but rejects Althusser's anti-humanism and holds that our socially formed consciousness is still capable of some degree of freedom and of free choice, within the parameters that shape it. In short, it agrees with Marx's dictum that, "Men [sic] make their own history, but they do not make it as they please; they do not make it under self-selected circumstances, but under circumstances existing already, given and transmitted from the past."

Another theorist who rejects the developmental approach is István Mészáros. His critique is based on a close reading of Habermas, who, as Mészáros correctly points out, discards practically everything that is important in Marx's critique of capitalism for fighting capitalism and class-based exploitation. The perhaps most important concept that Habermas discards in this regard is the concept of class conflict because, according to Habermas, "state-regulated capitalism, which emerged as a reaction against the dangers of the system produced by open class antagonism, *suspends class conflict*." Mészáros goes on to quote Habermas as writing, "in advanced capitalist society deprived and privileged groups no longer confront each other as socioeconomic classes."[36]

---

[36] Quoted in Mészáros (2005, p. 136).

Mészáros thus does not challenge Habermas's use of developmental psychology directly but rather does so indirectly by pointing out that the whole of Habermas's approach, to achieve emancipation through the gradual achievement of undistorted communication, involves an analysis of contemporary society that ignores class conflict and class antagonism. That is, by emphasizing the development of cognitive and moral capacities, which aims toward the eventual achievement of undistorted communication, Habermas loses sight of class oppression and class struggle.

I would agree with Mészáros that Habermas's analysis of contemporary society is naïve in the sense that he believes that class conflict has been overcome with the achievement of the welfare state. Habermas wrote this analysis during the height of the German welfare state, in the mid-1970s, and has maintained this analysis up until his most recent work. However, with the advance of neoliberalism in the 1980s and 1990s, class conflict has become more prominent again all around the world. More than that, class conflict in more or less functioning welfare states, such as in the Scandinavian countries, is merely a form of appeasement that does not alter the class-based nature of capitalism, whose essence continues to rely on the dichotomy between owners of capital and wage earners.

Paying attention to the centrality of class thus remains essential for an understanding of contemporary capitalism and my developmental psychological approach to socialism does not mean to undermine or avoid class analysis in the least. Actually, part of the argument of this approach is that class conflict, as well as other types of social conflict between the powerful and the marginalized (such as those involving gender, race, ethnicity, sexual orientation, etc.), drive advances in cognitive and moral development—not automatically or every time, but quite often. That is, it is crises, which emerge out of a variety of types of social conflicts, often class-, gender-, or race-based (or ecological), that cause advances to higher stages of consciousness. This means that I agree with Habermas to a limited extent when he points out that class is not the primary driver of social change and consciousness development, but I also agree with Mészáros, that Habermas goes too far in ignoring the importance of class struggle.

Conclusion

If we take all the foregoing criticisms of developmental socialism into account, one could summarize these as embodying a series of false assumptions either about developmental socialism, as a social theory, or about individuals and society. Beginning with the criticism that developmental socialism commits an ontogenetic fallacy where the theory simply assumes that social evolution recapitulates individual psychological development, I tried to show that this criticism actually is the one making a false assumption, namely that the relationship between individual and societal development is simply assumed in this theory. Rather, developmental socialism makes the connection between individual and social development based on empirical verification and a logical argument.

The Eurocentrism critique makes the highly questionable assumption that either there is no progress or that all that might be called progress is inherently Eurocentric. Instead, I argued that we can generally identify progress as an increase in human freedom and that this should be the non-Eurocentric basis for any emancipatory project.

Next, the criticism that developmental socialism embodies a totalitarian project makes the false assumption that the theory claims to know exactly what a future society looks like. While this theory might say something about the general trajectory or directionality (increasing complexity and increasing freedom, for example), it makes no claims about the specific organization of a future society, nor about the inevitability of society's future development in the direction that it has developed so far. Reversals and setbacks are always possible. The same response applies to the criticism that the theory is teleological and too linear, where an additional complicating factor that was mentioned was the false assumption that progress means only improvement. Instead, it makes more sense to think of it as a "dialectic of progress," where every step forward also implies the emergence of new problems.

The criticism that there are no real stages of psychological development or, if there are, that these stages are culturally specific, involves the false assumption that the theory of developmental socialism is making empirically unverifiable claims. That is, this approach finds the arguments in favor of developmental psychology to be compelling but does not say that these should be assumed as unquestionable facts. Actually, the opposite is true; we need more research into developmental psychology and its relationship to societal development.

Similarly, the rejection of developmental psychology as an essential component for a theory of socialism often embodies the false assumption that human development comes to an end with the onset of adulthood and that therefore developmental psychology has nothing to offer a theory of socialism. As I have tried to argue in this chapter and in Chapter 2, however, this assumption has largely been proven to be false by research that demonstrates that all humans are capable of continued development, throughout their lifetimes, and that there is no specific end point, as far as we can tell, to this development.

Finally, the rejection of developmental socialism on the basis that it leaves out materialism, class conflict, and power relations more generally is false too. Rather, the aim of this approach is to complement materialism, class conflict, and power considerations with an "interior" dimension to these issues by pointing out that the ways our consciousness makes sense of the world and changes—because of conflict and crises— are essential elements for a more complete understanding of how we might bring about a more just and more emancipated society.

Now that I have outlined the theory and defended it against common objections, we will take a closer look at how this theory might be applied to our current situation, which is governed by what I call neoliberal digital capitalism.

5

The Challenge: Neoliberal Digital Capitalism

If the approach outlined so far is considered useful for charting an empirically and theoretically grounded approach to social emancipation, then it makes sense to now turn our attention to what is preventing us, as a society, from realizing this project. My main argument here is that while there are a wide variety of social forces and belief systems in place that present obstacles to the further development of consciousness and of social systems, every social formation in history has presented obstacles to development that tend to be specific to a particular time and place. Given the globalized world that we live in,[1] however, there is a greater degree of homogenization in terms of the social factors that impinge on everyone's lives, no matter where they live in the world. The main differences between people no matter where in the world they live that continue to affect us are distinctions of class—which also overlap to a large degree with distinctions of race, ethnicity, and gender. Nationality, however, plays less of a role now than it did in previous

---

[1] There is some debate as to exactly how globalized our world is and whether it truly is more globalized than it was in other epochs. I cannot review this literature here, but I take the side of those who argue that our world is more globalized now than it has ever been, culturally, economically, politically, and socially, particularly if globalization is distinguished from internationalization. That is, the term globalization refers to the global integration of production and consumption processes (both of material and of cultural goods), which is qualitatively different from the internationalization of trade. See, in particular, Robinson (2004).

epochs.[2] The predominant—or hegemonic—social formation of our times can be called neoliberal digital capitalism.[3]

Usually, when we think of neoliberalism, we think of it mainly as an ideology or set of beliefs that have to do with the economy. However, it makes sense to make a distinction between neoliberalism the ideology, as a set of beliefs and a particular rationality, and neoliberalism the set of policies and practices (just as we often do with the term capitalism). There might be a large degree of overlap between the ideology and the practice, but, as I will outline in a moment, the differences can be substantial. Both the ideology and the practice of neoliberalism present a wide variety of obstacles to the further development of consciousness and of new social formations. But they can also present new opportunities for breaking through to new forms of consciousness and new social formations to the extent that they cause significant crises.

The potential crises that neoliberalism provokes take on a different character when combined with contemporary digital technologies, such as smartphones, social media, media on demand, surveillance technology, and artificial intelligence, to name a few. It is not only that digital technology combines with neoliberalism, but both enter our lives with a particular culture or worldview, which in some ways intensifies the potential crises we face, but also presents new and perhaps unexpected ways of overcoming them. All these aspects of neoliberal digital capitalism and how it presents obstacles, crises, and possible breakthroughs will be examined in this chapter.

As we will see, the crises that neoliberal digital capitalism is causing can be divided into two categories: eternal or objective and internal or

---

[2] This is not to say that nationality does not continue to play a significant role in the elites' construction of global differences, precisely to distract those with less power from targeting those elites in the class conflict. I will discuss the role of nationalism in this context in greater detail later in the chapter.
[3] In the wake of the COVID-19 pandemic there has been a lot of speculation that we might be moving beyond neoliberalism now. However, as will become clearer in the following pages, I argue that while this might be true on the level of explicit ideology, it is far less true on the level of economic institutions and their effects on people's lives.

subjective. On the external side, we see the unprecedented growth in inequality, environmental destruction, surveillance, and repression. On the internal side, we see a steady growth of individualization (despite the ubiquity of digital networks), loneliness, depression, anxiety, and addiction.

A Brief History of Neoliberalism

Before we look at how neoliberal digital capitalism shapes our current world and creates obstacles and opportunities for a new consciousness, it makes sense to take a brief look at how we got here. When looking at the history of neoliberalism, though, the aspect of neoliberalism as an ideology or belief system quickly becomes confused with neoliberalism as a policy or set of practices. Another source of confusion has to do with how neoliberalism came about. Analysts of neoliberalism tend to focus on three main causal factors: (1) a group of elite academic economists who managed to successfully promote neoliberalism in academia and in governments around the world,[4] (2) a response to the economic crisis of the 1970s, which was perceived as a crisis of the Keynesian welfare state,[5] (3) powerful elites who promoted the neoliberal ideology of neoliberal thinkers in a wide variety of institutions because it was best suited to expanding their material interests and power.[6] These three explanations are not mutually exclusive and all of these factors were no doubt in evidence in the historical development of neoliberalism. I would add a fourth causal factor, rooted in developmental psychology, which has—to my knowledge—not been considered, but which helps explain why neoliberalism managed to become a sort of common sense. That is, as a belief system it represents a radicalization of world-centric

---

[4] Dardot and Laval (2014) are representative of this approach.
[5] Cahill and Konings (2017) are representative of this approach.
[6] Harvey (2005) is representative of this approach.

individualistic consciousness.[7] In what follows I will summarize the history of neoliberalism, paying attention to all three of the main causal factors that economic analysts usually consider.

As the term neoliberalism would suggest, it represents a further development of classical liberal economics, whose founder was Adam Smith (1723–1790). Classical liberal economics predominated economic thought in the Western world for the entire nineteenth century and into the early twentieth. It generally advocated in favor of free markets and mostly against government intervention, which it saw as being oppressive and harmful to economic development. At least, this was its self-justification. However, when classical liberal economics was applied, it would only appeal to these principles when it was convenient for those in power. For example, the leading economic power of the nineteenth century, the UK, only adopted liberal economics once it was in a position of unrivaled power to argue why other countries should open their relatively weaker and less developed economies to that of the UK. At the same time, the UK did not hesitate to impose its economic power with the brutal force of the British state in its colonies.[8]

The appeal of liberal economics, however, began to decline in the early twentieth century with the Russian Revolution of 1917 and especially with the Great Depression of the 1930s. The main alternative approach to economics during this time was the liberalism of John Maynard Keynes (1883–1946), also known as Keynesianism. Keynes's reworking of classical liberal economics tried to understand the business cycle and how state intervention could smoothen its ups and downs. Keynes's emphasis on reducing unemployment also provided crucial policy justifications for social democratic parties around the world, which were gaining influence due to increased democratization, unionization, and decolonization after the Second World War. Another

---

[7] There are, of course, plenty of thinkers who have related the emergence of capitalism more generally to world-centric rationalistic consciousness, beginning with Max Weber and more recently via George Ritzer (2020).

[8] Ha-Joon Chang (2002, 2008) provides a detailed overview of the hypocrisy of dominant powers in his books.

key factor of this period was the Bretton Woods conference of 1944, where representatives from the forty-four allied nations hammered out a post-war economic order that sought to avoid the economic instability of the 1930s and was thus mostly based on Keynesian principles. Key among these policies was the fixing of exchange rates between the world's currencies, the pegging of the dollar to the gold standard, and the creation of the International Monetary Fund (IMF) and the World Bank (called IBRD at the time). These policies gave governments a greater degree of independence in their economic management because they did not have to be too concerned about the impact of currency speculation on their domestic policies. As a result, the global economy grew more during the Keynesian period (1945–1975) than during any other time in world history.[9] Also, the growth was marked by a far more even distribution of wealth than at any time since then.

Several factors, though, conspired to bring the Keynesian period to an end in the 1970s. The perhaps most important development was the economic crisis of the 1970s, which began with the 1973 OPEC oil embargo. However, already before this, US President Richard Nixon set the stage for neoliberalism when he decided in 1971 that the United States would no longer convert the dollar to gold on demand. He made this decision, under the advice of Milton Friedman—one of neoliberalism's main economic theorists—when the United States sought to gain more economic maneuverability due to the cost of the Vietnam War and when the United States was rapidly losing its gold reserves to other countries because of the Bretton Woods fixed exchange rate system.[10]

The decision to remove the gold standard undermined one of the main pillars of the Bretton Woods era because it placed pressure on all countries to abandon the fixed exchange rate system. This, combined with the enormous flow of petrodollars from the OPEC oil embargo and the Eurodollars that countries had earned when the US trade balance

[9] Weisbrot (2015, chap. 3).
[10] Cahill and Konings (2017, p. 34).

favored Europe, meant that financial transactions and speculation were unleashed upon the world. With the clout of the financial sector behind them, the world's capitalist class was in a better position than ever before to argue in favor of and to push for the implementation of neoliberal policies around the world, a project that would reestablish their preeminence everywhere.

Neoliberal Reorientation (1975–95)

The application of neoliberal ideas to economic policy marks the beginning of the period of neoliberalism, which itself has undergone three phases until now. The first phase, which can be called the phase of "neoliberal reorientation,"[11] already began in the United States with President Jimmy Carter, who took the first steps toward neo-liberalization in the late 1970s, when he deregulated air traffic, railroads, trucking, and gas prices. Shortly before that, Chile, under the dictatorship of Augusto Pinochet, was probably the first real experiment in neoliberal economics and was directed by Milton Friedman's "Chicago Boys."

However, the election of Margaret Thatcher in the UK in 1979 and of Ronald Reagan in the United States in 1980 represented the real breakthrough for neoliberalism on a large scale. Thatcher and Reagan, among other leaders in this period, proceeded to break the back of the union movement, which made the implementation of neoliberal policies far easier. They weakened organized labor by, first, allowing unemployment to rise to unprecedented levels since the Great Depression. This was done first and foremost by the US Federal Reserve, which, under Fed Chair Paul Volcker, raised interest rates to over 20 percent in 1981, to halt rising inflation and causing a serious recession. Second, they broke a series of key strikes (mining in the UK and air traffic control in the United States). Third, they facilitated new

---

[11] Davidson (2023) calls it "Vanguard Regimes of Reorientation" and William Davies (2016) calls it "combative neoliberalism."

manufacturing plants in nonunionized low-wage areas, such as in the US South and in developing countries.

One of the neoliberal intellectuals' main arguments in support of these policies was that the state had become "overburdened" with demands from a wide variety of interest groups and that it needed to become more independent and autonomous. In other words, there was "too much democracy" and economic policy ought to be turned over to technocrats and be more insulated from the democratic process according to neoliberal intellectuals. In practice, this meant giving more power to the bankers and to finance capital.

Third Way Neoliberalism (1995–2007)

This first phase of neoliberal reorientation lasted more or less until the mid-1990s, by which time it had become the predominant or hegemonic economic philosophy of the world. Neoliberalism had become so common sense that even once nominally leftist parties, such as the UK's Labour Party and Germany's Social Democratic Party, came to accept neoliberalism's main assumptions. US President Bill Clinton was one of the first to pursue what came to be known as the so-called third way. Tony Blair in the UK and Gerhard Schroeder in Germany joined Clinton in this project soon thereafter.[12] This phase could thus be called "third way consolidation of neoliberalism."[13] In addition to accepting neoliberalism's main precepts, this third way approach argued it was necessary to soften the blow of neoliberalism by maintaining the rudiments of a welfare state. This, however, did not stop the center-left governments of the time from continuing the dismantling of the welfare state, as Bill Clinton did with the Personal

---

[12] Also instrumental was Jacques Delors, of France's Socialist Party, who pursued what amounted to third way neoliberalism on the level of the European Union, with the formation of the single market under the Maastricht Treaty of 1993, while he was president of the European Commission. Eventually, this led to the highly neoliberal Economic and Monetary Union of the European Union.

[13] This is a term provided by Dardot and Laval (2014), but Davies (2016) calls it "normative neoliberalism" and Davidson (2023) calls it "social regime of consolidation."

Responsibility and Work Opportunity Reconciliation Act (PRWORA) in 1993, which turned welfare from a right into a conditional benefit. UK's Prime Minister Tony Blair followed suit shortly thereafter, with his welfare/workfare reform of 1997. Germany's Gerhard Schröder implemented a similar policy change in 2002.[14]

A second aspect of the consolidation of neoliberalism involved the gradual acceptance of so-called free trade treaties, such as the signing of NAFTA (North America Free Trade Agreement) in 1994 (negotiated and signed by Clinton), the creation of the World Trade Organization (also in 1994), and the signing of the European Union's (EU's) Maastricht Treaty of 1993. All these agreements institutionalized neoliberal policies of free trade in goods and services while consolidating monopoly rights for intellectual property. The EU treaty went even further by limiting member governments' flexibility in the areas of fiscal and monetary policy.

Third, the developing world had neoliberal policies imposed on it during this consolidation period with the help of a reoriented IMF and World Bank (WB). That is, although these institutions were originally founded to act as guarantors of global Keynesianism, the Western governments that ultimately controlled these institutions redirected them in the 1980s and 1990s toward providing loans for developing countries only if they adopted neoliberal policy reforms as a condition for these loans. Developing world countries had become highly dependent on IMF and WB loans during the 1980s because of the Third World debt crisis that the high interest rates of the Volcker Shock had caused. Eventually, private banks saw the advantage of allowing the IMF and WB to lead the way so that private lenders would only give loans if a country already had a neoliberal IMF Structural Adjustment Program (SAP) in place. These SAPs involved the privatization of public utilities and other government-owned enterprises, fiscal austerity, the dismantling of social programs, and the deregulation of worker, health, and environmental protection.

[14] Cahill and Konings (2017, p. 48).

Finally, China's turn toward market economics (already in the late 70s) and the former Soviet Union's and Eastern Europe's abandonment of state socialism (in the early 1990s) in favor of neoliberal capitalism represented yet another consolidation of and victory for neoliberalism.

There was one major exception to third way neoliberalism, however, which took place in Latin America with its so-called pink tide and which lasted more or less from 2003 until 2012. Hugo Chávez was elected president of Venezuela in 1998, but it wasn't until after the failed coup and the oil industry shutdown in 2003 that he began to radicalize and oppose neoliberalism in all of its forms. Also in 2003, Workers Party leader Luis Inácio "Lula" da Silva was elected as president of Brazil and Nestor Kirchner in Argentina, a few years later Tabaré Vázquez in Uruguay (2005), Evo Morales in Bolivia (2006), Michelle Bachelet in Chile (2006), Manuel Zelaya in Honduras (2006), Rafael Correa in Ecuador (2007), Daniel Ortega in Nicaragua (2007), Fernando Lugo in Paraguay (2008), and Mauricio Funes in El Salvador (2009). To varying degrees these presidents worked on reintroducing welfare state policies in their countries, which involved expanding social programs, redistributing wealth, and, in some cases, nationalizing industries. At least part of the reason these policies enjoyed initial success is that a global "commodities boom" took place during this time, in which the price of raw materials, such as oil (Venezuela, Ecuador, and Brazil), copper (Chile), and natural gas (Bolivia, Brazil), among others, rose significantly.

However, when the commodities boom turned into a slump in the early 2010s and Hugo Chávez died in 2013, the pink tide gradually came to an end. One country after the other either elected conservatives or went through a right-wing coup and the governments returned to neoliberalism in one form or another (with the exception, so far, of Venezuela, Cuba, and Nicaragua).[15] Ultimately, the economic pressure that global financial markets place on left-leaning governments, in the

---

[15] Neoliberal restorations via the ballot box took place in Argentina (2015–2019), Ecuador (2017), Chile (2018), El Salvador (2019), Uruguay (2020). Military and/or legislative coups in favor of neoliberalism took place in Honduras (2009), Paraguay (2012), Brazil (2018), Bolivia (2019), and Peru (2022). As of this writing (2025), however, most of these restorations were cut short, with center-left or leftist parties regaining control in all of

form of capital flight, higher risk ratings and lower bond ratings, and declining foreign direct investment makes it extremely difficult for these countries to maintain extensive welfare state policies for longer periods of time in the absence of a commodities boom.[16]

Institutionalized Neoliberalism (2008-2025)

The Great Recession or Great Financial Crisis of 2007-2008 at first seemed like neoliberalism's most definitive and damaging crisis. Numerous major banks either went bankrupt or were bailed out, unemployment soared to over 10 percent in the United States, and, for a moment, it seemed as if the economy might collapse entirely.[17] Ultimately, though, the economy was not only rescued but seemed to recover. Still, neoliberalism as a belief system and ideology lost most of its legitimacy because of this crisis.

Following 2008, one could argue that neoliberalism entered its third phase, of being on autopilot. That is, it no longer needed the support of broad ideological legitimacy because it is deeply institutionalized

---

South America—except in Paraguay and Peru—but under far more difficult economic circumstances than during the first pink tide.

[16] The cases of Venezuela and Bolivia represent a very interesting contrast in this context because Evo Morales was able to maintain a strong economy in Bolivia, while Nicolas Maduro, in Venezuela, was not. I would argue that the Bolivian and the Venezuelan cases represent interesting exceptions from the rest of Latin America, in that these two countries are far more dependent on commodity export earnings than the others are. Venezuela and Bolivia pursued somewhat different economic policies, which, in the case of Bolivia, led to sustained economic growth, despite the decline in commodity prices, while in the case of Venezuela has led to an economic downturn. Venezuela also had to confront a series of crippling US-imposed sanctions, which further deepened its economic crisis. However, it is possible that US sanctions would not have been imposed on Venezuela, had it succeeded economically the way Bolivia did. In other words, it is probable that the sanctions were imposed on Venezuela because of its economic weakness. Bolivia succeeded economically (but not politically, when Morales was overthrown in late 2019) whereas Venezuela failed mainly because, unlike Bolivia (which saved a portion of its export earnings for times when these earnings declined) Venezuela pursued the pro-cyclical economic policy, of spending aggressively when earnings were up and followed austerity policies when earnings were down. See Rojas (2018, 2020) for a detailed analysis of these dynamics.

[17] Fed Chair Ben Bernanke allegedly told members of Congress that they must pass the $700 billion rescue bill and added, "If we don't do this tomorrow, we won't have an economy on Monday." (https://www.pbs.org/wgbh/pages/frontline/meltdown/etc/script.html)

in everyday habits, rules, laws, treaties, and common sense that it is implemented without any real self-awareness about what is being implemented. I thus call this third phase of neoliberalism "institutionalized neoliberalism."[18] Later I will say more about why I add the modifier "digital" to this phase, but for now, I want to highlight that this phase begins the same year that Apple's iPhone was first released and when Facebook came into its own as the world's main social media platform and these digital developments further contributed to the un-self-conscious institutionalization of digital neoliberalism.

The institutionalization of neoliberalism has taken on numerous forms, many of which were initiated in the previous phase, but which became solidified or even intensified following the Great Recession. The perhaps most important forms of institutionalization have taken place in the ever-expanding power of global financial capital. For example, foreign exchange transactions rose from US$1.5 trillion per day in 2001 to US$7.5 trillion per day in 2022—five-fold increase.[19] Similarly, the global derivatives market was valued at around US$730 trillion in 2024, seven times as high as in 2000.[20] Meanwhile, in comparison, global GDP tripled between 2001 and 2023, from US$33 trillion to US$106 trillion.[21] In short, the greater the volume of financial transactions and investments, the greater the power of those who control these transactions. During the Bretton Woods regime of fixed exchange rates countries had far more leeway in determining their economic policy. But now, as Cahill and Konings (2017) note, "Increasingly, the operation of international financial markets worked at odds with the ability of states to maintain social protective institutions, forcing them

---

[18] Davies (2016) calls it "punitive neoliberalism."
[19] Bank for International Settlements: https://www.bestbrokers.com/forex-trading/forex-daily-trading-volume/
[20] 2000 - IMF: https://www.elibrary.imf.org/display/book/9781557759993/ch03.xml
2024 - ISDA: https://www.isda.org/a/GpbgE/Key-Trends-in-the-Size-and-Composition-of-OTC-Derivatives-Markets-in-the-First-Half-of-2024.pdf
[21] Statista: https://www.statista.com/statistics/268750/global-gross-domestic-product-gdp/

to use their policy instruments to instead enforce compliance with market forces."[22]

The second reason for the institutionalization of neoliberalism has been the increasing size and power of corporations. First and foremost, this affects the banking sector, which is now even more concentrated than it was before the Global Financial Crisis of 2008. In the US the total number of banks declined from 8,305 in 2008 to 5,913 in 2016, while in Europe the number of banks declined from 6,097 to 4,385 in the same period.[23] More importantly, in 2023, the world's twenty largest asset management firms managed US$128 trillion—significantly more than the world's annual GDP—in assets.[24] In addition, these asset management firms are highly interconnected because they invest heavily in each other's companies. Further indicating the extent of financialization and concentration is the fact that, in 2025, of the world's twenty largest corporations, in terms of assets, seventeen are banks.[25] Similar patterns of increasing concentration exist in almost every other branch of business, whether auto manufacturing, agriculture, pharmaceuticals, software, mass media, and so on.[26] These megacorporations that exist in all areas of life are thus more powerful than ever and use that power to push governments toward neoliberal policies in all areas of life.

The third development that has put neoliberalism on autopilot is the increasing indebtedness of states, corporations, and individuals around the world. Both public and private indebtedness have increased significantly since 2008. According to the 2018 IMF Fiscal Monitor report, "At $164 trillion—equivalent to 225 percent of global GDP—global debt continues to hit new record highs almost a decade after

---

[22] Cahill and Konings (2017, p. 56).
[23] BIS (p. 83): https://www.bis.org/publ/cgfs60.pdf
[24] See https://www.thinkingaheadinstitute.org/content/uploads/2024/10/PI-500-2024.pdf (accessed July 8, 2025).
[25] Forbes: https://www.forbes.com/lists/global2000/ (accessed July 8, 2025).
[26] Phillips (2018) provides a detailed summary of these developments.

the collapse of Lehman Brothers."[27] More specifically, private household debt has been one of the main factors in rising debt levels. For example, US private household debt in 2017 reached its highest level since the 2008 Global Financial Crisis, at US$13 trillion—and by 2024 it reached US$18 trillion.[28] A large part of the reason for the constantly increasing levels of private household indebtedness is that while wages and benefits have remained mostly the same over the past forty years, the costs of housing, education, and medical care have risen continuously.[29] The main means for dealing with rising expenses when incomes remain the same is to go into debt. This is good for keeping consumption up and the economy going in the short term, but in the long term it is unsustainable. Ultimately, as far as neoliberalism is concerned, debt represents a powerful force for "disciplining" the individual. According to the neoliberal ethos, debt represents a moral failure for which the individual bears full responsibility. As William Davies notes, "[E]conomic dependency and moral failure become entangled in the form of debt, producing a melancholic condition in which governments and societies unleash hatred and violence upon members of their own populations," adding, "Research on public attitudes to austerity confirms a[n] ... internalization of financial morality, which produces the sense that we 'deserve' to suffer for credit-fueled economic growth."[30]

Fourth, as the previous point indicates, individuals living in neoliberal societies have come to internalize the neoliberal ethos. I will explore the meaning of this in greater detail later. Briefly, though, this means that instead of splitting our activities up into different spheres,

---

[27] IMF (2018, p. 30). All countries increased their private and public debt, but the country with the fastest rise was China's, increasing from US$4.9 trillion in 2007 to US$25.5 trillion in 2016.

[28] Reuters, Aug. 14, 2018, "U.S. household debt rises to $13.3 trillion in second quarter," (https://www.reuters.com/article/us-usa-fed-debt/u-s-household-debt-rises-to-13-3-trillion-in-second-quarter-idUSKBN1KZ1QZ). For 2024: https://tradingeconomics.com/united-states/debt-balance-total (accessed July 8, 2025).

[29] See, for example, New York Times, July 13, 2018, "Paychecks Lag as Profits Soar, and Prices Erode Wage Gains" (https://www.nytimes.com/2018/07/13/business/economy/wages-workers-profits.html).

[30] Davies (2016, p. 130).

such as work, politics, family, leisure, and friends, we see all spheres under the overarching context of their economic impact on our lives. In other words, we have become "entrepreneurs of the self," where all our capacities, networks, identities, and affinities can be valorized as "human capital" for our one-person enterprise of the self.[31] The implication is that all successes we achieve in our lives are thanks to our entrepreneurial skills and any failures are also wholly our responsibility.

Finally, the fifth reason for neoliberalism's hegemonic commonsense nature has to do with our digital technology of smartphones and social media. On the one hand, these technologies are historically unprecedented tools for networking and for being in constant communication with everyone in our social networks. On the other hand, numerous studies show that this technology, despite its networking power, also isolates us.[32] This sense of isolation, alienation, and loneliness further contributes to the sense that we are alone in the neoliberal economic world and must rely only on ourselves for economic success. In other words, the sense of altruism and solidarity, which is antithetical to neoliberalism, is lost in the process.

External Consequences of Neoliberal Digital Capitalism

I will now examine the external consequences of digital neoliberalism and then, in the next section, its internal consequences. By external consequences I mean the ways it manifests itself objectively to an outside observer. By internal consequences I mean the ways it manifests itself subjectively, on an experiential level—how those who are caught up in the dynamics of neoliberalism perceive the world of digital neoliberalism as participants in it.

One can describe the external consequences along at least four primary aspects: oligarchic, financialized, privatized, and social

---

[31] Foucault (2008) was one of the first to highlight this feature of neoliberalism.
[32] The one who has perhaps done the most work in this area is Sherry Turkle (2017).

media-based. Each of these features overlaps and reinforces the other, which makes it at times difficult to identify clear distinctions between them. What they all have in common, though, is that in different ways they present obstacles to the development of post-neoliberal consciousness and practices. These obstacles, in turn, express themselves in terms of ever-increasing inequality, ecological destruction, surveillance, and neo-imperialism.

Oligarchical

Corporations, in the neoliberal phase of capitalism, have not only become larger but have also taken on more areas of social life than ever before. As mentioned earlier, the percentage of GDP that is controlled by the public sector has declined in almost all countries of the world. Meanwhile, also as pointed out above, corporations have become ever larger, with fewer and fewer megacorporations controlling various branches of industry. In some industries, particularly those involved in digital technology, these corporate behemoths are practically monopolies, such as Google in the Internet search and advertising sector and Amazon in the online shopping sector.

Capitalism has in the past gone through phases of monopolization, but eventually, these monopolies were broken up, with the argument that they were hurting the consumer. Under neoliberal digital capitalism, though, the arguments and laws in favor of breaking up monopolies have been dismantled, making the prevention of monopoly formation more difficult. In the United States, for example, courts began applying a new standard known as "consumer welfare" instead of competition to evaluate whether a corporation should be broken up under antitrust law. That is, previously the main objective of the law was to maintain competition in any given market. Since the 1980s, however, under the principle of consumer welfare, the judgment was based on whether a megacorporation offered greater efficiencies of scale that would benefit the consumer. As we will see later, this principle is increasingly applicable to so-called digital platforms, where the corporation acts as an intermediary between the consumer and various smaller enterprises. The larger the platform in which a corporation such as Amazon can provide access to all the goods and services of distributed and competing enterprises, the greater the ultimate choice and efficiency for the consumer. This principle thus acts as a key argument against antitrust law and the breaking up of monopolies.[33] I will return to this issue later when looking at the implications that so-called digital platforms have for capitalism and for a post-capitalist future.

Digital–Financial

The second major trend of contemporary capitalism is its extreme degree of financialization. There are three compelling explanations for why capitalism has become so financialized in the early twenty-first century. One of these is an economic explanation, which has to do with capital's problems in making a profit in the "real" (nonfinancial) economy. The second explanation is ideological and has to do with the neoliberal transformation of the political-economic context in which corporations operate. And the third explanation has to do with the digitalization of finance. One could thus say that the economic factor was the driver, and the ideological and technological factors were the enablers of financialization.

It is well-known among economists of all political persuasions that so-called mature economies stagnate over time. The clearest evidence for this is that in every decade since the 1950s economic growth has been steadily slower for the United States, Europe, and Japan. For example, while economic growth in the 1960s averaged nearly 10 percent per year in Japan and about 5 percent per year in the United States and Europe, annual growth decreased a whopping 63 percent in the United States and a similar amount in Europe from 2000 to 2011. In Japan, it declined by 90 percent.[34] It is the increasing stagnation of major

[33] See Crouch (2011, p. 55).
[34] Foster and McChesney (2012, p. 4).

economies that drives the financialization of the economy.³⁵ A key reason for the increasing economic stagnation is the dual phenomenon of growing inequality and growing centralization and concentration of capital, which are key tendencies that Karl Marx also highlighted.

That is, with every business cycle the more powerful companies buy up the weaker ones, thereby creating greater centralization and concentration of capital. As fewer and fewer companies and corporations dominate the market, each one has ever-greater power and creates an oligopolistic context where competition between corporations is no longer based on price. Instead, they maintain relatively high prices and high profit margins by competing against each other based on advertising, lowering labor costs, and obtaining political favors from governments. The high prices and profit margins and the political maneuvering for policies that benefit capital, in turn, mean that inequality increases. As Foster and McChesney explain,

> [T]he rise of the giant monopolistic (or oligopolistic) corporations had led to a tendency for the actual and potential investment-seeking surplus in society to rise. The very conditions of exploitation (or high price markups on unit labor costs) meant that both inequality in society increased and that more and more surplus capital tended to accumulate actually and potentially within the giant firms and in the hands of wealth investors, who were unable to find profitable investment outlets sufficient to absorb all of the investment-seeking surplus. Hence, the economy became increasingly dependent on external stimuli such as higher government spending (particularly on the military), a rising sales effort, and financial expansion to maintain growth.³⁶

The main reason capital turns to financial expansion as an outlet for investment is that such investment easily turns into an upward spiral in that greater investment in financial assets means asset price

---

[35] Foster and McChesney (2012, p. 9) give primary credit for this insight to the post-Keynesian economist Hyman Minsky and to the Marxist economist Paul Sweezy.
[36] Foster and McChesney (2012, pp. 11–12).

inflation and hence the potential for greater capital gains. In short, capital creates financial bubbles that function as a sort of Ponzi scheme. One of the main side effects of such financial bubbles is frequent financial crashes. As Foster and McChesney point out, at least fifteen major financial crises occurred between the 1970s and the Great Financial Crisis of 2008, where each subsequent financial crisis was larger and more serious than the last. Another consequence is that each financial crisis makes the surviving financial institutions fewer and larger than before the crisis. For example, in 1990 the twenty largest US financial institutions held only 12 percent of total financial assets. After the 2008 crisis, they held 70 percent of all financial assets.[37] We have thus seen a transition to the financialization of the economy since the 1970s, and this has been reflected in the following five developments:

> (1) increasing financial profits as a share of total profits; (2) rising debt relative to GDP; (3) the growth of FIRE (finance, insurance, and real estate) as a share of national income; (4) the proliferation of exotic and opaque financial instruments; and (5) the expanding role of financial bubbles.[38]

In addition to the pursuit of capital gains (the profits gained by buying financial assets at a lower price and selling them later at a higher price), finance capital also manages to maintain a steady profit rate via the collection of interest. Interest-bearing capital thus forces debtors who make profits in the real economy to maintain a high rate of exploitation of labor to pay off their loans. This could be the exploitation of others' labor (when a company's owners borrow in order to expand or modernize their own business) or of one's own labor (as when a household borrows to maintain its standard of living). As a result, inequality continues to grow. The most glaring example of this process is how real wages hardly increased at all ever since 1980, while

---

[37] Foster and McChesney (2012, p. 43).
[38] Foster and McChesney (2012, p. 50).

productivity grew at a steady rate.[39] Meanwhile, inequality in the United States (as well as in almost all the rest of the developed world) has grown steadily. The result of the ever-growing inequality is what Marx called the "realization problem," where capital finds it increasingly more difficult to find buyers for the products that an ever-larger proportion of the population cannot afford to buy. This further contributes to economic stagnation and to even greater financialization.

While the centralization and concentration of capital in developed economies push it toward ever more financialization, it is the recent developments in digital technology and in neoliberal public policy that have enabled financialization to a far greater extent than before. For example, on the technological front computer technology has been essential for the development of new financial "instruments," such as Collateralized Debt Obligations (CDOs) and Credit Default Swaps (CDSs). Computer technology has also been instrumental in networking banks and for calculating prices and hiding the complexities of these instruments.[40] Another important technology-enabled financial innovation is high-frequency trading (HFT), which uses sophisticated algorithms to make rapid stock market trades to take advantage of small price differences or shifts. According to one estimate, up to half of all US stock trades are now conducted via HFT algorithms.[41]

Another crucial development that digital technology has helped support is bank lending to private households. Banks have always done this, but with automated calculation of credit risks and credit scores the process of providing household loans, usually via credit cards—but not only—has become increasingly simple and more efficient for banks.[42]

While digital technology provided the material infrastructure for financialization, neoliberal economic policy provided the regulatory

---

[39] According to the Economic policy Institute (EPI), "The Productivity-Pay Gap" has meant that productivity increased 3.7 times as much as wages between 1980 and 2021. (See https://www.epi.org/productivity-pay-gap/).
[40] Staab (2019).
[41] Nasdaq (2016).
[42] Lapavitsas and Dos Santos (2008).

framework, as we covered in the previous section. This regulatory framework involves both a dismantling of old financial regulations, such as the Glass-Steagall Act of 1933 (repealed in 1999), which placed limits on financial institutions, or the provision of new international rules for financial transactions, such as those embedded in the World Trade Organization's (WTO's) founding,[43] which give financial institutions and corporations the power to sue governments to force national economies to become more neoliberal.

"Platform" Capitalism and Privatized Markets

Another dimension of neoliberal digital capitalism is the development of what some have called "platform capitalism."[44] The global economy is not only governed by financial corporations and institutions but is also increasingly under the sway of digital technology companies, such as Google (Alphabet), Amazon, Apple, Facebook, and Microsoft. As a matter of fact, of the world's ten largest publicly traded corporations in the second quarter of 2025, in terms of market capitalization, the top eight spots were held by digital technology companies.[45] All of these major digital technology companies, including many more, aim to be "platforms" on which other companies and individuals (often as self-employed one-person companies) offer their own services. For example, Amazon is a platform not only for Amazon's products but also for tens of thousands of other businesses to sell their goods using Amazon's search and fulfillment services. Facebook is a platform for news media, social media posts, and advertisers. Apple's operating

---

[43] The push for increasing the power of transnational finance capital continues in many other trade agreements, such as TRIPS (Trade-Related Aspects of Intellectual Property Rights) and TRIMS (Trade-Related Investment Measures).
[44] Srnicek (2017).
[45] See https://en.wikipedia.org/wiki/List_of_public_corporations_by_market_capitalization - 2025 (Retrieved July 8, 2025). The eight largest were, in order: Nvidia, Microsoft, Apple, Amazon, Alphabet, Meta, Broadcom, and TSMC (Taiwan Semiconductor Manufacturing). If we were to include investment management companies, though, according to the volume of assets under their management, then the largest would all be financial companies, such as Black Rock, Vanguard, Charles Schwab, and UBS. (See https://en.wikipedia.org/wiki/List_of_asset_management_firms)

system universe (Mac OS, iPhone OS, iPad OS, Watch OS) is a platform for software companies and their applications. As Srnicek observes,

> At the most general level, platforms are digital infrastructures that enable two or more groups to interact. They therefore position themselves as intermediaries that bring together different users: customers, advertisers, service providers, producers, suppliers, and even physical objects. More often than not, these platforms also come with a series of tools that enable their users to build their own products, services, and marketplaces.[46]

One could argue that the term "platform" is actually a euphemism for a private market.[47] After all, the above description of the so-called platforms fits precisely into what markets do: provide an infrastructure to bring together customers and suppliers. The main difference, though, is that normally markets are supposed to be public and neutral. The digital platform companies, though, are private and can exert total control over everyone that participates in them. In the process, they not only siphon off rents for the usage of their private markets, by charging access fees (usually to the suppliers, but sometimes also to the customers), but they can also siphon off the data of anyone who trades or participates in them. The data then represents another potential source of income, either by selling it to advertisers or by using it to the competitive advantage of the products that the platform itself has to offer.

It is interesting to note here that privatized markets are in a sense a further radicalization of neoliberalism's effort to privatize everything. However, privatized markets also represent a stark contradiction to the neoliberal principle that markets should be neutral.

Several trends are responsible for the evolution of capitalism toward this platform model. First, as manufacturing profitability declines around the world, the services sector seeks new realms of profitability,

---

[46] Srinek (2017, p. 41).
[47] Staab (2019) makes this argument very effectively in a book-length treatment.

which are now found in data mining, intellectual property (IP), and the accompanied extraction of rents from both data and IP.[48] Platforms, by their nature, gather tremendous amounts of data about both the consumers and the producers who use their platforms, thereby putting themselves—the platform or privatized market—at an advantage with respect to both consumers and producers. This data is then used for surveillance purposes and sold to other companies and governments in their efforts to target and manipulate consumer and citizen behavior (more on this later).

Second, platforms, to the extent that they function as digital networks, take advantage of so-called network effects that enable the formation of monopolies. That is, once a platform reaches a certain critical size, users (both the consumers and the producers) gain additional usefulness from the platform, which in turn causes the platform to become increasingly valuable, creating an upward spiral between value and use.[49] The trend toward privatized markets is making itself felt not only among digital technology companies but even in more traditional manufacturing companies, as they focus mainly on developing their intellectual property and their branding while outsourcing all other aspects of their business, such as manufacturing and marketing. This is not to say that digital platform companies do not need physical infrastructure. Quite the opposite: the most dominant of these digital platform companies have enormous infrastructures, but these consist mainly of physical and/or digital warehouses (such as Amazon's warehouses and Google's data processing centers).

---

[48] Christophers (2010) argues that rentier capitalism has become the single most important type of capitalism in the twenty-first century. Rents, according to Christophers, is "income derived from the ownership, possession or control of scarce assets under conditions of limited or no competition." (Kindle loc. 377) It thus includes interest, dividends, capital gains, licensing fees for intellectual property, subcontracts, and ground rent.

[49] For example, as more and more people use Uber as their ride hailing service, Uber drivers and Uber riders have an increasing advantage from using Uber instead of a smaller competitor, which would be less useful in terms of delivery speed of the service, since a smaller platform would take longer to match drivers with riders.

Mass Communication via Social Media

Finally, the fourth aspect of neoliberal digital capitalism is the dominance of social media as the means of communication in contemporary society. Of course, social media, such as Facebook, X (previously known as Twitter), YouTube, LinkedIn, and Instagram, also are digital platforms and private markets par excellence. However, their societal importance goes well beyond the market aspect described in the previous section because they have replaced traditional means of communication (such as telephone and mail) and traditional mass media outlets (such as TV and newspapers) as the primary means by which members of society receive their information not only from friends and family, but also about important social, political, economic, and cultural developments. According to Pew Research Centers, social media as the primary source of news has been climbing steadily over the past decade. It is particularly pronounced among those who are eighteen to twenty-nine years old, where, according to a 2018 survey, they consume news via social media (36 percent) more than any other news source (news websites 27 percent, TV 16 percent, radio 13 percent, and newspaper 2 percent).[50] Social media use for news consumption has no doubt continued to increase since then. Meanwhile, worldwide, 3.6 billion people use social media of one kind or another.[51]

Negative External Consequences of Neoliberal Digital Capitalism

The foregoing aspects of neoliberal digital capitalism combine to produce a variety of negative consequences for people's material life conditions, as well as for their psyche. In other words, for their external-objective dimension and their internal-subjective dimension.

---

[50] Shearer (2018)
[51] Statista (2025)

First, regarding the negative economic consequences of neoliberal digital capitalism, the most glaring one is the dramatic rise in inequality over the past fifty years in all countries of the world once they implemented neoliberal economic policies. For example, in the United States—the country with the greatest growth in income inequality among developed countries—the top 20 percent of households increased their share of national income from 44 percent to 52 percent between 1968 and 2018. Meanwhile, the poorest 20 percent of households decreased their share of income from 4.2 percent to 3.1 percent.[52] Expressed as a ratio of richest to poorest 20 percent of households, this meant the ratio went from 10:1 to 17:1. Similar trends have been present in all countries and all regions.[53] According to Alvaredo et al. (2018), "all these world regions went through a relatively egalitarian phase between 1950 and 1980. For simplicity, and for the time being, this relatively low inequality regime can be described as the 'post-war egalitarian regime,' with obvious important variations between social-democratic, New Deal, socialist, and communist variants."[54]

For the United States, the growth of income inequality has been so pronounced that MIT economist Peter Temin has argued that the US situation ought to be seen from the perspective of the economic development concept of a "dual economy,"[55] a concept that originated with the analysis of the economies of developing countries. That is, according to this concept, some segments of a dual economy prove to be quite dynamic and wealthy, growing at a steady rate,

---

[52] Income and Poverty in the United States (2018, Table A-4, p. 35–9).
[53] For example, Alvaredo et al. (2018, p. 41–2) write: "[T]he evolution of the top 10% income share in Europe (Western and Eastern Europe combined, excluding Ukraine, Belorussia, and Russia), North America (defined as the United States and Canada), China, India, and Russia ... has increased in all five of these large world regions since 1980. The top 10% share was around 30–35% in Europe, North America, China, and India in 1980, and only about 20–25% in Russia." "Top 10% income shares then increased in all these regions between 1980 and 2016, but with large variations in magnitude. In Europe, the rise was moderate, with the top 10% share increasing to about 35–40% by 2016. However, in North America, China, India, and even more so in Russia (where the change in policy regime was particularly dramatic), the rise was much more pronounced. In all these regions, the top 10% share rose to about 45–50% of total income in 2016."
[54] Alvaredo et al. (2018, p. 41–2).
[55] Temin (2017).

while other segments of the economy remain mired in poverty and stagnation for decades. The two economies are separate in many ways but are linked mainly via the labor market so that the poorer sector (known as the "subsistence sector") provides cheap labor to the wealthier sector (known as the "capitalist sector"). According to Temin, the two sectors distinguish themselves in that the wealthier one involves people who are mainly engaged in finance, technology, and electronics (the "FTE sector"), making up roughly the top 20 percent of incomes, while the poorer sector involves everyone else who is engaged in a low-wage job (the "low wage sector") and make up roughly the bottom 80 percent of the population in terms of income.[56] The causal connection between the neoliberal economy and the dual economy is that neoliberalism unleashes the power of the economically powerful, enabling them to accumulate more wealth steadily because of lower taxation rates and fewer regulations to constrain their political and economic activities.

Another crucial negative external consequence of neoliberal digital capitalism is that an ever-increasing number of those in the bottom 80 percent income bracket are precariously employed, meaning that they lack job security and are often employed part-time or on temporary work contracts, earning income from one "gig" to the other. The reason the precarious workforce (also known as the "precariat"[57]) has grown has to do both with the process of neoliberal deregulation of labor markets, which has made unionization more difficult and reduced employment benefits, and the digitization of the economy, which has reorganized labor to make work from home and the previously discussed platform business model more feasible. The precarious employment model fits with the previously discussed neoliberal concept of the "entrepreneur of the self." In other words, precarious employment is ideologically justified in neoliberalism as an opportunity for greater personal freedom

---

[56] According to Temin, the FTE sector consists mostly of whites, while the low wage sector is about 50% whites and 50% people of color. (Temin, 2017, p. 9)

[57] A term coined by Standing (2011).

and self-reliance, while at the same time exposing the individual to the vicissitudes of the market more than ever.

Next, neoliberal digital capitalism further exacerbates the ecological crisis that industrial capitalism first brought about. Of all the many dimensions of this crisis, which includes air pollution, water pollution, and topsoil erosion, among others, global warming and the accompanying climate crisis are the most dramatic. Neoliberal economic policy, which aims to deregulate the limited environmental policies of industrial capitalism, makes efforts to limit carbon emissions and global warming practically impossible. As the environmental economist Robert Pollin stated,

> Neoliberalism is a driving force causing the climate crisis. This is because neoliberalism is a variant of classical liberalism, and classical liberalism builds from the idea that everyone should be granted maximum freedom to pursue their self-interest within capitalist market settings.[58]

It is a matter of controversy among critics of neoliberalism whether regulated capitalism, which strictly limits environmental impacts of production and consumption, could avoid ecological catastrophe or whether capitalism is inherently anti-ecological and that a regulated, so-called green capitalism, is impossible. Regardless of which of these positions might be true, there is a consensus that neoliberalism is fundamentally incompatible with ecological sustainability. The more pressing problem, as previously mentioned, is that neoliberalism is no longer "just" an ideology whose doctrines some governments have chosen to follow, but that it has become institutionalized and now functions on "autopilot" on international and national levels, which makes it very difficult (and in some cases practically impossible) to introduce environmental regulations. Free trade agreements, such as the USCMA (previously known as NAFTA) and the World Trade Organization, often consider environmental regulations to be a form of

---

[58] Pollin and Chomsky (2020, p. 20).

protectionism and impose hefty fines and sanctions on countries that try to apply them.[59]

Finally, neoliberal digital capitalism also has detrimental effects on political involvement by hollowing out democratic governance and imposing police surveillance and repression. Concerning the hollowing out of democratic governance, this happens on the level of neoliberal ideology, which aims to remove democratic participation from anything that could affect so-called free market exchange. However, as the political theorist Wendy Brown has pointed out, neoliberal thinkers argue that practically all realms of human activity can be seen from the point of view of economic exchange, which means that political (let alone democratic) governance should not intervene practically anywhere.[60] We thus see not only the deregulation of environmental and workplace protections, but also the marketization and privatization of education, healthcare, criminal justice, warfare, and even politics itself. What is left of politics and the state is limited to figuring out how to enable competition in all spheres of social activity.[61]

Such a perspective on politics only further exacerbates inequality, since in the context of market exchanges the rich and better-off are always in a more powerful position to outcompete (and outbid) the poor and the not-so-well-off. As inequality increases, so do the number of revolts and rebellions against this situation. It is no coincidence that right-wing populism, as well as progressive and leftist protest movements, have been on the rise in recent years. Both represent rejections of declining standards of living and of growing inequality in society, even though their political analyses of what has caused this situation are completely different.

---

[59] Global Trade Watch of the organization Public Citizen has documented many examples of such cases (see https://www.citizen.org/topic/globalization-trade/).

[60] "All conduct is economic conduct; all spheres of existence are framed and measured by economic terms and metrics, even when those spheres are not directly monetized. In neoliberal reason and in domains governed by it, we are only and everywhere homo oeconomicus, which itself has a historically specific form." Brown (2015, p. 10).

[61] However, as mentioned earlier, neoliberalism has now turned against itself when it enabled the privatization of markets in the form of platform capitalism, which limit free market competition.

Governments around the world have reacted to these revolts and rebellions by augmenting the state's surveillance and repressive capacities.[62] For example, the whistleblower Edward Snowden revealed in 2013 that the US government's National Security Agency (NSA) has for a long time been illegally monitoring practically all private internet and telephone communications, in cooperation with intelligence agencies of many other countries and all major information technology companies (such as Verizon, Vodafone, Apple, Google, Facebook, and Microsoft). Supposedly this surveillance is used to prevent terrorism, but it is well-known that activist groups and individuals are to a large extent also the targets of this surveillance.[63]

The effort to control rebellions and protest movements goes far beyond mere surveillance, though, into direct repression. This repression can take a wide variety of forms, whether coups against rebellious governments, such as in Latin America,[64] direct police repression against social movements, such as the Occupy and the Black Lives Matter movements in the US, mass incarceration of minority populations, or immigrant detention and deportation. Evidence for the increasing repression of potentially and actually rebellious populations can be found in the ever-increasing state budgets devoted to surveillance, warfare, policing, and detention. For example, the US military budget increased by 91 percent in real terms between 1998 and 2011. Meanwhile, total global defense spending increased by 50 percent between 2006 and 2015.[65] Prison and police spending have similarly grown by leaps and bounds during this period.[66]

---

[62] It should be noted that state repression and surveillance is usually directed far more forcefully against movements of the left than of the right, since the left is correctly perceived to be a far more dangerous threat to the status quo than the right.

[63] See, for example, Choudry (2018) and Lemieux (2019).

[64] The US-supported coups against Haiti's president Bertrand Aristide in 2001, against Venezuela's president Chávez in 2002, Honduras's president Manuel Zelaya in 2009, and Bolivia's president Evo Morales in 2019 are all examples of US efforts to repress popular movements just in the twenty-first century (not to mention the numerous efforts in the twentieth century).

[65] Figures taken from Robinson (2020, p. 74).

[66] Federal, state, and local inflation-adjusted spending on law enforcement and corrections increased from $79 billion in 1980 to $267 billion in 2020—a 330 percent increase in 40 years, while the population grew by 150 percent during that time. In other words,

As William Robinson (2020) points out, the steady increase in surveillance, military, police, and incarceration spending serves a dual purpose. It is not only designed to prevent or subdue the increasing number of rebellions but also serves to maintain capitalist accumulation. That is, as the living standards and disposable income of the vast majority of the population decline, due to the increasing inequality that neoliberal digital capitalism causes, corporations have an ever more difficult time maintaining profits. One way that profits can be maintained in the aggregate is via "military Keynesianism," which Robinson calls accumulation by repression, meaning ever-increasing spending on surveillance, military, police, and incarceration.[67]

Negative Internal Consequences of Neoliberal Digital Capitalism

While neoliberal digital capitalism impinges on people's lives externally, in terms of economic polarization, precarity, environmental destruction, surveillance, and repression, it also has profound negative effects on the psyche, on their internal dimension. These internal effects are perhaps best summed up in terms of an ever-growing sense of isolation, anxiety, depression, distraction, and addiction. But how does it come to this? One could simply assume that the external effects of neoliberal digital capitalism cause them. However, as numerous social thinkers have pointed out, these internal effects might have a more complicated source, having to do with a variety of sociocultural transformations that have taken place in most societies over the past fifty years. These transformations included a cultural development, the rise of the counterculture, and an economic-technological one, which

---

justice system spending increased at approximately twice the rate as the population (source: https://usafacts.org/state-of-the-union/crime-justice/, accessed January 2, 2024).

[67] Robinson (2020, chap. 3).

is the emergence of a postindustrial digital economy, in the context of neoliberalism.

The German sociologist Andreas Reckwitz describes the consequences of these transformations very well in his book, *The Society of Singularities*.[68] According to Reckwitz, the counterculture of the 1960s and 1970s pushed for post-materialist values, in reaction against the materialism of their parents, as well as for a focus on improving the quality of life instead of one's standard of living. This post-materialist quality of life focus was also a turn against standardization and conformity, which had become the norm in most Western societies since the introduction of Fordism[69] at the start of the twentieth century. Focusing on quality-of-life issues meant living a life that is attuned to one's own unique desires, preferences, talents, and creativity. This countercultural trend influenced (and was also influenced by) the launch of the digital revolution in the early 1980s, which increasingly gave each individual the ability to harness digital technology—via the PC—for the expansion of a wide variety of private endeavors, from networking with remote peers, to deploying creative potentials on a mass scale, to increased access to information and education, to the launch of creative new business ventures, among many other things.

The main consequence of these changes is a process that Reckwitz calls "singularization," whereby individuals, things, lives, places, and collectives are all singularized in the sense that these all undergo a process of becoming unique, extraordinary, and special. Singularization is distinct from individualization in that the latter is a simpler and more antisocial process than singularization. In contrast, singularization depends on cultural valuations for what constitutes being unique or special. As Reckwitz states:

---

[68] Reckwitz (2017).
[69] Fordism, as introduced by the Ford Motor Company, involves the standardization of product lines, the use of assembly lines in production, large-scale production, and an accompanying effort to pay workers' wages that are high enough so that they can participate in the mass consumption of the products that they helped assemble.

In the mode of singularization life is no longer simply lived, but it is curated. The late-modern subject *performs* their ... special self in front of the other, which becomes its audience. Only when it is authentic is it attractive. The ubiquitous social media with their profiles are one of the main arenas of this work on the creation of specialness.[70]

In effect, singularization is an exacerbation of differences, which thus also individuates and isolates, but does so in a different way than individualism because singularization is an eminently sociocultural process of constant valuation and devaluation of individuals, goods, services, places, and collectives. In addition, this process necessarily takes place in the context of the networked society, which allows for a constant process of valuation by anyone of anyone or anything. Another consequence of singularization is that everything that is singularized is also lifted out of its traditional cultural context, in the hope that this decontextualization will give it a new unique marker of attractiveness. World music, world food, world dance, and so on, come out of this ongoing search for uniqueness, creating what Reckwitz calls a "hyperculture." Finally, since everyone and everything is in a state of intense competition among each other, it becomes increasingly difficult for each singularity to stand out, which means that the ability to attract attention becomes ever more important.

The singularization process thus involves not only the creation of uniqueness but also the careful management of reputation and of acquiring attention—a process that today's digital media, especially social media, are only too eager to amplify. The constant exhortation to "be oneself" (or to "be the best version of oneself") is exemplary of the singularization pressure.

In addition, while digital technology enables the singularization of lives it also singularizes our environment. In the pre-digital era, technology was far more context-bound, in that we would use it when

---

[70] Reckwitz (2017, p. 9; my translation). This interpretation of the performative role of the individual in late-modern society echoes the observations of other social theorists, such as those of Agger (2003) and Poster (2006), among others.

and where we needed it and were free from it when we didn't. Digital technology, though, has become our environment all the time, since we are always involved with our computers, smartphones, tablets, or smart appliances. More than that, this technology customizes itself to our specific habits, search histories, technology usage, and demographic, so that this environment becomes singular as well.

Meanwhile, in the world of work, as individuals set about creating a singular life, this means trying to work in an area that provides fulfillment while also being attuned to market forces and public demands. If one is unlucky these two areas fail to coincide, and the individual suffers from devaluation and loss of employment. This potentially contradictory situation creates a large amount of uncertainty, pressure, stress, and anxiety for the individual. One way to cope with these contradictory pressures is to develop what Reckwitz calls one's "psycho-physical capital,"[71] that is, to constantly work on one's psychological and physical well-being to establish the foundation for a successful singular lifestyle. However, the potential for disappointment, when the lifestyle is unsuccessful always remains, especially when one's life is exposed to the public eye, as it usually is via social media.

The sense of being left behind is especially intense for the lower classes, who do not generally share in the curation of a singular lifestyle and who have lost the sense of pride and class consciousness that the working class previously enjoyed because of the increasing precarity and uncertainty in which the lower class now lives. This lower class makes up roughly one-third of the population in developed economies and consists of simple service sector employees, semi-qualified industrial labor, precarious employees, the unemployed, and welfare recipients. What distinguishes the lifestyles and life chances of this new lower class relative to the new creative middle class is that the new lower class has less cultural capital, they do not singularize their lifestyles, and they are exposed to an intensified cultural devaluation (as opposed to mainly a material devaluation, as in previous epochs).

---

[71] Reckwitz (2017, p. 305).

In effect, the society of singularities produces individuals that have less and less in common with each other, are thus isolated, dependent on unpredictable cultural and market valuations of their lifestyles, and are exposed to constant conditions of competition with everyone else.[72] It is thus no wonder that anxiety and depression have come to be the defining mental illness of our times.[73] For example, anxiety is currently considered to be the most prevalent mental disorder, affecting at least 33 percent of the US population during their lifetime[74] and depression increased significantly between 2005 and 2015.[75]

It is important to note, though, as many analysts of digital media have, that while we may become more isolated because of the technology, we are not necessarily lonelier because digital media embeds us into networks of friends and associations of the like-minded. However, this embeddedness or networking does not have the same emotional resonance for us as real face-to-face encounters. That is, they are emotionally flatter and more impoverished and thus do not give us the same satisfaction that real-life connections provide. As one observer writes, "We have thus traded in 'real' relationships for simulated ones."[76]

As mentioned earlier, individuals in neoliberal digital capitalism are forced to create their own "startups of one," not only as a job, but as a lifestyle project, and their success or failure is dependent on social perception and cultural valuation. So, instead of becoming revolutionaries who revolt against the system, as workers once did when they saw their employer and the larger economic system as being

---

[72] Numerous other studies of the effect of the digital era have also echoed this problem of increasing isolation, most notably perhaps Turkle (2017) and Ugolik Phillips (2020).
[73] A very important meta-study conducted by Curran and Hill (2019) shows that an increasing sense of perfectionism is linked to the increase in the prevalence of neoliberal economic conditions in the US, Canada, and the UK, between 1989 and 2016. It is well established in the psychological literature that feelings of perfectionism are positively correlated with an increased incidence of depression and anxiety. For example, in Flett and Hewitt (2014) and Hewitt and Flett (1990).
[74] Bandelow and Michaelis (2015).
[75] Weinberger et al. (2018).
[76] Pettman (2016, loc. 260).

responsible for their troubles, now, being self-employed, they feel they can only blame themselves.[77]

Finally, since individuals in neoliberal digital capitalism are becoming increasingly isolated, depressed, and anxious, they seek new ways to "fill the void."[78] Constant engagement in social media is one way to fill this emotional void. It provides, first, a source of distraction.[79] And those who refuse to participate in the distraction of the digital environment run the danger of falling "out of sync with the flow of life."[80] Unfortunately, as we seek the distraction of digital media, this tends to "further aggravate the conditions which make it so difficult to cope with in the first place."[81]

The consequences of distracting ourselves from our emotional problems and of the constant battle for attention, however, include increased development of attention deficit disorder[82] (ADD or ADHD), as well as addictions to social media use itself. Since social media companies depend on capturing our attention and holding it, albeit in a constant flow of new and unrelated posts, they engage in a variety of techniques for keeping our attention on their platforms. These can be positive rewards in the form of "likes," "shares," and friends' positive comments or they can be negative comments or criticisms of our statements, thereby requiring a new reaction to maintain our social standing. While negative comments are hardly addictive, the satisfaction of having provided a snappy comeback that one's friends "like" and one's opponents dislike is highly satisfying.[83]

In short, neoliberal digital capitalism is a process that radicalizes individuation and singularization, as well as increases the power of the powerful. It was the result of a confluence of four main factors: (1)

---

[77] Byung-Chul Han (2017) makes this argument succinctly and powerfully.
[78] This term is taken from Gilroy-Ware (2017).
[79] Pettman (2016).
[80] Pettman (2016, loc. 1216).
[81] Pettman (2016, loc. 1640).
[82] This is something that Stiegler (2010) emphasizes in his work.
[83] Seymour (2020) provides an excellent analysis of this social media dynamic and its addictive nature.

neoliberal ideology, as an effort of the upper classes to regain control over the capitalist accumulation process following an extended period of social-democratic Keynesianism, (2) the unleashing and growth of the power of global financial capital, following the breakdown of the Bretton Woods system, (3) the development of digital technology that simultaneously isolates as well as connects individuals in a complex and contradictory dynamic, and (4) a merging of the 60s counterculture's post-materialism with neoliberalism's ever-increasing market competition and dependence. Externally, this process produced unprecedented levels of inequality, ecological destruction, and the dismantling of liberal representative democracy. Internally, it has produced unprecedented levels of anxiety, depression, loneliness, and addiction. In other words, on all fronts, this system is heading toward multiple crises. Whether we can overcome these crises depends on whether they will provoke a transformation to a newer and higher level of social organization and of consciousness.

6

Commonist Consciousness and Commonist Institutions

The perhaps most pressing question of the moment is, how do we get from here to there, from the current neoliberal nightmare to a post-capitalist commonwealth? That is, what forms of struggle and organizing and what types of social and psychological processes will bring about the new society that we so desperately need? And what would this post-capitalist commonwealth and its accompanying post-capitalist consciousness look like? These are all questions I will attempt to briefly outline in this chapter, based on the analysis presented so far.

Within the Marxist school of thought, which is one of the few that has attempted to answer these questions systematically, there are generally two types of responses to these questions. The first type we could call revolutionary theories, in that while they acknowledge the seriousness of the crises we face, they emphasize the will to fight for change among certain segments of the population—usually, the working class and other marginalized sectors (also known as the "revolutionary subject") as being the decisive factor for bringing about a post-capitalist or socialist society. The second type we could call crisis theories, which focus on how the crises we face will be resolved via certain institutional, psychological, and societal transformations that the crises themselves provoke.

This is not to say that revolutionary theories and crisis theories do not recognize the importance of the other, but that they tend to emphasize one factor as being more important than the other. Among the more recent proponents of revolutionary theories, we could count Antonio Negri and Michael Hardt, as well as Michael Lebowitz,[1] who argue that it is through the process of revolutionary struggle for a post-capitalist society that new forms of consciousness and new institutions will come about. For example:

> Through their struggles against capital, workers develop their capacities. They make themselves fit to undertake new struggles. In this dialectical relation of acts and capacities, acts create capacities.[2]
>
> Struggles valorize existing subjectivities but also create new ones; subjectivities are radically transformed by their participation in political organizing and political action. Struggle too is a terrain of the production of subjectivity.[3]

While this process of social struggle and self-change is no doubt crucial for the creation of a new subjectivity or consciousness, these theories do not theorize the exact relationship between struggle and the creation of a post-capitalist society. They emphasize how class struggle is cooperative and how this would presumably result in more cooperative institutions, but this is a very loose connection, especially when one considers that many revolutionary efforts throughout history depended on top-down and authoritarian leadership for their success and did not always result in particularly cooperative institutions once the revolution was achieved.

We, therefore, need to combine the observation that the struggle for better social conditions changes the people engaging in that struggle with the type of crisis that this struggle hopes to overcome. That is, I would suggest that a struggle to overcome a crisis of feudalism or fascism will not lead to the same type of self-transformation (a new consciousness or subjectivity) as a struggle against the multiple crises of neoliberal digital capitalism. This is why it is so important for us to understand the nature of neoliberal digital capitalist crises and where

---

[1] For example, Hardt and Negri (2017), Lebowitz (2020).
[2] Lebowitz (2020, p. 82).
[3] Hardt and Negri (2017, p. 224).

the consciousness that this type of social system creates can lead when it faces and resolves its crises.

In general systems theory, a crisis can lead to two possible outcomes—either a reorganization of the system at a higher level of complexity or a reorganization towards an earlier and simpler level of complexity.[4] Thus, if we want to know what the options are, we need a clear analysis of what would be the current, previous, and possible higher forms of complexity of organizations and of consciousness. In this context, it is useful to refer to the previously mentioned work of Jürgen Habermas (Chapter 3). According to Habermas, Marx's conception of a capitalist crisis—a mismatch between the relations of production (social relations) and the forces of production (technology)—does not consider the needed change in consciousness for resolving that crisis. Habermas goes on to outline the necessary transformations in consciousness when societies resolve different crises due to the contradictions inherent in different types of society, such as in the transition from feudal to capitalistic societies.

We thus return to an examination of the psychological effect that the neoliberal crises have on individual consciousness and what the most likely positive option is for resolving these crises towards a new and higher form of consciousness, that is, to take consciousness from the pluralistic-rational stage to the integral stage. This is not to say that this is the only possible response to the crises that neoliberal digital capitalism would provoke, but that this would be a positive and probable higher-level resolution to the crisis, based on what we know about the further reaches of consciousness development after the pluralistic-rational stage.

The four crises that we are confronting are of an existential nature, which force all members of society except the most oblivious among us to find a way to cope with them and to hopefully overcome them. The first and most basic is one of survival, which is the climate crisis and—potentially, to the extent people are aware of it—the possibility

---

[4] One of the classical statements on this is Jantsch (1980).

of nuclear war. The second most basic crisis is one of justice, due to the growing inequality within and between nations. The third, which is exacerbated by the previous two, but also has its own sui generis causes, is of legitimacy, due to the ongoing processes of de-democratization. And finally, there is the psychological crisis, which the previous crises also exacerbate, but which the growing trends towards individualization and singularization intensify. All these crises, put together, can only be resolved via a combined institutional/societal and psychological resolution towards a higher level of development: the integral stage.

If indeed consciousness development builds on and integrates past experiences and learning, developing through qualitatively different stages, often as the result of negotiating and overcoming crises and conflict, and if all of this happens in a social–historical context that shapes and is shaped by consciousness development, via a process of enactment, then we can begin to ask ourselves the question of how a "better" and "more advanced" consciousness and society might look like. In Chapter 2, I presented six levels of consciousness development, which—in Chapter 3—I roughly aligned with four stages of societal development (tribal, feudal, modern-industrial, and postmodern/postindustrial). That is, for the sixth level of consciousness, which I called integral, I did not present a corresponding fifth form of social organization. The reason, of course, is that there is no such society in existence yet and the purpose of this chapter is to speculate about what kind of social organization might result when a critical mass of individuals at this integral level of consciousness organize society (and are organized by that society), based on what we know of this stage of consciousness.

Once we see how this sixth level of consciousness fits with what could be called post-capitalist, socialist, or commonist institutions, the link between integral consciousness and commonism is not only logical and natural but also necessary. That is, although integral consciousness, especially as different developmental psychologists describe it, does not embody an explicit critique of capitalism, I would argue that its worldview and values imply a post-capitalist society and commonist institutions whenever the opportunity to enact these views and values presents itself. Exactly how this might happen will be explored in the following pages. But before we get into the details of this relationship, we need to go into greater depth as to exactly what integral consciousness—which I also call commonist consciousness—looks like.

Integral/Commonist Consciousness Revisited

Practically every developmental psychologist has their own designation for the different levels, including the integral. However, while the names might be different, the descriptions of each level roughly correspond to one another. In this review of the integral level of consciousness, I will summarize how some of the most important developmental psychologists have described the integral level: Robert Kegan, Susan Cook-Greuter, Jane Loevinger, Lawrence Kohlberg, Carol Gilligan, and Ken Wilber.

Fifth Order/Inter-Institutional: Robert Kegan

The heart of Kegan's approach to consciousness development is one in which at each stage that which was the subject of the previous stage becomes the object in the next stage. So, for example, in what Kegan calls the third order (what I call the ethno-centric stage), one's role is at the center of subjectivity or identification, meaning that we completely identify with our roles as "parent," "teacher," "husband," "teenager," and so on. At the next stage, though, this role identification becomes an object of analysis, leading one to question and examine these roles and to develop a subjectivity that Kegan calls self-authorship. Similarly, in the transition from fourth order (world-centric) to fifth order (integral), the subjectivity of self-authorship becomes an object of understanding, that is, understood in the context of societal institutions and society as a complex system. As Kegan says, fifth order consciousness requires "that the epistemological organization of system, form, or theory be relativized, moved from subject to object in one's knowing."[5] In other words, the subject is now dialectical, inter-institutional, and self-transformative, while the object is abstract systems, ideology, institutions, relationships, and self-formation.

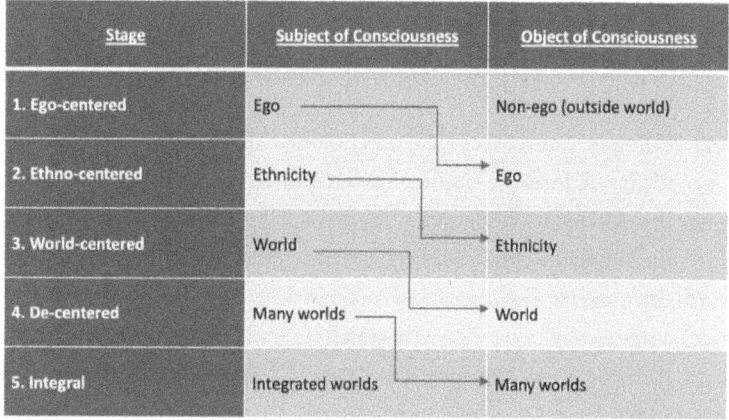

Figure 1. repeated.

Kegan also calls this form of consciousness postmodern but divides it into two different phases: deconstructive (which is strongly anti-modernist) and reconstructive (which is more trans-modern). The reason for using this terminology is that postmodern philosophy exhibits many of the key characteristics of this stage of consciousness. For this discussion, though, I am more interested in the reconstructive postmodernism, which Kegan describes as follows:

> Reconstructive postmodernism thus reopens the possibility that some kinds of normativeness, hierarchizing, privileging, generalizing, and

---

[5] Kegan (1994, p. 321).

universalizing are not only compatible with a postideological view of the world, they are necessary for sustaining it.[6]

Strategist/Autonomous: Jane Loevinger and Susan Cook-Greuter

Loevinger and Cook-Greuter focus on self-identity, that is, on what Kegan refers to as the subject. Loevinger thus writes, "Where the Conscientious [stage 5] person tends to construe the world in terms of polar opposites, the Autonomous [stage 6] person partly transcends those polarities, seeing reality as complex and multifaceted."[7] For Cook-Greuter the autonomous stage also means reintegrating disparate subidentities that have become complex:

> Persons at the Autonomous stage realize that they may notice different conflicting aspects of themselves at different times but, unlike [Individualists] who may despair about ever knowing who they really are, Autonomous individuals become able to "own" more of the contradictory parts of themselves. They can integrate previously compartmentalized subidentities of the self into a coherent new whole or core identity.[8]

An essential element of the Strategist/Autonomous stage is that individuals recognize life as a developmental process and thus strive to develop themselves and others:

> They are convinced that higher development is better and closer to truth (…). They are therefore often invested in helping others to grow. Higher is believed to be better because the more differentiated and the more autonomous persons become, the more they can claim that they have a nondistorted (true) and realistic view of themselves and the world.[9]

---

[6] Kegan (1994, p. 331).
[7] Loevinger (1976, p. 23).
[8] Cook-Greuter (1999, pp. 83–4).
[9] Cook-Greuter (1999, pp. 83–4).

Universal Ethical Principles: Lawrence Kohlberg, Carol Gilligan, Susanne Cook-Greuter

According to Cook-Greuter, individuals at this stage feel outrage against social injustice:

> Strategists genuinely feel *principled anger* and righteous indignation towards the injustices of the world. They will stand up against society to express their personal convictions or to uphold their higher, overarching principles regarding human rights and well-being. They are willing to go on the barricades and risk their lives and reputations in order to fulfill the aims of their convictions. Their anger does not usually seek a victim but is geared towards rectifying perceived ills.[10]

The principled anger against injustice is also a result of being guided by universal ethical principles. Rights are an inherent aspect of these principles, which are also correlated to obligations or duties. Carol Gilligan, in her critique of Kohlberg's analysis of moral development, modified Kohlberg's analysis by saying that moral development is different for males and females in that females go through these stages more oriented by conceptions of care, responsibility, and relationship, while in males the development is marked by a more individualistic approach. At the integral level, these masculine and feminine tendencies tend to become integrated, though.

As mentioned in Chapter 2, if we combine the notions of development and universal ethical principles, we can easily reach the conclusion at this level that one of the most basic ethical principles is to promote the greatest development for the greatest number of beings (which Wilber calls the "basic moral intuition").

Integral: Ken Wilber

Like Kegan, Wilber argues that each step in the developmental process is a process of dis-identification and reintegration. Thus, in the transition

---

[10] Cook-Greuter (2014, p. 89).

from the world-centric consciousness to the integral, the self begins to dis-identify from the ego:

> As consciousness begins to transcend the verbal ego-mind, it can—more or less for the first time—integrate the ego mind with all the lower levels. That is, because consciousness is no longer identified with any of these elements to the exclusion of any others, all of them can be integrated: the body, the persona, the shadow, the ego—all can be brought into a higher-order integration.[11]

In terms of the cognitive capabilities at this level, Wilber states:

> [W]hereas the formal mind [world-centric] establishes relationships, vision-logic [integral] establishes *networks* of those relationships. .... Such vision or panoramic logic apprehends a mass network of ideas, how they influence each other and interrelate. It is thus the beginning of a truly higher-order synthesizing capacity, of making connections, relating truths, coordinating ideas, integrating concepts.[12]

At another point Wilber describes this stage as "integral-aperspectivism" (borrowing from Jean Gebser's work), saying:

> This integral-aperspectivism—this unity-in-diversity, this universal integralism—discloses global interconnections, nests within nests, and vast holarchies of mutually enriching embrace, thus converting pluralistic heapism into integral holism.[13]

Integral/A-Centric Culture

The foregoing represents some of the psychological approaches to the integral/a-centric form of consciousness. However, there are numerous

---

[11] Wilber (1996, p. 53).
[12] Wilber (1999, p. 86).
[13] Wilber (2000a, p. 172). Wilber's reference to holarchies borrows from Aldous Huxley's coining of the term, which highlights that all of being consists of wholes that are part of a larger whole (nested wholes). For example, atoms are wholes that are part of molecules, which are wholes that are part of compounds, etc. Similarly, in consciousness development, the ethno-centric level is a whole that eventually becomes part of the world-centric, which is a whole that becomes part of the integral.

social theorists and sociologists who have identified a transition from the world-centric to the a-centric perspective in the general culture as well, except that most refer to it as a transition from modernity to postmodernity. I will review some of the more empirically based approaches here as they apply to the areas of social theory, science, and society in general. As we will see, there is a rough correspondence between the transition that the above-named psychologists describe and the transition that some sociologists identify.[14]

From Modernity to Postmodernity

In my opinion, one of the best and most comprehensive summaries of the cultural transition from modernity to postmodernity is the work of Douglas Kellner and Steven Best (1997), *The Postmodern Turn*.[15] In analyzing the postmodern turn Kellner and Best focus on the realms of philosophy, art, science, and politics. According to them, postmodern thinking emerged almost immediately after the first modern thought appeared, in the form of Enlightenment philosophy. It has thus become a bit difficult to separate the two, since they emerged so close together. The fact, though, that one emerged as a reaction to the other and that they are somewhat different paradigms allows us to distinguish them. The first truly postmodern philosopher was Friedrich Nietzsche. He reacted against the culture of modernity, with its deterministic logic, universalism, optimistic belief in progress, and individualism. Nietzsche, according to Best and Kellner,

---

[14] There are countless other social theorists and sociologists who have studied the evolution of consciousness and of culture, but the vast majority have focused on the evolution from hunter-gather societies to modern capitalism, but not beyond. The focus of this book, though, is to look beyond modern capitalism.

[15] There are many others, of course, such as Anderson (1998), Bauman (1992), Denzin (1991), Featherstone (1991), Harvey (1989), and Jameson (1991). As can be seen from this list, there have been practically no significant new publications on the topic since 2000. There are several possibilities for this, such as that postmodernity was just a fad or trend that has passed, that culture has moved past postmodernity since then, or that everything that needed to be said about it has been said. I would argue that the most likely explanations are the second and third one. The first, that the analysis of postmodernity was a passing and presumably meaningless fad, is unfounded if we look at the evidence.

"anticipated postmodern theory both in its sociological explorations of mass society and in his critique of the subject and reason, his deconstruction of modern notions of truth, representation, and objectivity, his perspectivism, his attacks on mechanism and determinism, and his highly aestheticized philosophy and mode of writing."[16]

Nietzsche's critique of the subject—which is so central to enlightenment philosophy—as being an illusory construct, parallels the pluralistic form of consciousness described by many developmental psychologists. That is, Nietzsche recognizes, just as individuals at the pluralistic stage, that one's subjectivity is not as unitary and coherent as originally thought. Rather, depending on the context, we occupy different subjectivities. Nietzsche thus also argued against universal reason and truth from a universal subject position, in favor of a more relativistic perspectivism.

Subsequent philosophers extended Nietzsche's line of thought, in varying ways—some in a conservative direction, critiquing modernity in favor of pre-modernity, such as Martin Heidegger, and others in a fatalistic embrace of postmodernity, such as the French thinkers Jean Baudrillard and François Lyotard. For the twentieth-century theorists of postmodernity, though, there is no clear line between their philosophy and their analysis of society. That is, consumer society in late capitalism has become so all-encompassing, fluid, and indeterminate that it creates forms of consciousness that is itself indeterminate, fluid, and decentered. The contemporary condition is one not only of postmodernity, but of hyperreality, according to Baudrillard:

> Thus, hyperreality signifies a rupture in the notion of the real brought on by techniques of mass reproduction. "Reality" implies something singular, sui generis, a touchstone by which to measure everything else. But in the conditions of reproduction, Baudrillard claims, all this is lost: Reality becomes what can be infinitely extended and multiplied

[16] Best and Kellner (1997, p. 59).

in series, through a reproductive medium. No longer sui generis, it infinitely resembles itself in identical copies.[17]

Lost in the funhouses of the hyperreal, the postmodern self dissolves in the realm of ersatz [replacement] experience, becoming itself a mutating set of signs whereby identity is defined in terms of look, style, and image.[18]

A key distinction that Best and Kellner make, just as the developmental psychologist Robert Kegan does, is between a deconstructive and a reconstructive postmodernism. These two versions of postmodernism parallel the stages of consciousness that I described as decentered/pluralist versus a-centric/integral. Best and Kellner describe this distinction in reference to postmodern science, where, "there is a major division in postmodern science between 'reconstructive' and 'deconstructive' approaches."[19] This difference is particularly visible with regard to their conception of objectivity. That is, deconstructive postmodernism sees objectivity as being altogether impossible because every effort to be objective is merely a contingent result of social construction and social power. Reconstructive postmodernism, though, recognizes the social contingency of objectivity, but insists nonetheless that better or worse descriptions of reality exist and that we can always strive for better or more effective descriptions, all the while remembering that our descriptions are not the same as reality.

Postmodern science is far more "reconstructive" than "deconstructive," as all of its main representatives firmly believe in the need for evidence and scientific research to make their points. What distinguishes postmodern science from modern science then is that it rejects the mechanistic, reductionistic, and deterministic worldview of modern science in favor of a more organic, holistic, and indeterministic approach. This approach is particularly noticeable in areas such as thermodynamics, general systems theory, quantum

---

[17] Best and Kellner (1997, p. 101).
[18] Best and Kellner (1997, p. 103).
[19] Best and Kellner (1997, p. 241).

mechanics, and chaos theory. For example, in thermodynamics, Ilya Prigogine showed how open systems—that is, systems that are open to receiving energy from outside their boundaries—are self-organizing, evolving, indeterminate, and dynamic.[20] This is in stark contrast to the modern Newtonian view, which is fundamentally mechanistic, static, and thus deterministic and predictable, and sees systems as generally winding down.

Similarly, quantum mechanics also makes a transition from the modern view of the determinism of all physical phenomena, to a radical indeterminism in the realm of subatomic particles. With regard to its epistemology, founders of quantum mechanics, such as Niels Bohr and Werner Heisenberg, relativized the possibility of objectivity when they recognized that the observer and the observed cannot be separated: "What we observe is not nature itself, but nature exposed to our method of questioning," said Heisenberg.[21]

The distinction between modern and postmodern politics also centers around their conceptions of universalism versus pluralism. For example, modern politics pursues universalistic principles, such as freedom, equality, and justice, for which the US Declaration of Independence and France's Declaration of the Rights of Man are prime examples. Postmodern politics, though, questions the utopianism of these universal principles as being excessively optimistic and for its ignoring of the history and context of marginalized minorities. Postmodern politics, which emerged particularly in the 1960s, eventually came to be identified with so-called identity politics, where the previously ignored identities of Black people, women, LGBT, Latinos, and others come forward in a multiplicity of movements and struggles for recognition and participation.

The more extreme form of postmodern politics, as represented by thinkers such as Michel Foucault, Jean Baudrillard, François Lyotard, Richard Rorty, and John Holloway reject utopian emancipatory

---

[20] Prigogine and Stengers (1984).
[21] Quoted in Best and Kellner (1998, p. 215).

projects altogether, arguing that these will only lead to new forms of totalitarianism and oppression. Instead, they advocate for more piecemeal and local forms of social change. This, in a sense, represents the deconstructive strand of postmodern politics.

A reconstructive postmodern politics—to which I see this book as belonging—agrees that modern politics is exclusive and that we need to be inclusive of all subject positions and identities in society. Also, it rejects the political vanguardism, absolutism, and class essentialism, as exemplified by some forms of Marxism, which argue that the masses do not know yet what they want and need to be pushed into the better society, even if it is against their will initially. Instead, the reconstructive postmodern approach insists on the absolute priority of real democracy and on the need to win over at least a majority of the population, especially the previously excluded, before instituting new institutions and new social relations.[22] The reconstructive approach thus holds on to the utopian emancipatory project, all the while realizing that it is a goal that functions as an ultimately unreachable horizon and that must be democratically approached. The writer and poet Eduardo Galeano expressed this sentiment best when he wrote:

> Utopia lies at the horizon.
> When I draw nearer by two steps,
> it retreats two steps.
> If I proceed ten steps forward, it
> swiftly slips ten steps ahead.
> No matter how far I go, I can never reach it.
> What, then, is the purpose of utopia?
> It is to cause us to advance.

Best and Kellner also take this position and summarize it as follows:

---

[22] In its perhaps more postmodern form this reconstructive approach is represented by thinkers such as Laclau and Mouffe (1985) and in its more moderate and modern-postmodern form it is represented by Habermas (1998). Habermas, though, would reject association with the postmodern paradigm because he sees it as being hopelessly anti-modern and thus essentially conservative (see Habermas, 1990).

A new society will never be attainable until it is experienced as a need, for new modes of community, work, experience, social interaction, and relations to the natural world that can never be satisfied within capitalism and therefore cannot be co-opted by economic reforms.[23]

The Expansion of Empathy

While Best and Kellner focus on the transition to postmodernity on the level of philosophy, social theory, and the cutting edges of science, art, and politics, Jeremy Rifkin has looked at cultural change from the perspective of the expansion of empathy.[24] That is, while Best and Kellner focus more on the cognitive dimension (how we make sense of and see the world), Rifkin focuses on the affective (how we feel and experience the world) dimension.

At the most basic level, our experience of the world is directly related to the extent to which we can interact with it. If we have means to expand our experience of the world, via expanded social networks, our consciousness and our ability to empathize expand to accommodate this expansion. This means that our communication and transportation technologies have a direct impact on the extent to which we can experience the world. Rifkin thus divides up the transitions in our consciousness and our ability to feel for fellow humans based on transitions in our communications technology. At first, humans had only verbal means for communicating, which meant that our worldview and our empathy were limited to the people we communicated with verbally daily, to the clan. The invention of script, of written language, expanded the sphere of our ability to empathize to the tribe, to the population with whom we shared the same language. This development was further deepened and expanded with the development of print and the standardization of

---

[23] Best and Kellner (1998, p. 278).
[24] Rifkin (2009). Rifkin, of course, is far from the first to examine the development of empathy in the process of individual and cultural change. There are too many studies to list here, beginning with Lawrence Kohlberg, perhaps. For a more recent in-depth study by a developmental psychologist, see Hoffman (2000).

language, enabling the creation of nation-states.[25] Next, the invention of electronic broadcast media further expanded and deepened our ability to empathize because we could see and hear people, instead of just reading about them. Finally, with the development of peer-to-peer social networks, primarily the Internet, our empathy can extend to the entire globe on a one-on-one basis. The foregoing does not mean that these technological developments are necessary for the expansion of empathy. Rather, what they do is facilitate the expansion.

Accompanying these transitions in the extent of empathy are qualitative changes in our consciousness, which Rifkin describes quite similarly to the transitions presented in Chapter 3. That is, with the printed mode of communication "ideological" consciousness predominates (termed "rational" in chap. 3), and with centralized electronic communication "psychological" consciousness predominates ("pluralist/postmodern" in chap. 3). Finally, with the development of peer-to-peer networks "dramaturgical" consciousness comes about ("integral" in chap. 3). It is this last form of consciousness that becomes necessary for a post-capitalist economy, which we will examine in greater detail shortly.

For social groups to maintain their organizational cohesion and integrity, though, they need not only a means for communicating information but also a steady supply of energy. Thus, the transitions are usually also accompanied by a new energy regime. Rifkin gives the example of how Europe descended into the Dark Ages when the energy resources of the Roman Empire became exhausted because of deforestation and soil erosion. According to Rifkin, "Maintaining its infrastructure and population in a non-equilibrium state required large amounts of energy. Its energy regime, however, was becoming exhausted."[26] Rifkin goes on to describe the process as one in which

---

[25] Anderson (1983) describes this process very well in his seminal work *Imagined Communities*.
[26] Rifkin (2009, p. 253). Nonequilibrium here refers to thermodynamic theory, which states that complex systems exist in a state of nonequilibrium, a state that requires a steady flow of energy in order to be maintained. If the system were in a state of equilibrium with its environment, it would dissolve into the environment (also known as "heat death")

an empathic expansion is not met with a corresponding increase in energy resources. Rather, until there is a new energy regime, the social organization is more likely to collapse and give in to entropy.[27]

> The change in human consciousness is played out in a dialectic between a rising empathic surge and a growing entropy deficit. As that dialectic unfolds, the empathic surge generally peaks at the height of the energy flow-through of the society, only to wane as the energy flow-through declines and the entropic deficit mounts. When the entropic externalities eventually exceed the values of the energy flowing through the society's infrastructure, the civilization withers and even occasionally dies. The empathic gains slow and even reverse as economic conditions worsen, political stability erodes, and desperation sets in. Social trust weakens and individuals draw in their emotional reserves to a smaller circle.[28]

The first industrial revolution was thus made possible with a transition not only to a new communications regime that was based on print, but with a new energy regime that was based on coal and the steam engine. This transition in communication and energy regimes helped bring about a new consciousness, the "ideological" (Rifkin) or "rational" (Gebser) consciousness, which was best represented by enlightenment philosophy. Universal literacy, the consolidation of the nation-state, and the emergence of democratic political structures were all tied into this transition.

Similarly, the second industrial revolution involved a transition to broadcast electronic media and to an oil and electricity-based energy regime that enabled the transition to "psychological" (or postmodern/de-centered) consciousness. Rifkin describes this as one in which "people began to think about their own feelings and thoughts, as well as those of others in ways never before imaginable. They became the psychic

---

because maintaining a system's boundaries and its internal organization requires a steady expenditure of energy.
[27] This is somewhat like Marx's idea that a crisis ensues when there is a mismatch between relations and forces of production.
[28] Rifkin (2009, p. 254).

explorers and analysts of the human mind. The new way of thinking opened the door to a great extension of empathic expression, which peaked in the 1960s and 1970s with the surge of the counterculture and social activism among the baby-boom generation."[29] The telephone, the radio, the television set, and the automobile further expanded people's social networks and the sphere of empathy.

> The anticolonial struggles, the civil rights movement, the antiwar movement, the antinuclear movement, the peace movement, the feminist movement, the gay movement, the disability movement, and the ecology and animal rights movements are all testimonials (at least in part) to the new psychological emphasis on intimate relationships, introspection, multicultural perspectives, and unconditional acceptance of others.[30]

Finally, Rifkin describes a third industrial revolution, which we are currently experiencing, and which involves the transition to a communications regime based on peer-to-peer networks (the Internet) and on an energy regime that is based on solar power and other renewable resources. This most recent transition brings about dramaturgical (or integral) consciousness. For Rifkin, "The shift from centralized top down, one-to-many connections to flat, open-source, many-to-many connections allowed a new generation to be the actors in their own scripts and to share a global stage with two billion other like-minded thespians—all performing for and with one another." In other words, Rifkin emphasizes a shift from psychological introspection, deconstruction, and a focus on difference, to self-creation and reconstruction. We thus see the parallel here to the shift that Kegan, as well as Best and Kellner, describe as a shift from deconstructive postmodernism to reconstructive postmodernism.

---

[29] Rifkin (2009, p. 366).
[30] Rifkin (2009, p. 414).

One of the most important aspects of dramaturgical (or integral) consciousness is the ability to think in terms of complex systems. Here Rifkin points out integral consciousness's relationship to the new complexity sciences. "Perhaps the most important aspect of the new science, with its emphasis on relationships and feedback, is how closely it mirrors the network way of thinking that is beginning to permeate the social and commercial realms and governance. The science of ecology and the notion of a self-regulating biosphere are all about relationships, feedbacks, and networks."[31] As we will see later, this aspect of the new consciousness is crucial as we try to develop a civilization that is more sensitive to living in harmony with the biosphere, and with our natural environment.

When looking at these transitions in consciousness, it is important not to fall into technological determinism, which one could say Rifkin tends to do. The transitions described above all seem to be preceded by a new communications technology and thus it would be logical to believe that it is the communications technology—with the help of a new technological energy regime—that drives the shifts in consciousness. I believe, though, that such an interpretation would be a misunderstanding. This is not to say that technology does not play a very important role in these transitions.

However, one must keep in mind, first, that the development and invention of new technologies necessitate a new form of consciousness itself in order to be invented. In other words, the consciousness shift and the invention of new technologies go hand in hand, in a dialectical or enactive process. Second, technological change facilitates changes in consciousness, but it is not necessary. That is, our social context and our home and formal education can also bring about changes in consciousness by themselves if the educators and the social structures are organized appropriately. New technologies make a change to a new form of consciousness easier and more likely but are not necessary preconditions.

---

[31] Rifkin (2009, p. 599).

Key Aspects of Integral/A-centric Consciousness

Summarizing the foregoing accounts of integral culture and consciousness, one can say that it is characterized by the following qualities (at a minimum):

1. *Integrative and multi-perspectival.* This means a rejection of the universalistic stance of the world-centric/modern, as well as of the relativistic de-centered/postmodern stance. Instead, it combines these two previous perspectives into a multi-perspectival or a-perspectival awareness that integrates many different perspectives, taking them into account and without sliding into either relativism or a closed-minded universalism. Another aspect is also the integration of mind and body, of rationalism and feeling, which it also sees as different perspectives that need to be integrated.
2. *Systems and network thinking.* The foregoing also means that individuals are much more capable of thinking in terms of complex systems and networks, taking into account the many different variables and relationships between the elements of a system. To quote Wilber again, "It is thus the beginning of a truly higher-order synthesizing capacity, of making connections, relating truths, coordinating ideas, integrating concepts."[32]
3. *Principle-based.* On the moral dimension, integral/a-centric consciousness is principle-based instead of rule- or role-based. The highest principle to be followed, based on this consciousness's global empathetic ability, is to facilitate and help the growth or development of all beings to their greatest potential.
4. *Globally empathetic.* This form of consciousness is generally able to empathize with all human beings, regardless of origin, class, status, ethnicity, race, religion, sexual orientation, and so on.

---

[32] Wilber (1999, p. 86).

The above characteristics of integral/a-centric consciousness and culture are not meant to be comprehensive. Rather, they highlight some of the most important characteristics of consciousness that are needed for a truly post-capitalist and commonist society. In what follows I will explore some of the institutions that various thinkers in this area have identified for a post-capitalist future and see in what way integral consciousness is needed to make these institutions work. This does not mean that this type of consciousness is a sufficient condition for post-capitalism. But a lack of a critical mass of individuals with the necessary consciousness is an important reason why such institutions would fail in the long run.

Post-Capitalist Institutions

In recent years writers and activists have raised the concept of the commons with increasing frequency.[33] There are probably three main reasons for why the commons has become one of the central issues of recent years. First, considering the global environmental crisis, we are increasingly realizing that the concept of the commons is one that can help us deal with and perhaps even resolve this crisis. That is, if the natural environment is something that belongs to all of us and that we share, then it is something that we hold in common. In short, it is a commons. However, we have lost the ability to manage this commons and so we need to (re-)learn how to manage the commons for the benefit of everyone.

Second, while we are rediscovering the natural commons as a concept, we have also been inventing new types of commons, particularly those that have emerged thanks to the rise of digital media. Digital commons such as Wikipedia, open-source software, creative commons licensing,

---

[33] Two of the most important texts of the past few years were probably Hardt and Negri's *Commonwealth* (2009) and *Declaration* (2012). Others include: Ostrom (1990, 2007), Bollier (2014), Bollier and Helfrich (2015, 2012), Dardot and Laval (2019), Linebaugh (2008), Patel (2010), Wall (2014), Walljasper (2010).

and blockchain, all represent important new innovations that in one way or another are based on commons principles.[34] These are only the best-known digital or knowledge commons projects, but there are countless more emerging all around the world every day.[35]

Third, as a society, we are increasingly aware that neither the market nor the state has been able to provide adequate solutions to the social, economic, political, and environmental problems that we face today. As a global society, we have all too often found that state solutions are inadequate because the state is too alienated or removed from its citizens. Generally, societies try to resolve this problem of state accountability by implementing representative democracy, but despite these efforts, even in what are often considered to be the most effective representative democracies in the world, in Western Europe, the population feels alienated and removed from their government.[36] We can point to many different explanations for this, which goes beyond the scope of this book, but the fact of the citizens' alienation from the state remains. An important negative consequence of the state's lack of accountability and responsiveness is that the state does not resolve the problems of the citizens and that lack of accountability to its citizens contributes to making the state increasingly more accountable to powerful elites.

The other solution, of resolving societal problems via the market, however, has not worked either, as we saw in the previous chapter on neoliberalism. Many, such as those who advocate neoliberal solutions to all social problems, continue to believe that the market will save us, but practical experience has shown that the so-called free market only contributes to more inequality and more environmental destruction.

---

[34] What blockchain is and to what extent it can be considered a commons will be explained later.
[35] Bollier and Helfrich (2015, 2012) and Walljasper (2010) have compiled large surveys of the different commons projects that exist around the world.
[36] One piece of evidence for the increasing alienation is the declining rate of voter participation. In almost all so-called Western democracies turnout has dropped steadily over the past fifty years (before the 1950s turnout was a less accurate measure of people's willingness to participate because in many cases certain groups of voters were disenfranchised). See International Institute for Democracy and Electoral Assistance (www.idea.int).

Finally, the effort to create a mix of state and market, in the form of social democracy, where the state intervenes in the market and corrects its shortcomings, has not been able to solve the problems either. The main reason for this, aside from the fact that social democracy has generally not solved the problem of citizens' alienation from the state, is that social democracy has proven itself to be highly unstable. That is, as long as the state exists in the context of a class-divided society, the market will generally create increasingly more powerful private economic actors who dominate the state and turn it to their advantage, dismantling policies that protect the less powerful from the more powerful.[37]

In short, we need to find an alternative beyond state and market. The concept of the commons, with its direct democratic and participatory practices and its emphasis on sharing instead of relying on private or public property could be the best solution. Hardt and Negri, referring to Nick Dyer-Witheford, redefine communism and summarize it as follows: "At a purely conceptual level, we could begin to define communism this way: what the private is to capitalism and what the public is to socialism, the common is to communism."[38]

The Centrality of Property Rights

It is all too easy to forget that when examining the merits of state versus market solutions that neither can do without the other. The modern state developed in the context of an emerging market society, and markets depend on the existence of the state to function. The key link between the state and the market is the contract. That is, the state is necessary to ensure adherence to an exchange contract. The main contract, in this context, is the contract that guarantees an individual the right to control and transfer a piece of property. Capra and Mattei

---

[37] Crouch (2011) provides a very important explanation for how this has happened over the past three decades. Along with most Marxists, I would argue that this is an inevitable consequence of capitalism, even when governed by social democratic policies.

[38] Hardt and Negri (2009, p. 273).

thus correctly point out that for modern society, "ownership and state sovereignty, respectively championed by John Locke and Thomas Hobbes, are the two organizing principles of legal modernity."[39] Similarly, Hardt and Negri make this point too, when they state, "In the dominant line of European political thought from Locke to Hegel, the absolute rights of people to appropriate things becomes the basis and substantive end of the legally defined free individual."[40] Overcoming capitalism and its limitations thus require overcoming what Hardt and Negri describe as the "republic of property." Capra and Mattei develop this point by calling for a transcendence of the atomistic legal notion of the individual and their property, in favor of a commons- and network-based community:

> This process requires that we now, as a consequence of our new ecological knowledge, displace the individual owner from the center of the legal system in favor of the commons. ... no mechanistic separation between subject and object; no individual atom, but community and relationships building blocks of the legal order.[41]

Capra and Mattei explicitly connect this transformation in legal understanding to a transformation of consciousness that has already been happening in the natural and social sciences, but which has not caught on in economics or jurisprudence. That is, as described earlier, the natural and social sciences (as well as philosophy and the arts) have undergone a significant conceptual transformation in the transition from modern to postmodern consciousness—a transition that has not yet happened in economics or in legal studies.[42] A key aspect of this

---

[39] Capra and Mattei (2015, p. 3).
[40] Hardt and Negri (2009, p. 13). They further make the important point that social democracy, which aims to mix state and market mechanisms, can never transcend capitalism precisely because of its stubborn adherence to modern notions of the republic of property.
[41] Capra and Mattei (2015, p. 12).
[42] Actually, there is a trend in legal studies, known as the Critical Legal Studies Movement, which has made such a transition from a modern to a postmodern conception of law. See, for example, Unger (2015). However, this movement is still rather marginal compared to situation of postmodern approaches in the sciences and the arts.

transformation, accordingly, is not only the form law takes, but also the ways they are made. Thus, "law is always a process of 'commoning' a long-term collective action in which communities, sharing a common purpose and culture, institutionalize their collective will to maintain order and stability in the pursuit of social reproduction."[43]

The idea of commoning as being central to the creation and maintenance of a commons is something that Massimo de Angelis emphasizes as well, when he writes,

> "[C]ommoning brings to life the essential social elements of the commons. The life sequence of commoning, its rhythms, pauses, cycles, draw on and craft anew networks of relationships turned into community by repetition of iterations, building expectations of reciprocal obligation of care and aid ... and shared understanding that are things that belong to all of us. On the other hand, commoning reproduces the community as well as resources, thus giving shape to the conditions of production of the next round of commoning.[44]

Another way de Angelis puts this is that the activity of commoning enacts the commons,[45] just as different cultural worldviews enact particular social formations—and the social formations (political and economic institutions), in turn, enact certain cultural worldviews (or forms of consciousness).

More than that, the commons is not just an alternative to both private and public property but represents property's antithesis, according to Hardt and Negri, who argue, "The common stands in contrast to property in a more radical way, by eliminating the character of exclusion from the rights of both use and decision-making, instituting instead schema of open, shared use and democratic governance."[46]

Hardt and Negri also make the connection between capitalism and modern philosophy, which depend on an individualized subject, and

---

[43] Capra and Mattei (2015, p. 14).
[44] de Angelis (2017, p. 203).
[45] de Angelis (2017, p. 104).
[46] Hardt and Negri (2017, p. 100).

how it is taken to extremes, as we saw in neoliberalism in the previous chapter. This subject is connected to private property and is undermined by the common:

> The modern theory of the subject, which emerged from capitalist ideology, is characterized by possessive individualism, to use C. B. Macpherson's formulation. The individual subject is defined by what it has. ... In contrast, subjectivities in the common are grounded not in possessions but in their interactions with and openness to others.[47]

And:

> Through cooperation [in struggle and in commoning] we realize the capabilities of the species in the sense that we create a world in which we are no longer forced to choose between our individual good and the good of humanity, between egoism and altruism, but instead can pursue them as one and the same project.[48]

Brief History of the Commons

Before we can get into the details of exactly how the post-capitalist commons could help us solve the problems caused by neoliberal digital capitalism and help create a better society and how it fits with integral consciousness, it makes sense to take a brief look at the history of the commons. After all, the commons, in one form or another, have been around for millennia. Why did they practically vanish and why should we believe that they could now represent a solution to the problems of postmodern societies?

We can divide the history of the commons into roughly three periods: pre-capitalist, capitalist, and currently emerging post-capitalist. Pre-capitalist commons existed (and still exist) in all parts of the world. Typical examples of these are the grazing and forest commons throughout Europe, the so-called *ayllú* of Peru and Bolivia,

---

[47] Hardt and Negri (2017, p. 105).
[48] Hardt and Negri (2017, p. 292).

the *ejido* of Mexico, and the *mir* or *obshchina* of Russia. The Nobel Prize-winning economist Elinor Ostrom studied many of these types of commons. She called them, "common pool resources," or CPRs, because the people who are members of these units share the resources of the commons, which are almost always renewable natural resources. Following an extensive analysis of these types of CPRs, as they exist today, she identified eight principles that they all share:

1. Clearly defined boundaries: Individuals or households who have the right to withdraw resource units from the CPR must be clearly defined, as must the boundaries of the CPR itself.
2. Congruence between appropriation and provision rules and local conditions: Appropriation rules restricting time, place, technology, and/or quantity of resource units are related to local conditions and to provision rules requiring labor, material, and/or money.
3. Collective decision-making: Most individuals affected by the operational rules can participate in modifying the operational rules.
4. Monitoring: Monitors, who actively audit CPR conditions and appropriator behavior, are accountable to the appropriators or are the appropriators.
5. Graduated sanctions: Appropriators who violate operational rules are likely to be assessed graduated sanctions (depending on the seriousness and context of the offense) by other appropriators, by officials accountable to these appropriators, or by both.
6. Conflict resolution mechanisms: Appropriators and their officials have rapid access to low-cost local arenas to resolve conflicts among appropriators or between appropriators and officials.
7. Minimal recognition of rights to organize: The rights of appropriators to devise their own institutions are not challenged by external governmental authorities.
8. For CPRs that are parts of larger systems: Nested enterprises: Appropriation, provision, monitoring, enforcement,

conflict resolution, and governance activities are organized in multiple layers of nested enterprises.[49]

The notion of private property was not all that well developed in feudal and pre-feudal times. As Derek Wall argues, "Legal theorists and historians have become increasingly aware that prior to the period of European colonialism, commons were the rule rather than the exception across much of our planet."[50]

Already during the Middle Ages land rights began to change, especially between AD 1000 and AD 1500, as kings, nobles, and the Church exercised ever-greater control over what had previously been commons. These developments of restricting the commons also took place in parallel in other parts of the world, such as throughout Asia during this time. Later, with the development of colonialism in Africa and in the Americas, commons were increasingly limited in these areas too.[51]

However, it wasn't until the development of capitalism in the seventeenth and eighteenth centuries that commons in Europe were almost completely eradicated through the process known as the enclosure. That is, enclosing or closing off commons lands for individual private use represented what Marx called primitive accumulation and set the stage for the development of capitalism.[52] The enclosure process, which was sanctioned in a series of laws in England between 1500 and 1800, created landless peasants, landlords, and private property—all elements that were necessary to begin the process of capitalist accumulation. Another aspect of this transformation of commons into private property was the process mentioned earlier, in which consciousness also changed, from group-centric to world-centric. That is, there was a shift from the idea that some people, because of their station in life, have no right to landownership, to the idea that everyone has a right to individual self-determination or sovereignty and to individual property. Whether they could afford to buy such

---

[49] Ostrom (1990, p. 90).
[50] Wall (2014, p. 9).
[51] See Wall (2014, chap. 1).
[52] Marx describes this process in *Capital*, vol. 1, chapters 27–29.

property was a different matter, but, in principle, all male citizens had the right. It is thus no coincidence that this was also the time of the French Revolution and of the Enlightenment, which sought to abolish the divine rights of the aristocracy and of the royalty.

However, some forms of commons survived the transition to capitalism. Usually, it was either land that was less valuable or where community ties were stronger than the capitalist accumulation process. Another option was for a group of people to join and purchase shares in a cooperative. The cooperative, as a form of commons, remained throughout the capitalist era and competed—often successfully—with private businesses, but always in a minority and always under threat of being wiped out.

In theory, one could also say that a publicly owned corporation is a sort of commons. The difference, though, between such a stock corporation and a traditional commons or a cooperative is that in a stock corporation the owners have shares that vary in number from one owner to the next, and they can sell these shares at any time. In a typical commons, however, all members have an equal right to participate in decision-making. Also, even though shareholders—in theory—determine the policies of the company and elect the management, in practice they have very little input in the running of the company. Finally, such corporations are not run by everyone who participates in them, as generally happens in a cooperative or a traditional commons, but corporations are formally run only by those who own the shares.[53]

While traditional (pre-capitalist) commons continued to exist during the capitalist era, alongside the newer cooperative type of commons, a new type of commons began to develop when societies began moving from the second to the third industrial revolution. That is, the shift from automobile and electricity-based society to computer and networking-based society brought about with it the development of a new consciousness and of a new type of commons. The first type of new commons to develop was the free and open-source software movement, which the software engineer Richard Stallman formally

---

[53] There are more differences, but these are probably the main ones.

launched in 1983. However, it had its first informal roots, long before that, with the first computers in the 1950s, when it was taken for granted that software was free to copy and modify among programmers. It was only when private companies began to apply and enforce intellectual property rights—copyright and patents—on software during the 1980s (with Microsoft leading the way), that a countermovement began in the form of the free and open-source software (FOSS). FOSS developed a new user license under which programmers could freely exchange and modify the software developments of others, in effect voluntarily rescinding intellectual property rights to the software code. Despite the freedom under which this happens, there still are collectively agreed-upon procedures and rules for exchanging and modifying software code. In this sense, FOSS resembles a commons as described by Elinor Ostrom.

Examining the eight design principles of commons that Ostrom outlined, we can see that FOSS applies six of the eight principles: boundaries on who may participate, collective decision-making, monitoring, sanctions, conflict resolution mechanisms, and noninterference from outside. The only principles that generally do not apply are #2 (congruence between appropriation rules and local conditions) and #8 (nested enterprises for applying the previous principles on a large scale). The reason #2 does not apply is that software is a "non-rival" resource. This means that because it can be copied with practically no material resource expenditure, as much of it as anyone likes can be provided without depriving anyone else of the resource. As a result, there is no need to make sure that there is congruence between resource appropriation and local conditions. The reason #8 does not apply (for the most part; there might be exceptions) is that the networked nature of software makes it possible to scale the commons to a global level, without needing "nested enterprises" for decision-making.

There are other important departures, though, from the traditional pre-capitalist commons. First, membership and participation in the FOSS or digital commons are much more loosely regulated. That is, participation is a matter of merit and collective monitoring rather than based on living in a particular geographical location or membership in a particular ethnic or tribal group, as is usually the case with pre-capitalist commons. Second, the digital commons is geographically global. I say "geographically" global because it can reach anyone who has the appropriate hardware and knowledge to participate. In other words, hardware and skill limitations prevent it from being truly global. Third, it is radically democratic. Everyone with the proper qualifications can participate, without an intermediary or representative.[54] This is also generally the case for pre-capitalist commons, except, as Ostrom's principle #8 indicates, when it spans a large geographical area. The digital commons, though, can span the entire globe and still does not require representatives or delegates for participation. Finally, given the number of people and issues that are involved, the digital commons tends to be far more complicated, in terms of management and monitoring, than the pre-capitalist commons ever was.

The ability to navigate and participate in the digital commons thus has different psychological prerequisites than participation in the pre-capitalist commons. That is, enabling potentially global participation requires a degree of empathy and acceptance of the other that was practically unheard of in the pre-capitalist era. Jeremy Rifkin's observation about entering into an age of global empathy points to the type of consciousness that is needed for participation in the global digital commons. The other quality of consciousness that is needed is the cognitive capacity to understand and make sense of this highly complex realm. Here I am not referring to the technological complexity of computer software, but to the complexity of the relationships or networks that are being built with the digital commons. In other words, it is the combination of the development of an a-centric/integral consciousness with the increasing accessibility to non-rival resources that makes the digital commons possible in the early twenty-first century.

---

[54] Of course, we must recognize that "having the proper qualifications" can be a major barrier to entry in a highly unequal and class-divided society.

Types of Post-Capitalist Commons

At the same time as we see the proliferation of different types of digital commons, this has inspired the development of various kinds of non-digital commons. We can identify three types of commons: natural, social, and cultural.[55] The natural commons is the same as the typical pre-capitalist commons, where land or other types of natural resources are managed collectively in accordance with the principles of commons management. Social commons refers to common resources that are collectively created, such as health care, education, and finished products of any kind. This is the type of commons that generally emerged at the same time as capitalism, in the form of cooperatives. Finally, cultural commons deal with the resources of knowledge and cultural creations that can be shared without limitation or expenditure because of their non-rivalrous nature. Natural and social commons, in contrast, generally deal with rivalrous goods because these are neither unlimited nor cost-free.

There is a fourth type of commons, though, which should not be forgotten, which is the one that is responsible for reproducing the very lives that the other three commons depend on: the household commons. That is, we should consider the family or nonfamily household to be a fourth type of commons, where household members share and collectively develop the rules for their household. It is important to take the household commons into account because it fulfills not only a crucial part in our daily lives but also in the life and functioning of the other three types of commons, especially since it overlaps with them to varying degrees.

---

[55] This is based on de Peuter and Dyer-Witheford's (2010) distinction between natural, social, and networked commons. However, I don't like the term "networked" for this type of commons mainly because all commons constitute a network of sorts. Natural and social commons are generally more limited and thus smaller in scope because of their boundedness to a particular geographic location, but they still constitute networks of people. However, as we will see later, natural and social commons are increasingly becoming far larger in scope than previously thought possible, thanks to digital technology.

A rough schematic of how these four types of commons could interact and exchange resources with each other could look like the following (see Figure 6):

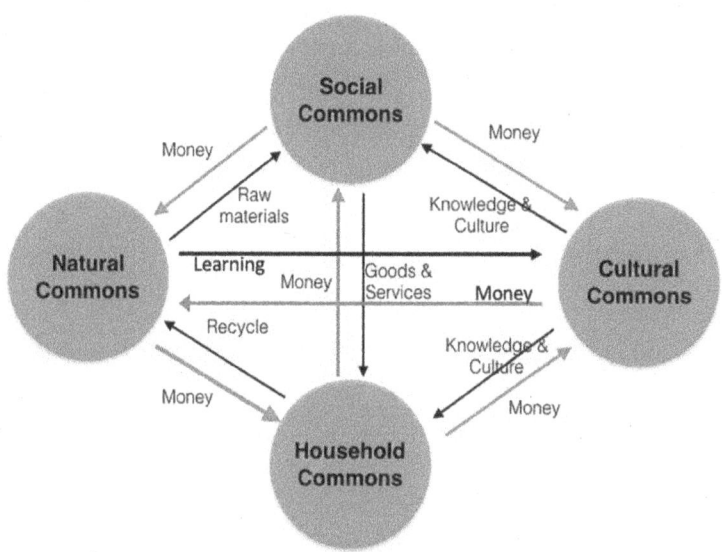

Figure 6. Circulation of money, goods, and knowledge between commons.

This is not the place to go into detail about the logic behind this model. It merely serves as a suggestive schematization of how the different types of commons might interact with each other, once these commons types have become prevalent throughout society. The key is that the circulation of money in this schema would not result in endless accumulation, as it currently does under competitive capitalism. Rather, the cooperative nature of the commons would strive to ensure equity and balance among all its members. Also, the distinctions between these types of commons are more conceptual than institutional, in the sense that individual participants in each of these types of commons could very well overlap with one another. For example, working-age members of a particular household commons would likely also be members of other types of commons.

The cultural commons, as many have pointed out, would need a new economic basis because, unlike the present system, the post-capitalist cultural commons would no longer rely on patent monopolies for income. It would, though, still need to receive some monetary resources from its users in the social commons and the household commons. Meanwhile, the cultural commons could provide monetary resources to the natural commons in exchange for learning about nature (whether through scientific research or the transmission of established knowledge about nature).

A Note on Commons Governance

The transition from neoliberal digital capitalism to post-capitalist commonism is not only an economic transition but also a political transition, in that it would fundamentally change the polity and governance systems that exist today. Earlier, when outlining Elinor Ostrom's eight principles of the typical commons I indirectly alluded to this, in that commons governance is quite different from both the governance systems that exist in the context of typical corporations as well as in state institutions. First, the commons would erase the distinctions between state, private enterprise, and nonprofit organizations,[56] in favor of a variety of forms of commons. However, to appreciate why such a transition is necessary not only in the economic realm, which I discussed extensively in the previous chapter, it makes sense to see why it would also be necessary for the realm of institutional governance more generally.

The area where it is probably clearest that such a transition would be beneficial is in most for-profit and not-for-profit institutions. These, after all, are overwhelmingly inherently autocratic and undemocratic, resulting in the types of problems Marx already discussed when analyzing the typical workplace, where alienation, exploitation, and commodification predominate.

---

[56] Another way this three-fold distinction, in terms of types of institutions, has been made is to refer to the public sector, the private sector, and civil society.

Although cooperatives should generally not be included in this critique of institutional governance, we need to recognize that cooperatives come in all sorts of varieties, where some types might very well expose their members to alienation, exploitation, or commodification. This is especially true of cooperatives that allow some members to amass far more power, by virtue of their position in the institution's culture (such as white men in a sexist and racist culture) or their institutional knowledge, which they then use to illegitimately dominate other members of the cooperative.[57]

The need for commons-based governance becomes a lot less obvious in the realm of the state. After all, most states are governed by the presumably democratic principles of representative democracy. However, neoliberal digital capitalism has not only brought the capitalist economic system to its breaking point, but it has also done so with liberal representative democracy. First, as already mentioned in the previous chapter, neoliberal digital capitalism has systematically hollowed out politics by removing political decision-making from the economic realm. A clear example of this has been the insistence that central banks be independent of the government so that they are free to control interest rates and the money supply based on neoliberal economic principles. This also goes for global and regional trade agreements, such as the World Trade Organization (WTO), the European Union (EU), and NAFTA/USMCA (United States–Mexico–Canada Agreement), which institutionalize free trade and neoliberalism within their respective areas of responsibility. As a result, governments have far less control over their national economies than

---

[57] This is why the model known as participatory economics ("parecon" for short), as developed by Michael Albert (2021) and Robin Hahnel (2022), argues in favor of "balanced job complexes," where all jobs within an organization are balanced so that no one type of job can accumulate illegitimate power by virtue of a job's access to specialized knowledge. The process by which such power is accumulated varies, but the class of individuals who acquire such power without everyone's approval Albert and Hahnel call the coordinator class. This class, is in many ways almost as powerful as the owning class, which is why any movement that strives for true equality and classlessness must take this class and its reproduction into account.

they did under the previous Bretton Woods system of fixed exchange rates and managed trade. Less control has translated into ever-greater disappointment with political leaders and ever-lower rates of political engagement and voter participation in elections.

Supporters of the liberal representative democratic system thus claim this system is legitimate, even as the average citizens themselves increasingly view their political systems as being illegitimate. Habermas already identified this tendency in the 1970s,[58] when he pointed out that the liberal democratic state is in a contradictory position, where it must appease both ordinary citizens—to get their vote—and capital—to maintain investment levels. Getting votes means appealing to citizens by making sure that there is a certain level of fairness or equality in the economy, via social programs, such as in health, education, and so on, and protection from exploitation and other harmful activities of the private sector. This, however, contradicts the state's simultaneous efforts to appeal to investment capital, by reducing the burden on capital as much as possible, via low rates of taxation and minimal regulation. As long as interest rates are not too high, the easiest way for a government to manage the fiscal contradiction is to engage in deficit spending, thereby avoiding the burdening of both individuals and corporations. Eventually, however, the debt burden can become too large, and the government engages in efforts to lower the debt via privatization, thereby removing more and more economic activity from the public's purview and turning it over to the private sector, increasing the power of capital and further eroding the legitimacy of the liberal democratic state.

Another highly problematic aspect of liberal representative democracy is closely related to the previous one, which is the alienation of citizens from their representatives. This is especially true of countries where there is no well-functioning system of public campaign financing, such as the United States, and candidates for public office are tempted to promise anything and everything to get elected, but then, once elected, do the bidding of

---

[58] Habermas (1975) and Offe (1984).

their financial backers who are disproportionately the wealthy and big business.[59]

Even though most people recognize the limitations of representative democracy, elites and mass media regularly try to impart the impression that there is no better alternative. It is thus no surprise that pundits who defend representative democracy love to quote Winston Churchill's maxim, "Democracy is the worst form of government—except for all the others that have been tried." This saying, however, embodies crucial false assumptions, which is, first, that representative democracy as it is practiced today is identical to democracy in general, thus implying that there is no other form of democracy.[60] Second, it implies that even if there are other forms of democracy, these are not worth considering or do not constitute real democracy. Once we come to see through the incredibly undemocratic nature of contemporary representative democracies, though, a willingness to try other—more direct—forms of democracy can develop.[61]

Commons governance is a more democratic alternative to representative democracy in that it is participatory and, depending on how it is organized, a form of direct democracy. Most accounts of the commons do not go into detail about exactly how its governance systems are organized since each can be somewhat different. But there are some general characteristics that a well-functioning commons would guarantee. For example, Alan Watkins and Iman Stratenous (2016) outline a few basic principles for what they call "crowdacracy," which for all intents and purposes is the same as a commons:

---

[59] In the United States this situation has become so extreme that a well-known Princeton University study concluded that ordinary citizens have no impact on policy decisions, while economic elites determine practically all policy outcomes (Gilens and Page, 2014). In other words, the US political system should be called a plutocracy and not a representative democracy.

[60] This equivalency is one that Herbert Marcuse focused on in his book, *One-Dimensional Man* (1964).

[61] One place where this was especially true is in Venezuela under President Hugo Chávez. I documented Chávez's effort to create a participatory democracy in my book, *Changing Venezuela by Taking Power* (Wilpert, 2007).

1. Individual participation: Each individual in a community (not company, organization, or group) can and should be encouraged to participate.
2. No delegation: For the system to be crowdocratic, the legislative, decision-making authority on a policy may not be delegated by the crowd. Thus, the crowd will always make the legislative decisions in that community rather than allowing an elite delegation to decide.[62]
3. Semi-anonymous: the crowdocracy platform will function on a semi-anonymous basis. As shapers and participating citizens, we will not use our own names. This will allow for a freer and more unbiased exchange of views—it takes much "ego" out of the system.
4. Constitutional: Every community and organization need to establish its ground rules, which govern the way the community members coordinate their actions, inside and outside the community.
5. Integrative: We need to learn how to integrate opposing views into our decision-making.

Watkins and Stratenous make a powerful argument that digital technology can help organize this type of commons democracy on all scales, including the global, without the need for nested decision-making bodies, where several smaller bodies name delegates to meet and make decisions at a higher level, as Ostrom suggests in her commons governing principles. They cite several cases where commons/crowdacracy principles have been deployed on large scales, such as Iceland's rewriting of its constitution in 2012 and the operation of the Wikipedia website. Whether this is necessary for very large

---

[62] Here the distinction between delegates and representatives is worth considering. Some supporters of direct democracy would argue that delegation, as long as it adheres to the instructions of the delegating group, is consistent with direct democracy. What is not consistent with real democracy, though, are representatives who decide for themselves what is best for their constituents.

commons ought to be an empirical question, though, to be decided via trial and error, and not ruled out as a matter of principle.

The basic point about why such governance structures would need a critical mass of members who are at an integral stage of consciousness development is that for individuals to function effectively in such a context, they would need to embody the main characteristics of the integral stage, such as the ability to:

- Take multiple perspectives into account and integrate them in ways that respect each individual perspective.
- See situations or conditions from a systemic perspective.
- Be oriented towards ultimate common, humanistic, and universal principles instead of societal norms or individual gain—principles that favor cooperation over competition and community over individualism.
- Have a scope of empathy that encompasses all human beings (and all life in general)—their human commonality, regardless of gender, ethnic background, nationality, race, sexual orientation, capacity, status, creed, and the like, without erasing or ignoring individual differences.

Toward a Definition of the Post-Capitalist Commons

Earlier I presented Elinor Ostrom's eight principles of the commons. However, based on the discussion above of the history of the commons it is necessary to rework her conception to consider the many new forms commons have taken in recent history. As the topic of the commons has gained in popularity, several analysts have outlined other dimensions that ought to be taken into account. Ostrom's original account of the commons focuses primarily on the ways by which a community establishes rules to govern the use of common pool resources—that is, limited and for the most part natural resources—so that they would not be overexploited. But, as we saw when we extend the concept of the commons to other types of activities, such as the sharing and production of knowledge, manufactured goods, services, and of the household, this ought to change the way we conceive of the commons.

I would suggest that one way to think of a new conception of the commons is by looking at three main aspects of the commons: its organizational form, its organizational culture, and its steering mechanism. Regarding the organizational form or structure of the commons, we can identify three main characteristics that most other theorists of the commons have also highlighted. First and foremost, the property that is involved in the commons, whether material or knowledge-based, is held in common by all members of the commons. This is primarily a legal designation, as discussed earlier, but has clear implications for decision-making and governance. Second, largely because of the first characteristic, all decision-making is democratic, participatory, and as nonhierarchical as possible.[63] Third, a commons has clearly defined boundaries for participation in the commons.

Regarding the organizational culture, I would mainly refer to the previous section in which I described the need for an integral consciousness to effectively implement the commons organizational structure. Boiling these down to their most important elements, though, I would say that such an integral commons culture needs, first, a scope of empathy with all of humanity and nature that emphasizes what we have in common instead of what divides us from each other. Second, it would have a profound understanding of complexity and ability to think in systems, which also means seeing the reality from a multi-perspectival and integral vantage point.

Finally, the third dimension is the "steering medium," which is a concept taken from Luhmann's systems theory. In Luhmann's systems theory, the steering medium is the "symbolically generalized

---

[63] This means that all types of power imbalances need to be taken account, not just those based on wealth and income, such as gender, race, sexual orientation, ability, age, knowledge, and competency. The implication of the last two imbalances means that tasks within a commons need to be rotated, to give everyone a more or less equal knowledge and competency base within the commons. Albert (2021) and Hahnel (2022) call these balanced job complexes.

communication media" that helps coordinate activity within its domain. In the case of the commons the steering medium is solidarity, which coordinates the activity that commons theorists call "commoning."[64] For example, according to de Angelis, "Commoning is the form of social doing (social labour) occurring within the domain of the commons, and thus is characterised by modes of production, distribution and governance of the commons that are participatory and non-hierarchical, motivated by the values of the commons (re)production, of the (re)production of commoners' commonwealth and of the affective, material, immaterial and cultural (re)production of the commoners and their relations."[65] Similarly, Bollier and Helfrich (2015) write, "The drama of commoning is an active, living process—a verb rather than a noun. ... Commoning involves so much idiosyncratic creativity, improvisation, situational choices, and dynamic evolution that it can only be understood as aliveness. It defies simple formulas or analysis."[66] Here too, the concept of enactment can be applied to the verb commoning, in that this activity both emerges out of and (re-)creates the commons at the same time.

---

[64] de Angelis (2017) and Bollier (2014), among others.
[65] de Angelis (2017, p. 121).
[66] Bollier and Helfrich (2015), Kindle loc. 366

7

Conclusion: Getting from Here to There

The history of social change efforts seems to revolve around a few key debates or dichotomies. First, there is the age-old debate about reform versus revolution. I addressed this dichotomy early on when I presented André Gorz's proposed synthesis in the form of "non-reformist reform,"[1] by which he meant that social change efforts ought to reform the existing system in such a way that it eases the path to more far-reaching transformative reforms, rather than merely addressing a problem in a way that appeases or coopts the constituency that is suffering a particular problem. For example, social democracy often focuses on nonrevolutionary reform when it introduces welfare measures to alleviate poverty or inequality, without fundamentally changing the power of the working class relative to the capitalist and coordinator classes. A revolutionary welfare reform, however, would increase workers' power in a way that also reduces the power of the capitalist class, such as by strengthening collective bargaining, giving workers strong representation on corporate boards, or increasing the sphere of democratic decision-making in the workplace. However, recognizing this distinction between revolutionary and nonrevolutionary reform is not that easy and requires a particular way of viewing the world, one that is systemic and sees a need for system change, rather than one that focuses on a merely material or monetary perspective.

[1] Gorz (1967).

Second, there is the dichotomy between local and national or global change. For example, the political theorist John Holloway, in his landmark book, *Change the World Without Taking Power* (2002), argues that it is pointless for movements to seek to change society on a national level because doing so—by taking national state power—would only lead to the cooptation of those seeking social change since the state is inherently capitalist and oppressive and would force those seeking change to act within that framework. Instead, he argues, social change efforts ought to be highly localized, to create local anti-capitalist and autonomous communities, such as the Zapatistas in Mexico have tried to do. I cannot get into the argument around this debate here, but I will simply state my perspective, which is that this is a question of strategy that needs to be resolved on a case-by-case basis. For example, not all states are equally capitalist and oppressive, and some lend themselves to transformation more than others. This means that taking state power to bring about social change can be highly effective, depending on the context.[2] On the other hand, local change efforts can also be effective, not only for the communities that are affected but also for everyone else, who might be looking for inspiration from positive social change examples.

Third, there is the dichotomy between relying on a social change movement's ability to effect change, and relying on the playing out of historical–social dynamics for social change. This dichotomy was already articulated by Friedrich Engels in his pamphlet, "Socialism: Utopian and Scientific,"[3] where he distinguishes the early socialists' efforts to establish socialism, whom he calls utopian socialists (such as Saint-Simon, Robert Owen, and François Fourier), from that of Karl Marx, whose approach is scientific socialism. According to Engels, utopian socialists are not connected to any class nor to a scientific (that is, based on contemporary reality) theory of social change. Utopian socialists

---

[2] My book on Venezuela under President Hugo Chávez was precisely an effort to illustrate such a situation. Wilpert (2007).
[3] Engels (1892).

"could not explain [the existing capitalistic mode of production and its consequences], and, therefore, could not get the mastery of them. It could only simply reject them as bad," argued Engels.[4] On the other hand, in the scientific socialism of Marx, "the final causes of all social changes and political revolutions are to be sought, not in men's brains, not in men's better insights into eternal truth and justice, but in changes in the modes of production and exchange. They are to be sought, not in the *philosophy*, but in the *economics* of each particular epoch." Marx and Engels's emphasis on the economic dynamics of social change and revolution is scientific, according to Engels, in that it looks at the real-life conditions of the different contending classes, instead of creating utopian castles in the air.

It is possible to dismiss Engels's distinction between the utopian and the scientific approach as one based on an outmoded economic reductionism and an outmoded conception of positivistic science. While there are elements of reductionism and positivism in his approach, I do think that the essence of his argument is valid, which is his concern that social change strategies ought to seriously consider and understand the trends and potentials in existing society, rather than working for change that is based purely on an idealistic conception of what an ideal society ought to look like, regardless of the objective conditions. This is not to say that there is no place for idealism and utopianism in social change efforts. On the contrary, as mentioned in the previous chapter, utopianism has a very important role to play in giving us an idea of where we want to go (as stated in the Eduardo Galeano poem I cited earlier). Rather, utopian conceptions ought to be integrated into a clear understanding of the potentials and dynamics in existing society.

This brings me, though, to Engels's apparent overemphasis on economic factors of social change. As outlined in Chapter 3, the materialist conception of history, which focuses on the contradictions within any given economic mode of production (feudalism or capitalism, for example), needs to be complemented by an understanding of

---

[4] Engels (1892).

the moral–practical belief systems that accompany each mode of production. As I have repeatedly stated, there is a match between belief systems or forms of consciousness and social–institutional arrangements, such as modes of production. One cannot change without the other and there is a dialectic between the two, which makes it very difficult, perhaps even impossible, to say which changes first: the institutional arrangements or the form of consciousness. Along with Habermas, though, I would argue that institutional crises, such as those that neoliberalism provokes (e.g., ecological and economic crises) contribute to psychological crises, which in turn provoke a new way of thinking—a new form of consciousness—and which then leads to new ways of acting and to new institutional arrangements, if (and only if) powerful vested interests can be overcome by those seeking transformative social change.

Finally, there is a fourth dichotomy that the emphasis on consciousness transformation brings up, which is the one between individual and societal transformation. That is, if we accept that consciousness transformation is an essential component of social transformation, then this could lead one to believe that it is the only thing that counts, and that real social transformation is only possible by promoting consciousness change one individual at a time. This is the argument that most religiously and spiritually oriented movements have generally made about how to achieve social change. It stands in sharp contrast with the more Marx-inspired social change movements, which argue that real social change only happens when the ruling class is removed from power, via a revolutionary movement of the marginalized vast majority. Similarly, the more social-democratic version of this approach is that the conservative ruling class could be removed from power via elections.

Once again, though, the solution to this dichotomy is not a taking of one side in the debate over the other but recognizing the validity of both sides and arguing for a social movement that both aims to remove the conservative ruling class from its position of power and also finding ways to transform people's consciousness. As stated earlier in this book, though, the Gramscian–Marxist approach of addressing the problem as one of developing class consciousness is insufficient because it deals with consciousness as a matter of ideology, which places the emphasis on developing a class analysis. While this is important, my argument about consciousness development and its transformation emphasizes the "deep structure" of consciousness, of how we make sense of the world, our place in it, and our values.

To some extent Marx (and later István Mészáros and Michael Lebowitz, among others) recognized this importance of consciousness development as being more than achieving class consciousness, but the lack of a clear understanding of the psychology of consciousness development—of its stages—leads to a rather simplistic assumption that the class struggle itself would develop the type of consciousness that is needed for socialism and communism. It might be true that some types of class struggle would contribute to the necessary type of post-capitalist consciousness, but it could just as well contribute to a wrong or inadequate type of consciousness. For example, a revolutionary movement could be organized in a very authoritarian way, which merely reinforces an authoritarian group/ethnocentric form of consciousness and upon taking power ends up creating authoritarian institutions that might be anti-capitalist and eliminate capitalist class domination, but it still would not emancipate the individual from the domination of a new ruling class. For real post-capitalist emancipation to happen, it is thus essential for consciousness to move beyond the stage that made capitalist domination possible.

If we look at the historical development of modes of production and their accompanying forms of consciousness, we can see quite clearly how these fit together. For the pre-capitalist feudal mode of production, which depended on the unquestioning acceptance of divine rule and the inherent superiority of the nobility, conventional, conformist, or group-centric consciousness was necessary because conventional consciousness does not question pre-given societal norms. Then, when this mode of production reached a crisis, in which a new class—the capitalists (or the bourgeoisie)—acquired significant economic power without commensurate political power, this class challenged the divine power of the king, the nobility, and the church. This challenge was largely possible not only because of a change in power relations but also due to a new form of consciousness—the rational or world-centric stage—which questioned the old societal and hierarchical norms, and insisted on the formal equality of all (white) men, and set up a rationalistic worldview in which every social arrangement had to be justified based on secular reason. This same consciousness transformation also enabled the emergence of the capitalist class in the first place, since it enabled rational calculation for increasing efficiency, innovation, and science and technology, all in the name of increasing productivity and profits. Eventually, further technological advances and further consciousness development brought about the digital information age, which was accompanied by various economic crises, and ultimately led to neoliberal digital capitalism as we entered the twenty-first century. This neoliberal digital capitalism was accompanied by pluralistic consciousness, which further radicalized the belief in the formal (not substantive) equality of all humans while it also individualized them to an unprecedented degree, creating a "society of singularities."

We have now reached the point at which neoliberal digital capitalism is in a multidimensional and existential crisis. This is, first, an economic crisis in that neoliberal economic policy has taken inequality to unprecedented levels so that capital has a hard time solving the "realization problem," as Marx called it, of finding profitable investment opportunities since an ever-larger portion of the world's population simply does not have enough disposable income to buy all the products that the system can produce. Every time there is a new financial crisis central banks inject more liquidity into the economy to keep it afloat, but this just ends up increasing the overall levels of indebtedness and inequality, further exacerbating the realization problem in the long run.

Second, there is the ecological crisis, which is currently mostly experienced via the climate crisis, but which has many other dimensions to it (such as declining freshwater levels, soil erosion, species extinction, and pollution, to name some of the main ones).

As capitalist businesses seek to maximize their profits—which they must—they consistently seek to find ways to "externalize" costs (dump them on others) whenever they can, which in turn means disregarding the ecological consequences of their activities as much as possible. As a result, the earth's atmosphere currently has a higher concentration of carbon dioxide than it has had in over 800,000 years, which is leading the world to countless catastrophes, such as ever-deadlier storms, droughts, and sea level rise.

Third, the foregoing two crises are producing a third crisis, one of political delegitimization. As the ecological and economic crises become more serious and the political class fails to resolve them, the population's trust and confidence in this class diminishes. Liberal representative democracy in the context of neoliberal digital capitalism simply no longer delivers what it had promised. The political sphere is bereft of any real majoritarian input because neoliberalism has removed the main policy issues from the political sphere. Meanwhile, the political class is far more beholden to wealthy donors in the capitalist class than it is to the average citizen, especially in the United States.

Fourth, neoliberal ideology and practice created a world of hyper-individualization, where the struggle for economic survival for the vast majority has become a constant war of competition of all against all. Everyone is encouraged or even forced to become unique self-employed "enterprises of one," which creates unprecedented levels of loneliness, anxiety, and depression. Every individual in this society of singularities struggles to find what makes them unique or different from anyone else, so they can succeed in the privatized market spaces of Amazon, Google, Facebook, X, and LinkedIn. Meanwhile, these companies hollow out our right to privacy as they mine our lives for data and allow the state to use this same data for potentially repressive purposes.

These four interlinked crises end up creating a situation where proceeding with the status quo is no longer tenable and an inflection point (or bifurcation point, as Ilya Prigogine and Erich Jantsch call it) is reached. Either the social institutions and individual consciousness reorganize at a new higher level of complexity or reorganize to an older lower level of complexity. That is, either toward a renewal of feudalistic institutions and conventional consciousness (although, with the help of digital technology, thereby making it more dangerous) or toward post-capitalist institutions and integral consciousness.[5]

One of the main factors that would cause consciousness to reorganize at a higher level, at the integral stage, is the realization that as we all become hyper-individualized and unique individuals, the only thing that we truly have in common is what we all have in common with all humans: our shared humanness and our shared planet. While neoliberal digital capitalism singularizes us to an unprecedented degree (whereby identity politics further contributes to this process), our capacity for empathy with others can be paradoxically broadened as we also become hyper-networked via digital technology. If this happens, the result would be a return to a new sense of community, but this time, due to the overcoming of parochial and local identities, community will transcend the local and national level, and come about on a global level.

Further, as we recognize the limitations of the pluralistic worldview, with its tendency to singularize and isolate, this worldview or consciousness itself becomes an object of our awareness and we see it in the contexts in which this worldview is embedded, giving us a new perspective on our lives, seeing where we fit in the context of systems within systems.[6] This capacity, together with the broadened scope of empathy also means that we begin to realize the need for our society to exist (once again, perhaps) in harmony with our larger ecological context. In other words, if consciousness develops to a higher level of complexity instead of a lower one, then the stage is set for us to develop new institutions, most likely in the form of the post-capitalist commons.

The institution of the commons and the practice of commoning have been around for thousands of years. How would the post-capitalist

---

[5] I might be stating the obvious, but the Trump presidency and similar far-right governments around the world represent effort to reorganize society around a lower level of complexity, in the direction of a fascistic feudalism governed by "enlightened" billionaires.

[6] This was Robert Kegan's insight into the transition to what he calls the fifth order of consciousness. (Kegan, 1994).

commons be different from the pre-capitalist version, and would it even need to be different? Pre-capitalist commons were characterized by a well-defined membership and were generally organized around what Ostrom called "common pool resources," that is, limited shared (usually renewable) resources that needed to be managed in common to preserve them for many generations.

With the development of capitalism and industrialization, a new type of commons came about, which was based on labor and production, and which represented a reaction against the typical capitalist enterprise: the cooperative, also known as the social commons (following Nick Dyer-Witheford's terminology). The capitalist social commons, which is capitalist in the sense that it developed during capitalism and thus had to operate and survive in a capitalist environment, also depended on a fixed membership, usually defined via a membership fee or stake, and with the primary resource being labor instead of nature. The capitalist context, though, makes it very difficult for cooperatives—the social commons—to operate according to commons principles because cooperatives face tremendous pressures to adapt to the capitalist context, which can mean changing their internal functioning so that it increasingly resembles those of typical capitalist enterprises.[7]

The post-capitalist commons become possible with the transition to the digital knowledge economy, which enables the development of an expanded cultural commons (or knowledge commons). Now, participation in the commons can be universalized for the first time to anyone who wants to join, since knowledge is an unlimitedly reproducible resource. Also, when combined with integral consciousness, digital technology can fundamentally change the functioning of both natural and social commons. That is, it is now conceivable for all types of commons to be upwardly scalable because their governance systems

---

[7] A good example of this tendency is seen with the Mondragon cooperatives of Spain, which serve as a shining example for cooperatives around the world, but which more recently changed their remuneration rules for managers, allowing for ever greater levels of inequality between managers and workers, and also began employing nonmembers on short-term contracts. (See Cheney (1999)).

can be deployed at any scale, from local to global. More than that, if the private digital platforms of today's tech giants (Amazon, Apple, Google, Facebook/Meta, X, etc.) were turned into commons, then we would see a transition from private markets and private information exchanges to socialized exchanges, which would mean an important break away from capitalist principles, making participatory economics on a large scale possible for the first time. Also, scaling up the commons to govern the global use of harmful resources, such as of carbon-based fossil fuels, would mean a significant step forward in humankind's ability to address the climate crisis.

I see two major obstacles, though, in the way of achieving such a transition: one social and one cultural. First, the social obstacle is that of powerful vested interests that benefit from maintaining the status quo. Even though most of the world's ruling elite ought to recognize that it is in their own survival interest to participate in a transition toward a post-capitalist society, their approach is predominantly governed by short-term thinking and the effort to maintain their exorbitant power. Worse yet, a significant part of this ruling elite would rather see a regression toward feudalism than an advance to post-capitalism, if these are the two options for resolving the crises.

Only a tiny minority among these elites occasionally see the light and make some efforts to help bring about a transition to an economic system that is less exploitative and damaging. As a result, the practically only way that this elite will be defeated, since rational arguments won't be enough, is through mass popular pressure. This elite will have to be either deposed from their position of power via elections or revolution, or it will see that holding on to their privileges will eventually cost them more than conceding power will.

However, the mobilization of mass popular pressure runs into the second obstacle: the cultural dominance of cynicism. Western culture has come to be imbued with the idea that the reason things are bad is because it is either due to human nature or that the powerful cannot possibly be dislodged from their positions of power. As a result, instead of trying to change the world, the average citizen tends to believe that they might as well make the best of the situation and play along in the competitive neoliberal struggle of all against all.[8] This general attitude is further reinforced by what Habermas once called, "the exhaustion of utopian energies."[9] That is, the demise of the social democratic welfare state, together with the apparent failures of Soviet-style state socialism have created a dearth of utopian thinking, leaving the overwhelming impression that "there is no alternative" (TINA), as the former British Prime Minister Margaret Thatcher once said.

The only way to overcome these two obstacles is to, first, reengage in "scientific"[10] utopian thinking, based on existing social and psychological possibilities and potentials, such as the ones I have outlined in this book. And second, to build social movements that strategically wield utopian imagination and the power of the vast majority to overcome the resistance of the power elite. Third, ideally, this movement would also consider the need to promote consciousness transformation in the direction of what I am calling integral consciousness. But how does a movement go about doing this?

The left has generally adopted two main approaches to consciousness transformation. First, there is the Gramscian approach, which focuses on the importance of educating the working class for class consciousness and, more broadly, the majority of the population for ideological hegemony in society in favor of socialism. In essence, the basic idea is that the party needs to disseminate socialist ideas via journalists, public intellectuals, and educators among the masses. The psychological theory behind this type of consciousness change is relatively simple in that it assumes that the individual adopts an ideology when they hear about it or becomes convinced by it. Resistance to the ideas only comes up when they contradict vested material interests, but since most of

---

[8] Sloterdijk ([1983] 1988) brilliantly outlines how this came about and what it means for society.
[9] Habermas (1985). Jacoby (1999) makes a similar argument.
[10] I do not want to fetishize the concept of science here. However, I do think it is essential for utopian thinkers to take seriously the question of how their utopian conceptions for a better society might come about, out of the potentials latent in existing society, including an understanding of the psychological dimension.

the population would stand to gain from socialism, resistance is not an obstacle to the dissemination of socialist ideas among the working class, according to this approach. A more sophisticated application of this approach would be the popular education model as promoted among many left parties in Latin America, which relies to some extent on Paulo Freire's pedagogy of the oppressed.[11]

The second approach has its origins in Marx and argues that the class struggle itself will change the consciousness of the working class.[12] According to this argument, the worker is the "second product" of the capitalist production process, with the first product being the commodity that the worker makes. During the production process, the workers are isolated and alienated, which creates a form of consciousness that allows for their continued exploitation because of their disunity and apathy. Their gradual resistance to oppressive circumstances, however, means that the workers develop a new practice, a revolutionary practice to change the system, and that this new practice also creates a new type of consciousness. That is, revolutionary practice is "the simultaneous change in circumstances and self-change."[13] The emphasis on this aspect of Marx's concept of revolutionary change is incredibly important because it focuses on how our circumstances shape our consciousness and how our consciousness shapes our circumstances via action on the circumstances. However, even though this approach clearly distinguishes between capitalist and socialist circumstances, it does not do the same for capitalist and socialist consciousness, other than perhaps arguing that socialist consciousness is a form of working-class consciousness. Paying attention to the logic involved in the development of consciousness as well as in the development of political–economic

---

[11] Freire (2007). While I consider Freire's critical pedagogy and its related offshoots to be a very important contribution for a more effective form of consciousness development, its emphasis on revealing power relations to the detriment of incorporating developmental psychology means that it runs the risk of failing to develop the other attributes that I have argued are necessary for a fully integral and post-capitalist consciousness.

[12] More recently, the theorists István Mészáros (2011) and Michael Lebowitz (2020) have recovered this very neglected aspect of Marx's thought.

[13] Lebowitz (2020, p. 73). Also, "Through its revolutionary activity, in short, the working class transforms itself" (Lebowitz, 2020, p. 76).

systems gives us a better idea as to how each of these might look when capitalism is overcome and how consciousness and circumstances fit together.

A third, non-Marxist approach to social and institutional change, via consciousness transformation, can be found in the work of Robert Kegan and Lisa Lahey.[14] The insight of their approach is that they use a sophisticated understanding of consciousness development and how it can be advanced and apply this understanding to organizational transformation. That is, they see each developmental stage of consciousness as one of increasing complexity, whereby each stage is one where the self identifies with a particular way of seeing the world—a particular perspective, such as group-centric, world-centric, and so on—and as it moves to the next stage it disidentifies from its old perspective, turning the old consciousness into an object of awareness, as it then becomes identified with (subject to) the more complex and higher new perspective. The process by which this happens is one that takes the form of crisis resolution but can also be guided by leaders who understand the consciousness transformation process. At the heart of that process of guiding such transformations lies the effort to get people to objectify their current identifications (or subjectivity), to question these, to disidentify from them, and to adopt a more encompassing identity (or subjectivity), which incorporates and transcends the old identity.[15] If this approach could be adopted in progressive social change movements, it would go a long way toward addressing the problem that all too often social change movements are completely unclear about what form consciousness transformation ought to take and how it could be brought about most effectively.

If social change movements were to combine all three of the above-mentioned consciousness transformation approaches, then the left would have a powerful tool in its hands for achieving lasting and real

---

[14] Kegan and Lahey (2009, 2016).
[15] Astute observers will recognize this as being in effect the core of G. W. Hegel's conception of dialectical development.

social change. In practice, this would mean that Gramscian efforts to develop ideological hegemony and Freireian critical pedagogy would both be informed by developmental psychology. Certainly, it is important for progressive social change efforts to inform and educate the public about how the current social arrangements favor the elite and harm the vast majority and nature. But such an approach is clearly not enough. Our minds are not arbitrarily shapeable via a one-to-one information dump but instead have certain grooves or inertia about them, which develop in accordance with certain patterns, and which need to be considered if we hope to achieve lasting social change. Similarly, the fight for social change cannot rely on a generalized faith that this fight will automatically generate a higher form of consciousness, as Marx, Meszáros, and Lebowitz argue. No doubt, it will probably create a greater understanding of social conditions, but an understanding of how consciousness develops would be needed to make sure that the movement does not lead toward a dead end, as has happened in so many social change movements.

Applying this understanding of consciousness development could mean that general education as well as training workshops for organizations could adopt, for example, the type of "deliberatively developmental" organizational change model that Kegan and Lahey describe in their work. This is but one example. Spiritual communities that focus on consciousness development, via meditation and other spiritual practices, could conceivably also be integrated into social change movements, to help people disidentify from their old and dysfunctional consciousness, which neoliberal digital capitalism helped create, and to develop a new consciousness, which will help create a post-capitalist commonism of the future. The hope is, for social change movements to realize that changing the world will require not only organizing people to challenge the powerful, but also that the creation of a new society and new institutions will require a systematic challenging of our way of making sense of the world.

Bibliography

Agger, Ben (1992). *The Discourse of Domination: From the Frankfurt School to Postmodernism*. Evanston, IL: Northwestern University Press.

Agger, Ben (2003). *The Virtual Self: A Contemporary Sociology*. Hoboken, NJ: Wiley-Blackwell.

Albert, Michael (2021). *No Bosses: A New Economy for a Better World*. Alreford: Zero Books.

Althusser, Louis (1969). *For Marx*. New York: Verso Books.

Alvaredo, Facundo, Lucas Chancel, Thomas Piketty, Emmanuel Saez, and Gabriel Zucman (2018). *World Inequality Report 2018*, published by World Inequality Lab. (Retrieved on October 10, 2022: https://wir2018.wid.world/files/download/wir2018-full-report-english.pdf).

de Angelis, Massimo (2017). *Omnia Sunt Communia: Principles for the Transition to Postcapitalism*. London: Zed Books.

Anderson, Benedict (1983). *Imagined Communities*. London: Verso Books.

Anderson, Perry (1998). *The Origins of Postmodernity*. London: Verso Books.

Bahro, Rudolf ([1987] 1994). *Avoiding Social and Ecological Disaster: The Politics of World Transformation*. Bath: Gateway Books.

Balibar, Etienne (1995). *The Philosophy of Marx*. New York: Verso Books.

Bandelow, Borwin, and Sophie Michaelis (2015). "Epidemiology of Anxiety Disorders in the 21st Century," *Dialogues in Clinical Neuroscience*, Vol. 17, No: 3, 327–35. doi:10.31887/DCNS.2015.17.3/bbandelow.

Bauman, Zygmut (1992). *Intimations of Postmodernity*. London: Routledge.

Benjamin, Walter ([1968] 2019). "Theses on the Philosophy of History." In Hannah Arendt (ed.), *Illuminations: Essays and Reflections* (pp. 196–209). New York: Schocken Books.

Best, Steven, and Douglas Kellner (1997) *The Postmodern Turn*. New York: The Guilford Press

Bhargava, Rajeev (1994). "Karl Popper: Reason Without Revolution," *Economic and Political Weekly*, Vol. 29, No. 53, 3313–14. https://www.epw.in/journal/1994/53/commentary/karl-popper-reason-without-revolution.html.

Blaut, J. M. (1993). *The Colonizer's Model of the World: Geographic Diffusionism and Eurocentric History*. New York: Guilford Press.

Blaut, J. M. (2000). *Eight Eurocentric Historians.* New York: Guilford Press.
Blunden, Andy (2012). *An Interdisciplinary Theory of Activity.* New York: Haymarket Books.
Bollier, David, and Silke Helfrich (2012). *The Wealth of the Commons: A World Beyond Market and State.* Amherst, MA: Levellers Press.
Bollier, David, and Silke Helfrich (2015). *Patterns of Commoning.* Amherst, MA: Levellers Press.
Bollier, David (2014). *Think Like a Commoner: A Short Introduction to the Life of the Commons.* Canada: New Society Publishers.
Bowles, Samuel, and Herb Gintis (2011). *A Cooperative Species: Human Reciprocity and Its Evolution.* Princeton: Princeton University Press.
Brown, Wendy (2015). *Undoing the Demos: Neoliberalism's Stealth Revolution.* New York: Zone Books.
Burman, Erica (1994). *Deconstructing Developmental Psychology.* New York: Routledge.
Cahill, Damien, and Martijn Konings (2017). *Neoliberalism.* Cambridge: Polity Press.
Capra, Fritjof, and Ugo Mattei (2015). *The Ecology of Law: Toward a Legal System in Tune with Nature and Community.* Oakland, CA: Berrett-Koehler Publishers.
Chalmers, David (1996). *The Conscious Mind: In Search of a Fundamental Theory.* Oxford: Oxford University Press.
Chang, Ha-Joon (2002). *Kicking Away the Ladder: Development Strategy in Historical Perspective.* London: Anthem Press.
Chang, Ha-Joon (2008). *Bad Samaritans: The Myth of Free Trade and the Secret History of Capitalism.* London: Bloomsbury Publishing.
Cheney, George (1999). *Values at Work: Employee Participation Meets Market Pressure at Mondragon.* Ithaca, NY: Cornell University Press.
Choudry, Aziz (ed.) (2018). *Activists and the Surveillance State: Learning from Repression.* London: Pluto Press.
Christophers, Brett (2010). *Rentier Capitalism: Who Owns the Economy, and Who Pays for It?* London: Verso Books.
Cook-Greuter, Susanne (1999). "Postautonomous Ego Development: A Study of Its Nature and Measurement." (Doctoral dissertation, Harvard University) *Dissertation Abstracts International*, Vol. 60, No. 6, 3000.
Cook-Greuter, Susanne (2014). "Ego Development: A Full-Spectrum Theory of Vertical Growth and Meaning Making." (Retrieved from ResearchGate

on October 10, 2022: https://www.researchgate.net/publication/356357233_Ego_Development_A_Full-Spectrum_Theory_Of_Vertical_Growth_And_Meaning_Making).

Commons, Michael L., and Francis A. Richards (2003). "Four Postformal Stages." In J. Demick, and C. Andreoletti (eds.), *Handbook of Adult Development* (pp. 199–219). New York: Kluwer.

Cornforth, Maurice (1968). *The Open Philosophy and the Open Society.* New York: International Publishers.

Crouch, Colin (2011). *The Strange Non-Death of Neo-Liberalism.* London: Polity Press.

Curran, Thomas, and Andrew P. Hill (2019). "Perfectionism Is Increasing Over Time: A Meta-Analysis of Birth Cohort Differences From 1989 to 2016," *Psychological Bulletin*, Vol. 145, No. 4, 410–29.

Dardot, Pierre, and Christian Laval (2014). *The New Way of the World: On Neoliberal Society.* London: Verso Books.

Dardot, Pierre, and Christian Laval (2019). *Common: On Revolution in the 21st Century.* London: Bloomsbury.

Davidson, Neil (2023). *What Was Neoliberalism?* Chicago: Haymarket Books

Davies, William (2016). "The New Neoliberalism," *New Left Review*, No. 101, Sept/Oct 2016.

Denzin, Norman (1991). *Images of Postmodernism: Social Theory and Contemporary Cinema.* London: Sage.

Doidge, Norman (2007). *The Brain That Changes Itself: Stories of Personal Triumph from the Frontiers of Brain Science.* New York: Penguin Books.

Durant, Will (1926). *The Story of Philosophy: The Lives and Opinions of the Greater Philosophers.* New York: Simon and Schuster.

Dux, Günter (2000). *Historisch-genetische Theorie der Kultur.* Weilerswist: Velbrück Verlag.

Dyer-Witheford, Nick (2007). "Commonism." *Turbulence – 1.* (Retrieved on July 28, 2025: https://www.turbulence.org.uk/turbulence-1/commonism/).

Eagleton, Terry (2021). "The Marxist and the Messiah," *London Review of Books*, Vol. 43, No. 17. https://www.lrb.co.uk/the-paper/v43/n17/terry-eagleton/the-marxist-and-the-messiah.

Elias, Norbert ([1939] 2012). *On the Process of Civilization.* Chicago: University of Chicago Press.

Ellner, Steven (2010). "The Perennial Debate over Socialist Goals Played Out in Venezuela," *Science & Society*, Vol. 74, No. 1, 63–84.

Engels, Friedrich (1892). "Socialism: Utopian and Scientific." *Marxists*. https://www.marxists.org/archive/marx/works/1880/soc-utop/.

Featherstone, Mike (1991). *Consumer Culture and Postmodernism*. London: Sage.

Federici, Silvia (2018). *Re-enchanting the World: Feminism and the Politics of the Commons*. Binghamton, NY: PM Press.

Flett, G. L., and P. L. Hewitt (2014). "Perfectionism and Perfectionistic Self-Presentation in Social Anxiety." In S. G. Hofmann, and P. M. DiBartolo (eds.), *Social Anxiety: Clinical, Developmental, and Social Perspectives*, Third Edition (pp. 160–83). London: Elsevier.

Foster, John Bellamy, and Robert McChesney (2012). *The Endless Crisis: How Monopoly-Finance Capital Produces Stagnation and Upheaval from the USA to China*. New York: Monthly Review Press.

Foucault, Michel (2008). *The Birth of Biopolitics: Lectures at the Collège de France, 1978–1979*. London: Palgrave Macmillan.

Freire, Paulo (2007). *Pedagogy of the Oppressed*. New York: Continuum.

Friedlmeier, Wolfgang, Pradeep Chakkarath, and Beate Schwarz (eds.) (2005). *Culture and Human Development*. New York: Psychology Press.

Gardiner, Harry, and Corinne Kosmitzki (2010). *Lives Across Cultures: Cross-Cultural Human Development*. Boston: Pearson.

Gardner, Howard (2006). *Multiple Intelligences: New Horizons*. New York: Basic Books.

Gebser, Jean ([1949/1953] 1985). *The Ever-Present Origin*. Athens: Ohio University Press.

Giddens, Anthony (1971). *Capitalism and Modern Social Theory: An Analysis of the Writings of Marx, Durkheim and Max Weber*. Cambridge: Cambridge University Press.

Giddens, Anthony (1984). *The Constitution of Society: Outline of the Theory of Structuration*. Cambridge: Polity.

Gilens, Martin, and Benjamin I. Page (2014). "Testing Theories of American Politics: Elites, Interest Groups, and Average Citizens," *Perspectives on Politics*, Vol. 12, No. 3, 564–81.

Gilroy-Ware, Marcus (2017). *Filling the Void: Emotion, Capitalism and Social Media*. London: Repeater Books.

Godelier, Maurice (1986). *The Mental and the Material*. New York: Verso Books.

Goleman, Daniel (1995). *Emotional Intelligence*. New York: Bantam Books.
Goleman, Daniel (2005). *Social Intelligence*. New York: Bantam Books.
Gorz, André (1967). *Strategy for Labor: A Radical Proposal*. Boston: Beacon Press.
Gould, Stephen Jay (1996). *Full House: The Spread of Excellence from Plato to Darwin*. New York: Harmony Books.
Graeber, David, and David Wengrow (2021). *The Dawn of Everything: A New History of Humanity*. New York: Farrar, Straus and Giroux.
Gramsci, Antonio ([1947] 2011). *Prison Notebooks, Vol. 1–3*. New York: Columbia University Press.
Guevara, Ernesto (2003). *The Che Reader*. New York: Ocean Press.
Gunder Frank, Andre (1998). *ReOrient: Global Economy in the Asian Age*. Berkeley: University of California Press.
Habermas, Jürgen (1975). *Legitimation Crisis*. Boston: Beacon Press.
Habermas, Jürgen ([1976] 1979). *Communication and the Evolution of Society*. London: Heinemann Educational Books.
Habermas, Jürgen (1985). *Die Neue Unübersichtlichkeit*. Frankfurt: Suhrkamp Verlag.
Habermas, Jürgen (1990). *The Philosophical Discourse of Modernity: Twelve Lectures*. Cambridge, MA: MIT Press.
Habermas, Jürgen (1998). *Between Facts and Norms: Contributions to a Discourse Theory of Law and Democracy*. Cambridge, MA: MIT Press.
Hahnel, Robin (2022). *A Participatory Economy*. Chico, CA: AK Press.
Hardt, Michael, and Antonio Negri (2009). *Commonwealth*. New York: Oxford University Press.
Hardt, Michael, and Antonio Negri (2012). *Declaration*. New York: Argo Navis.
Hardt, Michael, and Antonio Negri (2017). *Assembly*. New York: Oxford University Press.
Harvey, David (1989). *The Condition of Postmodernity: An Enquiry into the Origins of Cultural Change*. London: Routledge.
Harvey, David (2005). *A Brief History of Neoliberalism*. Oxford: Oxford University Press.
Han, Byung-Chul (2017). *Psychopolitics: Neoliberalism and New Technologies of Power*. London: Verso Books.

Hewitt, P. L., and G. L. Flett (1990). "Perfectionism and Depression: A Multi-Dimensional Analysis," *Journal of Social Behavior and Personality*, Vol. 5, No. 5, 423–38.

Hoffman, Martin L. (2000). *Empathy and Moral Development: Implications for Caring and Justice*. Cambridge: Cambridge University Press.

Holloway, John (2002). *Change the World Without Taking Power: The Meaning of Revolution Today*. London: Pluto Press.

Hook, Sidney (1951). "From Plato to Hegel to Marx." *New York Times*, July 22.

IMF (2018). *IMF Fiscal Monitor: Capitalizing on Good Times*. (Retrieved on October 5, 2025: https://www.imf.org/-/media/Files/Publications/fiscal-monitor/2018/April/pdf/fm1801.ashx).

Ingelhart, Ronald (2018). *Cultural Evolution: People's Motivations Are Changing and Reshaping the World*. Cambridge: Cambridge University Press.

Ingersoll, R. Elliott, and Susanne R. Cook-Greuter (2007). "The Self-System in Integral Counseling," *Counseling and Values*, Vol. 51, No. 3, 193–208. John Wiley.

Jacoby, Russell (1999). *The End of Utopia*. New York: Basic Books.

Jameson, Frederick (1991). *Postmodernism, or, the Cultural Logic of Late Capitalism*. Durham, NC: Duke University Press.

Jantsch, Erich (1980). *The Self-Organizing Universe: Scientific and Human Implications of the Emerging Paradigm of Evolution*. Oxford: Pergamon Press.

Kastrup, Bernardo (2024). *Analytic Idealism in a Nutshell*. Winchester, UK: IFF Books.

Kegan, Robert, Gil G. Noam, and Laura Rogers (1982). "The Psychologic of Emotion: A Neo-Piagetian View." *New Directions for Child and Adolescent Development*, Vol. 1982, 105–28. doi.org/10.1002/cd.23219821606.

Kegan, Robert (1994). *In over Our Heads: The Mental Demands of Modern Life*. Cambridge, MA: Harvard University Press.

Kegan, Robert, and Lisa Laskow Lahey (2009). *Immunity to Change: How to Overcome and Unlock the Potential in Yourself and Your Organization*. Boston: Harvard Business Review Press.

Kegan, Robert, and Lisa Laskow Lahey (2016). *An Everyone Culture: Becoming a Deliberatively Developmental Organization*. Boston: Harvard Business Review Press.

Kohlberg, Lawrence (1981). *The Philosophy of Moral Development: Moral Stages and the Idea of Justice (Essays on Moral Development: Vol. 1)* (1st ed.). San Francisco: Harper & Row.

Kołakowski, Leszek (2005). *Main Currents of Marxism.* New York: W. W. Norton.

Laclau, Ernesto, and Chantal Mouffe (1985). *Hegemony and Socialist Strategy: Towards a Radical Democratic Politics.* New York: Verso Books.

Lapavitsas, Costas, and Paulo L. Dos Santos (2008). "Globalization and Contemporary Banking: On the Impact of New Technology," *Contributions to Political Economy,* Vol. 27, No. 1, 31–56.

Laszlo, Ervin (1996). *Evolution: The General Theory.* New York: Hampton Press.

Lebowitz, Michael (2004). Unpublished manuscript of "The Rich Human Being: Marx and the Concept of Real Human Development," a talk given at the "Marx Conference," 4–8 May 2004 in Havana, Cuba.

Lebowitz, Michael (2010). *The Socialist Alternative: Real Human Development.* New York: Monthly Review Press.

Lebowitz, Michael (2020). *Between Capitalism and Community.* New York: Monthly Review Press.

Lemieux, Frederic (2019). *Intelligence and State Surveillance in Modern Societies: An International Perspective.* Bigley: Emerald Publishing.

Lenin, Vladimir ([1902] 1961). "What Is to Be Done?" In *Lenin's Collected Works,* Volume 5 (pp. 347–530). Moscow: Foreign Languages Publishing House.

Lenski, Gerhard (2005). *Ecological-Evolutionary Theory: Principles and Applications.* Boulder, CO: Paradigm Publishers.

Linebaugh, Peter (2008). *Stop, Thief!: The Commons, Enclosures, and Resistance.* Oakland, CA: PM Press.

Loevinger, Jane (1976). *Ego Development: Conceptions and Theories.* San Francisco: Jossey-Bass.

Lovejoy, Arthur ([1936] 2009). *The Great Chain of Being: A Study of the History of an Idea.* New York: Routledge.

Marcuse, Herbert (1964). *One-Dimensional Man: Studies in the Ideology of Advanced Industrial Society.* Boston: Beacon Press.

Martinez, Carlos, Michael Fox, and Jojo Farrell (2010). *Venezuela Speaks! Voices from the Grassroots.* Oakland, CA: PM Press.

Marx, Karl ([1885] 1963). *The Eighteenth Brumaire of Louis Bonaparte.* New York: International Publishers.

Marx, Karl ([1846] 1970). *The German Ideology.* New York: International Publishers.

Marx, Karl ([1859] 1970). *A Contribution to the Critique of Political Economy.* New York: International Publishers.

Marx, Karl (1977). *Capital, Volume I.* New York: Vintage Books.

Marx, Karl ([1852] 1978). *The Marx-Engels Reader*, Second Edition, edited by Robert C. Tucker. New York: W.W. Norton.

Marx, Karl (and Frederick Engels [1848] 1998). *The Communist Manifesto.* London: Verso Books.

Mészáros, István (2005). *The Power of Ideology.* London: Zed Books.

Mészáros, István (2011). *Social Structure and Forms of Consciousness, Volume 2: The Dialectic of Structure and History.* New York: Monthly Review Books.

Ministerio de Comunicación e Información (2004). "Taller de Alto Nivel," p. 17, November 12–13, 2004. (Retrieved on June 1, 2023: https://www.minci.gob.ve/wp-content/uploads/downloads/2013/01/nuevomapaestrategico.pdf).

Ministerio de Comunicación e Información (2007). "Líneas Generales del Plan de Desarrollo Económico y Social de la Nación 2007–2013." (Retrieved on June 1, 2023: https://www.nodo50.org/plataformabolivariana/Externos/LineasGenNacion.pdf).

Nasdaq (2016). "High Frequency Trading." (Retrieved on October 5, 2025: https://www.nasdaq.com/investing/glossary/h/high-frequency-trading).

Offe, Claus (1984). *Contradictions of the Welfare State.* Cambridge, MA: MIT Press.

Ollman, Bertell (n.d.). (Retrieved on May 23, 2012: https://www.nyu.edu/projects/ollman/docs/class_consciousness.php).

Osterdiekhoff, Georg (2009). *Die Geistige Entwicklung der Menschheit.* Weilerswist-Metternich: Velbrück Wissenschaft.

Ostrom, Elinor (1990). *Governing the Commons.* Cambridge: Cambridge University Press.

Ostrom, Elinor, and Charlotte Hess (2007). *Understanding Knowledge as a Commons: From Theory to Practice.* Cambridge, MA: MIT Press.

Owen, David S. (2002). *Between Reason and History: Habermas and the Idea of Progress*. Albany: SUNY Press.

Patel, Raj (2010). *The Value of Nothing: How to Reshape Market Society and Redefine Democracy*. New York: St. Martin's Press.

Pettman, Dominic (2016). *Infinite Distraction: Paying Attention to Social Media*. Cambridge: Polity Press.

de Peuter, Greig, and Nick Dyer-Witheford (2010). "Commons and Cooperatives," *Affinities: A Journal of Radical Theory, Culture, and Action*, Vol. 4, No. 1, 30–56.

Phillips, Peter (2018). *Giants: The Global Power Elite*. New York: Seven Stories Press.

Piaget, Jean (1995). *The Essential Piaget*. New York: Basic Books.

Pollin, Robert, and Noam Chomsky (2020). *Climate Crisis and the Green New Deal*. London: Verso Books.

Popper, Karl (2013). *The Open Society and Its Enemies*. Princeton: Princeton University Press.

Poster, Mark (2006). *Information Please: Culture and Politics in the Age of Digital Machines*. Durham, NC: Duke University Press.

Prigogine, Ilya, and Isabel Stengers (1984). *Order Out of Chaos: Man's New Dialogue with Nature*. New York: Bantam Books.

Ratner, Carl, Daniele Nunes, and Henrique Silva (eds.) (2017). *Vygotsky and Marx: Toward a Marxist Psychology*. New York: Routledge.

Reckwitz, Andreas (2017). *Die Gesellschaft der Singularitäten: Zum Strukturwandel der Moderne*. Frankfurt: Suhrcamp.

Reuters (2018). "U.S. household debt rises to $13.3 trillion in second quarter." (Retrieved July 8, 2025: https://www.reuters.com/article/us-usa-fed-debt/u-s-household-debt-rises-to-13-3-trillion-in-second-quarter-idUSKBN1KZ1QZ/).

Rifkin, Jeremy (2009). *The Empathic Civilization: The Race to Global Consciousness in a World in Crisis*. New York: Tarcher/Penguin.

Ritzer, George (2020). *The McDonaldization of Society: Into the Digital Age*, Tenth Edition. Los Angeles: Sage Publications.

Robinson, William I. (2004). *A Theory of Global Capitalism*. Baltimore: Johns Hopkins University Press.

Robinson, William I. (2020). *The Global Police State*. London: Pluto Press.

Rojas, René (2018). "The Latin American Left's Shifting Tides," *Catalyst*, Vol. 2, No. 2, 7–71.

Rojas, René (2020). "The End of Progressive Neoliberalism," *Catalyst*, Vol. 4, No. 2, 141–224.

Sanderson, Stephen K. (2007). *Evolutionism and Its Critics*. Boulder, CO: Paradigm Publishers.

Seymour, Richard (2020). *The Twittering Machine*. London: Verso Books.

Siegler, Robert S. (1996). *Emerging Minds*. New York: Oxford University Press.

Shearer, Elisa (2018). "Social media outpaces print newspapers in the U.S. as a news source." Pew Research Center. (Retrieved on October 5, 2025: https://www.pewresearch.org/fact-tank/2018/12/10/social-media-outpaces-print-newspapers-in-the-u-s-as-a-news-source/).

Sloterdijk, Peter ([1983] 1988). *Critique of Cynical Reason*. Minneapolis: University of Minnesota Press.

Srnicek, Nick (2017). *Platform Capitalism*. Cambridge: Polity Press.

Staab, Philipp (2019). *Digitaler Kapitalismus: Markt und Herrschaft in der Ökonomie der Unknappheit*. Frankfurt: Suhrkamp Verlag.

Standing, Guy (2011). *The Precariat: The Dangerous New Class*. London: Bloomsbury.

Statista (2025). "Number of social media users worldwide from 2019 to 2029." (Retrieved on Oct 5, 2025: https://www.statista.com/statistics/278414/number-of-worldwide-social-network-users/).

Stiegler, Bernard (2010). *Taking Care of Youth and the Generations*. Stanford, CA: Stanford University Press.

Strydom, Piet (1992). "The Ontogenetic Fallacy: The Immanent Critique of Habermas's Developmental Logical Theory of Evolution," *Theory, Culture & Society*, Vol. 9, No. 3, 65–93.

Temin, Peter (2017). *The Vanishing Middle Class*. Cambridge, MA: MIT Press.

Thompson, Evan (2007). *Mind in Life: Biology, Phenomenology, and the Sciences of Mind*. Cambridge, MA: Harvard University Press.

Trotsky, Leon ([1937] 2004). *The Revolution Betrayed*. Mineola, NY: Dover Publications.

Turkle, Sherry (2017). *Alone Together: Why We Expect More from Technology and Less from Each Other*, Third Edition. New York: Basic Books.

Ugolik Phillips, Kaitlin (2020). *The Future of Feeling: Building Empathy in a Tech-Obsessed World*. Seattle, WA: Amazon Publishing.

Unger, Roberto Mangabeira (2015). *The Critical Legal Studies Movement*. New York: Verso Books.

Varela, Francisco, Evan Thompson, and Eleanor Rosch (2016). *The Embodied Mind: Cognitive Science and Human Experience*. Cambridge, MA: MIT Press.

de Vos, Cato M. H., Natasha L Mason, and Kim P C Kuypers (2021). "Psychedelics and Neuroplasticity: A Systematic Review Unraveling the Biological Underpinnings of Psychedelics," *Frontiers in Psychiatry*, Vol. 12, No. 724606. doi:10.3389/fpsyt.2021.724606.

Wall, Derek (2014). *The Commons in History: Culture, Conflict, and Ecology*. Cambridge, MA: MIT Press.

Walljasper, Jay (2010). *All that We Share: How to Save the Economy, the Environment, the Internet, Democracy, Our Communities, and Everything Else that Belongs to All of Us*. New York: The New Press.

Watkins, Alan, and Iman Stratenous (2016). *Crowdacracy: The End of Politics*. Chatham, Kent: Urbane Publications.

Weinberger A. H., M. Gbedemah, A. M. Martinez, D.Nash, S. Galea, and R. D. Goodwin (2018). "Trends in Depression Prevalence in the USA from 2005 to 2015: Widening Disparities in Vulnerable Groups," *Psychological Medicine*, Vol. 48, No. 8, 1308–15.

Weisbrot, Mark (2015). *Failed: What the "Experts" Got Wrong about the Global Economy*. New York: Oxford University Press.

Wexler, Bruce E. (2006). *Brain and Culture*. Cambridge, MA: MIT Press.

Wilber, Ken (1981). *Up from Eden: A Transpersonal View of Human Evolution*. Wheaton, IL: Quest Books.

Wilber, Ken (1999). *The Collected Works of Ken Wilber, Volume 4*. Boulder, CO: Shambhala.

Wilber, Ken (2000a). *The Collected Works of Ken Wilber, Volume 6: Sex, Ecology, Spirituality*. Boulder, CO: Shambhala.

Wilber, Ken (2000b). *Integral Psychology*. Boulder, CO: Shambhala Publications.

Wilber, Ken (2000c). *A Brief History of Everything*. Boulder, CO: Shambhala Publications.

Wilber, Ken (n.d.). "The Many Ways We Touch." (Retrieved on June 19, 2025: https://integrallife.com/many-ways-touch/).

Wilpert, Gregory (2006). "The Dimensions of Political Ideology and Integral Politics," *AQAL: Journal of Integral Theory and Practice*, Vol. 1, No. 2, 72–90.

Wilpert, Gregory (2007). *Changing Venezuela by Taking Power: The History and Policies of the Chávez Government*. London: Verso Books.

Zelik, Raul (2011). *Nach dem Kapitalismus. Perspektiven der Emanzipation oder: Das Projekt Communismus anders denken*. Hamburg, VSA: Verlag.

Index

a-centric consciousness *see* integral consciousness
Adorno, Theodor 2n2, 4n3
affective development 25
agency, individual 21, 39
Albert, Michael 132n1, 165n57, 170n63
alienation in capitalism 5, 52–3
 from the state 152, 165–6
 in neoliberal digital capitalism 108, 128, 164
Althusser, Louis 2n2, 89–91
Alvaredo, Facundo 118
anarchism 61–2
Anderson, Benedict 148n25
Angelis, Massimo de 155, 171
anxiety 97, 123, 127, 129, 179
Aristide, Bertrand 122n64
Aristotle 35n1
artificial intelligence 96
attention deficit disorder 128
authoritarianism 77–80, 144, 177
autonomous stage (Loevinger/Cook-Greuter) 137
Axial Age 73

Bahro, Rudolf 7n10, 51n25, 66
Baldwin, James Mark 21–2
Bandelow, Borwin 127n74
base and superstructure 36–41
Baudrillard, Jean 141–3
Benjamin, Walter 80n20
Bernanke, Ben 104n17
Best, Steven 140–5, 148
Biden, Joe administration 96n3
biology, consciousness and 13–21, 84–9
Blair, Tony 101–2
Blaut, J. M. 73n6, 76n12
blockchain 152

Bohr, Niels 143
Bollier, David 151n33, 171
Bolívar, Simón 10
bourgeoisie *see* capitalist class
brain development 16–19
 neuroplasticity 17–19, 30
Bretton Woods system 99–100, 103, 105, 166
Brown, Wendy 121
Buddhism 15, 49n22, 50n22
Burman, Erica 77
Bush, George W. administration 99n11

Cahill, Damien 97n4, 105–6
capital gains 112
capitalism
 contradictions of 1–2, 175
 development stunted by 5
 digital *see* neoliberal digital capitalism growth and stagnation 110–12
 ideology 52–8
 industrial 48–9
 late 50–1
 platform 114–16
 property rights central to 153–6
 rentier 116n48
 surveillance 122
capitalist class 49, 63, 100, 177–8
Capra, Fritjof 153–4
Carneiro, Robert 87
Carter, Jimmy administration 100
Chalmers, David 14n2
Chang, Ha-Joon 98n8
chaos theory 143
Chávez, Hugo 7–9, 103–4, 122n64, 167n61, 174n2
Cheney, George 181n7
childhood development 25–30

concrete operational stage 27–9
preoperational stage 26–7
sensorimotor stage 25–6
Chile 100, 103
China 99, 103, 116n48
Chomsky, Noam 120
Christophers, Brett 116n48
Churchill, Winston 167
class
  consciousness 53–4, 62–5, 183
  coordinator 165n57, 173
  lower 126–7
  middle 126
  struggle 38, 62–5, 91–3, 177, 184
  working see working class
climate crisis 120, 133–4, 178–9, 182
Clinton, Bill administration 101–2
cognition see cognitive development
cognitive development 25–33
  concrete operational stage 27–9
  formal operational stage 29–30
  integral stage 31–3, 139
  pluralistic stage 31
  preoperational stage 26–7
  sensorimotor stage 25–6
Collateralized Debt Obligations (CDOs) 113
commodification 52–3, 164
Commons, Michael 29n37, 32
commons
  capitalist 181
  cultural 162–3, 181
  definition 169–71
  digital 159–61, 181–2
  governance 164–9
  history of 156–63
  household 162–3
  natural 151, 162–3, 181
  post-capitalist 151–71, 180–2
  pre-capitalist 156–9, 161, 181
  social 162–3, 181
commonism 133–71
consciousness see integral consciousness

definition 153
institutions 131–71
communication
  empathy and 145–8
  mass 117
  technology 145–8, 149
communism socialism versus 10–11
  Soviet-style 10–11, 41, 48–9, 99, 103, 183
  totalitarianism and 77–80
  utopian 174–5
Communist Manifesto (Marx and Engels) 5, 33
competition 61, 109–10, 125, 127, 129, 179
complexity
  consciousness 185
  science 149
  societal 44, 179–80
concrete operational stage 27–9
consciousness
  a-centric see integral consciousness
  autonomous 137
  biology and 13–21
  capitalist 38–9, 52–8
  class 53–4, 62–5, 183
  commonist see integral consciousness
  crises and 36, 41–3, 66, 133–4, 176
  de-centered see pluralistic consciousness
  definition 13–15
  deconstructive postmodern 142, 144, 148
  development see consciousness development
  dramaturgical 146, 148–9
  ego-centric see ego-centric consciousness
  enlightened false 57–8
  ethno-centric see ethno-centric consciousness
  false 2, 53, 55–6
  feudal 177

Index

fifth order (Kegan) 135–6
fourth order (Kegan) 135
group-centric *see* ethno-centric consciousness
ideological 146–7
integral *see* integral consciousness
lines of development 24–5, 30, 44, 75, 83–4
material reality and 15, 19–21, 36–41, 86–9
modern rational 48–9
mythic 47
neurobiology of 16–19
one-dimensional 54–6
pluralistic *see* pluralistic consciousness
postmodern 31, 49–51, 136, 140–5
pre-conventional 36
psychological 146–8
psychology of 21–34
reconstructive postmodern 142, 144, 148
revolutionary 132, 184
self- 13–14, 27–9, 32
singularization and 124–7
socialist 6, 11, 66, 184
socio-centric *see* ethno-centric consciousness
stages *see* stages of consciousness development
trade union 53
transformation 134, 176–7, 183–6
universal 63
world-centric *see* world-centric consciousness
consciousness development
adulthood 6–7, 30–3
childhood 25–30
lines of 24–5, 30, 44, 75, 83–4
logic of 22–4
psychology of 21–34
social evolution and 35–67, 70–2
stages *see* stages of consciousness development

conservatism 59, 61
consumer welfare standard 109–10
consumption 55, 107
conventional consciousness *see* ethno-centric consciousness
Cook-Greuter, Susanne 25, 29, 31–3, 135, 137–8
cooperatives 159, 165, 181
coordinator class 165n57, 173
Correa, Rafael 103
counterculture 123–4, 129, 148
COVID-19 pandemic 96n3
creative commons licensing 152
Credit Default Swaps (CDSs) 113
crisis theories 131–4
critical legal studies 154n42
critical pedagogy 184n11, 186
critical theory 2n2, 4, 7, 89
Crouch, Colin 153n37
crowdacracy 167–9
Cuba 10
cultural commons 162–3, 181
Cultural Revolution (China) 10n18
culture
  capitalist 54–6
  commons 170
  integral 139–51
  political 8–9
  postmodern 140–5
Curran, Thomas 127n73
cynicism 58, 182–3

Dardot, Pierre 97n4, 101n13, 151n33
Darwin, Charles 82
Davies, William 100n11, 101n13, 105n18, 107
debt 106–7, 178
de Bretteville, Sheila 6
decision-making
  collective 157, 168, 170
  commons 164–9
  democratic 49, 170
Declaration of Independence (US) 143

Declaration of the Rights of Man (France) 143
decolonization 98
Deleuze, Gilles 2n2
Delors, Jacques 101n12
democracy
  direct 161, 167–9
  liberal representative 48–9, 165–7, 179
  participatory 8, 152, 167
Denzin, Norman 140n15
depression 97, 123, 127, 129, 179
derivatives 105
determinism
  economic 37, 78–9, 175
  technological 149
development
  affective 25
  cognitive *see* cognitive development
  consciousness *see* consciousness development
  economic 6
  forces of production 11, 37, 41, 133
  individual 4–6, 35, 70–2
  interpersonal 25, 30
  lines of 24–5, 30, 44, 75, 83–4
  moral *see* moral development
  psychological *see* psychological development
  relations of production 37, 41n9, 133
  self-identity 25, 28, 30–1, 137
  social *see* social evolution
  societal *see* social evolution
  technological 6, 74, 145–9
  values 25
developmental psychology 3–4, 6–7, 21–34, 70–94
  adulthood development 30–3
  childhood development 25–30
  criticisms of 69–94
  cross-cultural research 24, 73
  idealism and 86–9
  lines of development 24–5
  neo-Piagetian 85–6
  stages *see* stages of consciousness development
  Vygotskian 86
dialectic
  base-superstructure 39–40
  consciousness-reality 15, 39
  progress 42, 66, 75, 81–2, 93
  subject-object 39
digital commons 159–61, 181–2
digital platforms 115–16, 182
digital technology 96, 107–8, 113, 125–6, 128–9, 149, 168, 179–82
discourse 56–7
discrimination 122
diversity 16, 148
Doidge, Norman 18n8
domination 2, 4, 11, 35, 43, 56, 62, 65, 86, 165, 177
dramaturgical consciousness 146, 148–9
Durkheim, Émile 153n40
Dux, Günter 71n4
Dyer-Witheford, Nick 151, 153, 162n55, 181

Eagleton, Terry 80n20
Eastern Europe 99, 103
ecological crisis 50, 65–6, 92, 120–1, 133–4, 151, 178–9, 182
  climate 120, 133–4, 178–9, 182
ecology 149
economic base *see* base and superstructure
economic crisis 97, 107, 110–12, 133, 178
  Great Depression 98, 100
  Great Financial Crisis 104–7, 112
  Great Recession 104
  oil embargo (1973) 99
  Third World debt 102
economics
  classical liberal 98

Keynesian 97, 98–9, 123, 129
neoclassical 154
neoliberal 97–129
participatory 9n14, 165n57, 182
education 10, 53, 152, 162, 166, 177, 183–4, 186
ego-centric consciousness 26–7, 45, 59–60
Elias, Norbert 35n1, 71n4
empathy 145–51, 161, 169, 180
global 150, 161
enclosure 158
enactment 20–1, 23, 39, 134, 155, 171
energy regimes 146–8
Engels, Friedrich 5, 33, 174–6
Enlightenment philosophy 48, 73, 141, 147, 159
entropy 147
environmental destruction 97, 107, 120–1, 123, 129, 152, 178–9
equality 11, 33, 59, 143, 166, 170n63, 178
ethno-centric consciousness 27–9, 45, 47, 73, 81, 83, 135, 177
Eurocentrism 69, 72–7, 86, 93
European Union (EU) 101n12, 102, 165
evolution
biological 82–3
social *see* social evolution
exploitation 62, 65, 76, 111–12, 132, 164–6, 184
externalization of costs 179

Facebook *see* Meta
Fanon, Frantz 2n2
fascism 6, 60, 132, 180n5
Featherstone, Mike 140n15
Federici, Silvia 46n20
feminism 148, 170n63
fetishism, commodity 52–3, 58
Feuerbach, Ludwig 39, 64, 88
feudalism 6, 36, 45, 47–8, 132, 153n40, 158, 177, 180

fifth order consciousness (Kegan) 135–6
financialization 100, 105–6, 110–14
Flett, Gordon 127n73
food 87, 157, 161
Fordism 124
formal operational stage 29–30
Foster, John Bellamy 110n34, 111–12
Foucault, Michel 2n2, 121n59, 143
Fourier, François 174
fourth order consciousness (Kegan) 135
Frankfurt School 2n2, 4, 89
free and open-source software (FOSS) 151, 159–60
freedom 1, 33, 61, 74, 83, 90–1, 93, 119
Freire, Paulo 184, 184n11, 186
French Revolution 48, 58, 159
Friedlmeier, Wolfgang 24, 73n5
Friedman, Milton 99–100
Fromm, Erich 2n2
Funes, Mauricio 103

Galeano, Eduardo 144, 175
Gandhi, Mohandas 33n51
Gardner, Howard 24
Gardiner, Harry 24, 73n5
Gebser, Jean 35n1, 44, 71n4, 139, 147
gender 2, 43, 62, 65–6, 77, 95–6, 126, 137, 150, 170n63
divisions 2
inequality 65, 95
Germany 75, 98, 101–2
Giddens, Anthony 39, 70
Gilens, Martin 167n59
Gilligan, Carol 77, 135, 138
Gilroy-Ware, Marcus 128n78
Glass-Steagall Act 114
global empathy 150, 161
global warming *see* climate crisis
globalization 1, 50–1, 95, 95n1
Godelier, Maurice 38n6
Goleman, Daniel 25

Index

Google 109, 114, 117, 122, 179, 182
Gorz, André 173
Gould, Stephen Jay 82
government spending 111, 122–3
Gramsci, Antonio 2n2, 4, 54, 177, 183, 186
Graeber, David 45n17
Graves, Clare 25, 32
Great Depression 98, 100
Great Financial Crisis 104–7, 112
Great Recession 104
Greece, ancient 48, 73
group-centric consciousness *see* ethno-centric consciousness
Guattari, Félix 2n2
Guevara, Ernesto "Che" 10, 79
Gunder Frank, Andre 77n13

Habermas, Jürgen 6–7, 35n1, 41–3, 44n16, 64, 71n4, 75, 81, 89, 91–3, 133, 144n22, 166, 176, 183
Hahnel, Robin 9n14, 165n57, 170n63
Hall, Stuart 2n2
Han, Byung-Chul 128n77
Hardt, Michael 132, 151n33, 153, 155–6
Harris, Kamala xi
Harris, Marvin 87
Harvey, David 97n4, 140n15
health care 162, 166
Hegel, Georg Wilhelm Friedrich 4–5, 37, 39, 77–8, 81n21, 154, 185n15
hegemony 52, 54, 183, 186
Heisenberg, Werner 143
Helfrich, Silke 151n33, 171
Hewitt, Paul 127n73
high-frequency trading (HFT) 113
Hill, Andrew 127n73
historical materialism 6, 36–41, 175–6
Hobbes, Thomas 154
Hoffman, Martin 145n24
holarchy 139, 139n13
Holloway, John 143, 174

Holocaust 80
Horkheimer, Max 2n2, 4n3
household commons 162–3
housing 107, 126
human nature 16–17, 182
human rights 74–5, 138
humanism
  Marxist 90–1
  socialist 90–1
hunter-gatherer societies 45–7, 82, 87, 89
Huxley, Aldous 139n13
hyperreality 141–2

idealism 14, 37, 39, 86–9
identity
  gender 143–4, 150
  politics 57, 143, 180
  self- *see* self-identity
ideology 36, 38, 52–62
  capitalist 52–8, 156
  critique 58
  libertarian 61
  Marxist 53–8
  neoliberal 96–8, 107, 113, 120, 165, 179
  political 58–62
imperialism 11, 109
incarceration 122–3
India 48, 73, 118n53
individualism 49, 141, 156
  possessive 156
individuation 177, 179
Indonesia 122n64
industrial revolution
  first 147
  second 147–8
  third 148
inequality 11, 42, 82, 97, 107, 109, 111, 118–19, 121, 123, 129, 134, 152, 173, 178, 181n7
  gender 65, 95
  income 118
  racial 65, 95

information technology *see* digital technology
Ingelhart, Ronald 98n7
Ingersoll, R. Elliott 29n38
institutionalized neoliberalism 104–8
institutions
  capitalist 38–9
  commonist 131–71
  feudal 38
  post-capitalist 151–71
  socialist 8, 38
integral consciousness 12, 31–3, 51–2, 62, 66, 134–51, 169, 176–7, 180, 183–6
  autonomous stage 137
  culture 139–51
  definition 135–9, 150–1
  fifth order (Kegan) 135–6
  strategist stage 137
intellectual property 102, 116, 160
intelligences, multiple 24–5
interest rates 99–100, 102, 105, 166
International Monetary Fund (IMF) 99, 102, 106–7
Internet 146, 148, 152
interpersonal development 25, 30
investment 105, 111–12, 166, 178
isolation 108, 123, 127–8, 180, 184

Jacoby, Russell 183n9
Jameson, Frederick 140n15
Jantsch, Erich 83n23, 179
Japan 110
Jaspers, Karl 73

Kegan, Robert 21–3, 25, 30, 73n7, 135–6, 138–9, 142, 148, 180n6, 185–6
Kellner, Douglas 140–5, 148
Keynes, John Maynard 98
Keynesianism 97, 98–9, 123, 129
King, Martin Luther, Jr. 33n51
Kirchner, Nestor 103

knowledge commons *see* cultural commons economy 181
Kohlberg, Lawrence 6–7, 25, 27–9, 31–2, 135, 138, 145n24
Kołakowski, Leszek 79
Konings, Martijn 97n4, 105–6
Kosmitzki, Corinne 24, 73n5
Kuhn, Thomas 4n3

labor
  exploitation 62, 111–12, 164, 184
  precarious 119–20
  productive 41
  reproduction 41
  social 171
  unions 98, 100, 119
Laclau, Ernesto 57n35, 144n22
Lahey, Lisa Laskow 73n7, 185–6
Lapavitsas, Costas 113n42
Laszlo, Ervin 83n23
Latin America 103–4, 122, 184
Laval, Christian 97n4, 101n13, 151n33
learning
  processes 42, 64
  social 35, 41, 64, 71, 74
Lebowitz, Michael 5, 132, 177, 184, 186
legitimation crisis 134, 166, 179
Lenin, Vladimir 53
Lenski, Gerhard 74, 87
liberalism 59, 61, 77
  classical 98
liberation theology 61
libertarianism 61
Linebaugh, Peter 151n33
Locke, John 154
Loevinger, Jane 25, 28, 30, 32–3, 135, 137
loneliness 97, 123, 129, 179
Lovejoy, Arthur 35n1
lower class 126–7
Lula da Silva, Luiz Inácio 103
Lukács, Georg 2n2, 53, 62

Lugo, Fernando 103
Luther, Martin 48
Lyotard, François 141, 143
Maastricht Treaty 101n12, 102
MacPherson, C. B. 156
magical worldview 45–6
Mao Zedong 10n18
Marcuse, Herbert 2n2, 4n3, 54–6, 66, 79, 167n60
marginalization 57, 62, 64–5, 131, 143, 176
market
  free 98, 120–1, 152, 165
  privatized 114–16, 121n61, 179
  rationality 49
  socialism 11
Marx, Karl 4–7, 15, 21, 33, 35–42, 49, 52–4, 62–4, 66, 73n6, 77–9, 81n21, 88, 111, 133, 147n27, 153n40, 154, 158, 164, 174–8, 184, 186
materialism 14, 37–41, 86–9, 94, 175–6
  dialectical 6
  historical 6, 36–41, 175–6
  post- 124, 129
Mattei, Ugo 153–4
McChesney, Robert 110n34, 111–12
media
  broadcast 146, 147
  mass 2, 122, 127
  social 96, 108, 117, 125, 127–9, 179
mental illness 127
Mészáros, István 37–8, 89, 91–3, 177, 184, 186
Meta (Facebook) 105, 114–17, 122, 179, 182
Mexico 103, 157, 174
Michaelis, Sophie 127n74
Microsoft 114, 122, 160
middle class 126
military spending 111, 122–3
Minsky, Hyman 111n35

modernization theory 11
monopoly 109–10, 116, 160
moral development 6–7, 25, 27–9, 31–3, 36, 41–3, 45, 49, 59, 64, 66, 75–6, 135, 137–8, 150, 176
Morales, Evo 103–4, 104n16, 122n64
Mouffe, Chantal 57n35, 144n22

NAFTA 102, 120, 165
nationalism 60, 96n2
nation-state 51, 146–7
Negri, Antonio 132, 151n33, 153, 155–6
neoliberal digital capitalism 7, 11, 49, 95–129, 133, 165, 176, 178–9, 183, 186
neoliberalism 50–1, 96–129, 152, 165, 179, 183
  consolidation phase 101–4
  consequences 97, 108–29
  definition 96
  external consequences 108–23
  history 97–108
  ideology 96–8, 107, 113, 120, 165, 179
  institutionalized 104–8
  internal consequences 123–9
  legitimation crisis 134, 166, 179
  oligarchical 109–10
  policy 97, 102, 113–14, 120, 165
  reorientation phase 100–1
  third way 101–4
neo-Piagetian psychology 85–6
networks 125, 139, 145–6, 148–51, 154, 161, 169–70
  digital 97, 146, 148
  neural 19
  peer-to-peer 146, 148
  social 124, 146
neuroplasticity 17–19, 30
neuroscience 3, 18
Nietzsche, Friedrich 49, 140–1
Nixon, Richard administration 99

North American Free Trade
  Agreement *see* NAFTA

objectivity 141–2
Offe, Claus 166n58
oil embargo (1973) 99
Ollman, Bertell 62–3
one-dimensionality 54–6, 66, 167n60
ontogenetic fallacy 69, 70–2, 87, 93
OPEC 99
open-source software *see* free and
  open-source software
oppression 36, 43, 56, 62, 65, 76,
  90–1, 132, 144, 166, 184
Ortega, Daniel 103
Osterdiekhoff, Georg 71n4
Ostrom, Elinor 151n33, 157–61, 164,
  168, 170, 181
Owen, Robert 174
Owen, David 89n32

Page, Benjamin 167n59
parecon *see* economics, participatory
Parsons, Talcott 82
participatory economics *see*
  economics, participatory
participatory society 51–2
Patel, Raj 151n33
pedagogy, critical 184n11, 186
Peru 157
Pettman, Dominic 127n76, 128
Peuter, Greig de 162n55
Phillips, Kaitlin Ugolik 127n72
Phillips, Peter 106n26
philosophy
  analytic idealism 14n1
  Eastern 14, 49, 50n22
  Enlightenment 48, 73, 141,
    147, 159
  postmodern 135, 140–2, 154
  Western 14, 35n1
Piaget, Jean 6–7, 21–2, 24–7, 29, 30,
  73, 77, 86, 135
Pinochet, Augusto 100

pink tide 103–4
platform capitalism 114–16
Plato 77–8
pluralistic
  consciousness 31, 49–51, 60–2,
    141, 176, 178, 180
  culture 140–5
    deconstructive 142, 144, 148
    reconstructive 142, 144, 148
    singularization and 124–7
police 122–3
political economy 6, 63
politics
  de-democratization 134, 165–7
  identity 57, 143, 180
  modern 143
  neoliberal 165–7
  postmodern 143–4
  representative democracy 48–9,
    165–7, 179
Pollin, Robert 120
pollution 178
Popper, Karl 23, 77–81
popular education 184
population growth 46, 82, 87
positivism 4, 55, 175
post-capitalism 10–11, 51–2, 131–71
  commons 151–71, 180–2
  consciousness *see*
    integral consciousness
  institutions 151–71
postcolonial theory 2n2
Poster, Mark 125n70
postindustrialization 50
postmodernism 49–51, 57,
  135, 140–5
  deconstructive 142, 144, 148
  political 143–4
  reconstructive 142, 144, 148
  scientific 142–3
post-structuralism 2n2, 56
poverty 42, 118
power 36, 43, 56–7, 62–5, 66, 87,
  89–94, 100, 106, 109, 142, 165,

165n57, 170n63, 173, 177, 182, 184n11, 186
precariat 119–20
preoperational stage 26–7
Prigogine, Ilya 143, 179
primitive accumulation 158
privatization 102, 114–16, 121, 166
production
  forces of 11, 37, 41, 133
  mode of 36–7, 47, 175–7
  relations of 37, 41n9, 133
productive forces *see* production, forces of
profit 105, 110–12, 116, 123, 178–9
progress 42, 48, 66, 74–6, 81–3, 93, 140–1
  dialectic of 42, 66, 75, 81–2, 93
proletariat *see* working class
property
  common 153–6, 170
  intellectual 102, 116, 160
  private 153–6, 158–9, 170
  public 153, 155, 170
  rights 153–6
  theory of 153–6
psychedelics 18n9
psychological development 3–4, 6–7, 21–34
  adulthood 6–7, 30–3
  childhood 25–30
  criticisms 84–6
  cross-cultural 24, 73
  lines 24–5, 30, 44, 75, 83–4
  stages *see* stages of consciousness development
  universal 24, 73
psychology
  biology and 19–21
  cognitive 6–7, 21–34
  developmental *see* developmental psychology
  neo-Piagetian 85–6
  Vygotskian 86

quantum mechanics 143

race 2, 28, 43, 62, 65–6, 86, 92, 95–6, 119n56, 137, 150, 170n63
rational consciousness *see* worldcentric consciousness
rationality 49, 55–6, 73, 141, 147
  market 49
  technological 56
Reagan, Ronald administration 100
realization problem 113, 178
Reckwitz, Andreas 124–7
reform, non-reformist 173
regression 45, 75, 80–1, 93, 133, 182
Reich, Wilhelm 2n2
reification 53–4, 58
relativism 31, 57, 141, 150
religion 47, 52, 58, 61, 150
  Christianity 48, 111, 158
rentier capitalism 116n48
representation 50n22, 141–2
repression 97, 109, 122–3, 179
revolutionary practice 64, 184
revolutionary theories 131–2
Richards, Francis 29n37, 32
Rifkin, Jeremy 145–9, 161
rights
  human 74–5, 138
  property 153–6
  universal 49, 138
Robinson, William I. 51n23, 95n1, 123
Rojas, René 104n16
Rorty, Richard 143
Russia 48, 99, 118n53, 157
  Revolution (1917) 8, 98

Saint-Simon, Henri de 174
Sanderson, Stephen K. 70, 87–9
Santos, Paulo L. Dos 113n42
science
  complexity 149
  empirical 4, 48
  modern 142–3

philosophy of 4, 55, 175
postmodern 142-3
positivistic 4, 55, 175
self-authorship 135
self-consciousness 13-14, 27-9, 32
self-identity 25, 28, 30-1, 137
   autonomous 137
   integral 32-3, 137
   pluralistic 31
   world-centric 28, 30-1
sensorimotor stage 25-6
services sector 50, 115, 126
Seymour, Richard 128n83
Shearer, Elisa 117n50
Siegler, Robert 85
singularization 124-7, 134, 178-80, 186
Sloterdijk, Peter 51n25, 57-8, 66, 183n8
smartphones 96, 108, 126
Smith, Adam 98
Snowden, Edward 122
social contract 32, 154
social democracy 1, 7, 49, 61-2, 98, 153, 154n40, 173, 176, 183
social evolution 35-67, 70-94
   consciousness development and 35-67, 70-2
   criticisms 69-94
   stages 44-52, 177-8
social learning 35, 41, 64, 71, 74
social media *see* media, social
socialism 1-12, 38, 60-2, 66, 131-86
   authoritarian 10, 177
   class consciousness and 62-5
   communism versus 10-11
   consciousness and 6, 11, 66, 184
   developmental approach 93-4, 173-86
   eco- 61-2
   failures 1-3, 8-11
   humanist 90-1
   institutions 8, 38
   market 11
   participatory 51-2
   scientific 174-5, 183
   state 11, 48-9, 60, 99, 103, 153, 183
   twenty-first-century 7-9, 11
   utopian 174-5, 183
socio-centric consciousness *see* ethno-centric consciousness
solidarity 42, 49, 61, 65-6, 108, 171
Soros, George 78
Soviet Union *see* communism, Soviet-style
Spencer, Herbert 35n1, 82
Spivak, Gayatri 2n2
Srnicek, Nick 114n44, 115
Staab, Philipp 113n40, 115n47
stages of consciousness development 22-34, 44-52
   a-centric *see* integral consciousness
   autonomous 137
   concrete operational 27-9
   criticisms 84-6
   de-centered *see* pluralistic consciousness
   dramaturgical 146, 148-9
   ego-centric 26-7, 45, 59-60
   ethno-centric 27-9, 45, 47, 73, 81, 83, 135, 177
   fifth order 135-6
   formal operational 29-30
   fourth order 135
   ideological 146-7
   integral 31-3, 51-2, 62, 66, 134-51, 169, 176-7, 180, 183-6
   pluralistic 31, 49-51, 60-2, 124-7, 140-5, 176, 178, 180
   preoperational 26-7
   psychological 146-8
   sensorimotor 25-6
   strategist 137
   universal 73
   world-centric 29-33, 48-9, 59-62, 71, 73, 75, 83, 97n7, 135, 146-7, 150, 158, 176-8, 180

stages of social evolution 44–52, 177–8
   agricultural 47–8
   feudal 47–8, 177
   horticultural 46–8
   hunter-gatherer 45–7, 82, 87, 89
   industrial capitalist 48–9
   industrial state-socialist 48–9
   magical-clan 45–7
   modern rational 48–9
   mythic-feudal 47–8
   neoliberal digital capitalist 49–51, 95–129
   pluralistic/postmodern 49–51
   post-capitalist 51–2, 131–71
Stallman, Richard 159–60
Standing, Guy 119n57
state
   alienation from 152, 165–6
   bureaucracy 8–9, 11, 49, 65
   socialism 11, 48–9, 60, 99, 103, 153, 183
   welfare 92, 98–9, 102, 120, 166, 173, 183
steering medium 170–1
Stengers, Isabel 143n20
Stiegler, Bernard 128n82
stock market 113
Stratenous, Iman 167–9
strategist stage 137
strikes 100
structuralism 2n2, 89–90
Strydom, Piet 70
subjectivity 20, 23, 90, 132, 135, 137, 141, 156, 185
superstructure *see* base and superstructure
surveillance 96–7, 109, 116, 122–3
Sweezy, Paul 111n35
systems theory 170
systems thinking 139, 150, 169–70

tabula rasa 3, 16–17
taxation 61, 119, 166

technology
   communication 145–8, 149
   development 6, 74, 145–9
   digital *see* digital technology
   information *see* digital technology
   rationality 56
   surveillance 96, 122
teleology 69, 80–3, 93
Temin, Peter 118–19
Thatcher, Margaret 100, 183
thermodynamics 142–3, 146n26
third way neoliberalism 101–4
Third World debt crisis 102
Thompson, Evan 20
Thompson, E. P. 153n40
TINA ("there is no alternative") 58, 183
totalitarianism 11, 69, 77–80, 91, 93, 144
trade
   agreements 102, 114, 120–1, 165
   free 102, 120–1, 165
   unions 53, 98, 100, 119
Trotsky, Leon 8
Trump, Donald administration 180n5
Turkle, Sherry 108n32, 127n72

Ugolik Phillips, Kaitlin 127n72
unemployment 98, 100, 104
Unger, Roberto Mangabeira 154n42
unions 53, 98, 100, 119
United Kingdom (UK) 98, 100–2, 127n73
United States (US) 2, 48, 100–5, 110, 112–13, 118–20, 122, 127, 127n73, 143, 165, 167n59, 179
universal consciousness 63
universal ethical principles 33, 138
universalism 30, 33, 49, 140, 143, 150
USMCA 120, 165
utopianism 143–5, 174–5, 183, 183n10

values 25, 59–61, 74, 76–7, 119, 124, 150
  development 25
  neoliberal 77
  post-materialist 124, 129
Varela, Francisco 20
Vázquez, Tabaré 103
Venezuela 7–11, 103–4, 104n16, 122n64, 167n61, 174n2
Vietnam War 99
vision-logic 139
Volcker, Paul 100, 102
Vos, Cato de 18n9
voting 55, 152n36, 166, 182
Vygotsky, Lev 86

wages 61, 107, 112–13
Wall, Derek 151n33, 158
Walljasper, Jay 151n33
war 50, 99, 111, 122, 134, 148, 179
Watkins, Alan 167–9
Weber, Max 48, 98n7
Weimar Republic 75, 81
Weinberger, Andrea 127n75
Weisbrot, Mark 99n9

welfare state 92, 98–9, 102, 120, 166, 173, 183
Wengrow, David 45n17
Wexler, Bruce 16–18
Wikipedia 151, 168
Wilber, Ken 7n10, 20–1, 24, 32–3, 35n1, 38, 41, 44n16, 59n38, 74–5, 135, 138–9, 141, 148
Williams, Raymond 2n2
work *see* labor
worker cooperatives *see* cooperatives
working class 2, 5, 11, 53–4, 62–5, 78, 126, 131, 173, 177, 183–4
world-centric consciousness 29–33, 48–9, 59–62, 71, 73, 75, 83, 97n7, 135, 146–7, 150, 158, 176–8, 180
World Bank 99, 102
World Trade Organization (WTO) 102, 114, 120, 165

X (Twitter) 117, 179, 182

Zapatistas 174
Zelaya, Manuel 103, 122n64
Zelik, Raul xn1